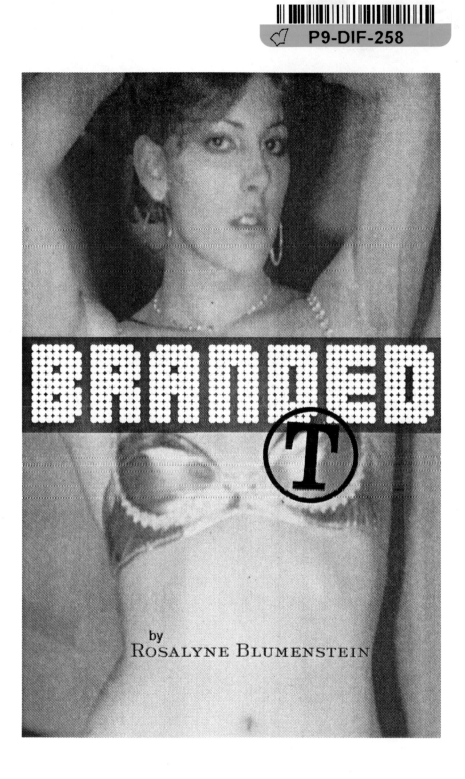

BRANDED

T

by
ROSALYNE BLUMENSTEIN

This book is a work of nonfiction. Some names and places have been changed to protect the privacy of all individuals. The events and situations are true.

Layout/artwork Jennifer Finch
WWW.BeeCharming.com

1stBooks – rev. 10/02/03

Dearest Kathy,

Wish you All the best

THxs 4 coming

This is a true story about a teenage runaway, her contact with suicide, gender identity issues, drug addiction, and the sex industry.

This is also the anecdote of how recovery opens the door to a healing process and alters the subjugators, <u>one day at a time</u>.

"Brassy, brainy, and buxom! Blumenstein pulls no punches and neither did her life on the mean streets. Wow, whatta wallop!"
-Loren Cameron, Photographer of Body Alchemy: Transsexual Portraits

"Rosalyne Blumenstein has gifted us with an astounding account of her life to date. It is a tale of sheer enduring spirit. She takes us from the flesh bars of pre-Giuliani Broadway to Graduate School, from New York to LA, from shame to self-confidence, from boy to girl. I hung on every word."
-Dallas Denny, Editor, Transgender Tapestry magazine

"This expansive, raw memoir offers a rare glimpse into the struggle for individual survival under the weight of transgender oppression. It's a story that must be heard."
-Leslie Feinberg, activist and author of
'Stone Butch Blues, Transgender Warriors, and Trans Liberation'

"An inspiring and triumphant story, part personal journey, part social history, about a woman who fought her way through physical, emotional and social challenges and the transformational power of educational and therapeutic communities.
A must read for teachers, counselors and therapists and anyone else who knows and loves someone dealing with trans issues."
-Suzanne Iasenza, PhD; Associate Professor, John Jay College-City University of New York.

"Rosalyne has come so far, but she not only remembers where she came from, she remembers exactly how she felt. She has survived and flourished against all odds, and it is clear that two of her sharpest tools are her wit and her ability to see the humor in the grimmest of events, even, and especially, at her own expense. Through her laughter and compassion, she brings a message of hope and recovery. One of the greatest gifts is to make a difference in just one life.
Roz, you are making a difference to so many. Thank you for your courage."
-Puma

"I loved this book! What an incredible journey! Not only is this the story of Rosalyne's life, but also the story of so many people whose lives

v

would have gone undocumented until now. Another fabulous aspect of the book is how it chronicles the history of a very exciting era in New York City. The perspective is fresh and enlightening, unique and empowering. Thank you for being gracious and selfless enough to share your experiences. It'll make a great movie!"

-Ru Paul Performer/Author 'Lettin it all hang out'

Table of Contents

THE JOURNEY OF RECOVERY

ACADEMIC RESCUE

REAL LIFE EXPERIENCE

THE ESSENTIALS: POLITICAL AND SOCIAL REORGANIZATION

Acknowledgements

What I would like to do is acknowledge everyone who has touched my life in one way or another. And that said I just did. I am usually bored with acknowledgements unless I am one of the 'acknowledged.' So I'd like to acknowledge all my hard work and support I have given me. Thank you, Rosalyne!

The LGBT Center in New York City provided me with many opportunities. I think I also got an ulcer from working there. To those special colleagues Carrie, Ray, Katie, David, David, Griffin, Lori, Alice, Rita, Arlene and Christopher, you were the reason I went to work every day. To those special mentors Barbara, David, Allan and Eleanor, I thank you. To you, dear Thom, without you I would've never survived the storms. To Carol, your input has always meant everything. To you Mr. Wheeler, HR means Healer Rescue. To the dearest Perina family, women like Melissa, Donna and Chloe, keep doing the work.

My NA friends, my family in 12 steps, without you guys there would be no me. We've buried so many since 1987. They live within us always. Brooklyn's in the house! To you, John, your old and new family, I will cherish you for the rest of my life. Bob, Leslie, Richie and Jessie, you are family. To Puma, we've watched each other grow. To Mickey and Joanne, the shiksa girls, you've fed me well.

Lynda, dearest Lynda, you always dressed me up and took care of me emotionally. I hope I returned some of that love and admiration. Please, may your soul and spirit rest in peace.

To Will Riley and crew, I miss my second home. Vincent, thank you for the gift of you and our time basking in the sun.

To my new friends on the West Coast, Susan and Esan, namaste!

And to you dear Precious, you have been more help than you will ever know. You were the first woman on the West Coast I trusted with all of 'me.' Thank you for eye and your artistry.

And to my family of origin, what's left of us, thank you for putting up with me. To my dearest nephew, be strong! You only have to live with him for another twelve years. And to you, my dear brother, I love you with all my heart and soul. You have always been an inspiration to me even when I hated your guts. You were always loved. Sound familiar?

And to those of you I did not acknowledge by name, know you were in the first part of my acknowledgement.

Hey, what do I think I am doing here, accepting an Academy Award?

Keep going girl!

A special thanks to you, Arlene. I remember when we first spoke, I thought I was meeting a Jew and you thought you were meeting an old lady. Boy, were you off! Your strength, courage and spirituality remain in my heart always.

To all of those people who have encouraged me and my work, I can never thank you enough for seeing in me things that I couldn't always see in myself. And for those of you who have had a difficult time with me and my character, thank you for sharing. I have learned even more about myself when the ridicule made sense.

Preface

For the past decade I've wanted to utilize my talents, my passion and my energy in the best possible way to create change, generate awareness and move folks away from a stereotypical analysis of a sexual, racial and cultural belief system. Stereotyping is a system all of us buy into. Oppression affects us all, the privileged as well as the disenfranchised. This was my priority for writing BRANDED...*T*. I wanted to challenge specific classifications.

My desire is for you to find within this collective 'truth.'

However, in addition to sharing my beliefs, my struggle with scotomas, my tools for working with and assisting in the process of recovery from addictions, recovery from oppressions, recovery from trauma and personal vicarious trauma, I want to share, celebrate and exhibit, as well as positively objectify, 'me.'

I want to share the opportunity to commemorate as well as advocate for those populations I've worked with, for, and am a component of. If it wasn't for many sub-cultural occurrences there would be no me, no work, no passion, no eclectic history, and no future. So many have struggled before me and unfortunately so many will struggle after I am gone. Hopefully this book, along with my energy, will be used by you as a light, an instrument, a channel towards less struggle for 'all.'

Yes this book is overflowing with me, self-centered, self-absorbed me.

Yes, this book exploits my history – the good, the bad, and the ugly – depending on perception, cultural background, personal morals and values.

And yes, this book is filled with hope, hope for me, hope for you, and hope for us!

Immerse yourself in these pages and you will find important progressive academic rhetoric in the vernacular.

Immerse yourself in these pages and you will understand the complexities of my ecosystem and my spirit. Immerse yourself in these pages and you will understand the complexities of your ecosystem and spirit.

I have received rare gifts and I must share them with others or they will rot within my self-centered, egotistical, unsure brain.

I wish to always be a student ... for in this role I obtain the ability to teach.

When I first began to write in 1999, I called this book "AIN'T NO WHITEBOY PRIVILEGE HERE, A Child's Confusion, a Woman's Conclusion." I believed I was a voice within a neo-movement that nobody wanted to listen to. They only cared to listen to those white women who were transexual and who spoke a language or lived a life that was unfamiliar to me.

I believed I had a voice that needed to be heard and the only voice people would listen to within 'Queer Academia' and/or the political arena were those white transexual women who transitioned later in life. After all, they had spent 30-50 years trapped in their white male privilege and had learned to play the game 'according to Garp.' They were college educated. They were established professionals. I was none of that.

I've learned so much about my stereotyping as well as my ignorance towards my own false privilege. I heard this amazing woman from Washington, D.C., Jessica Xavier, sing a song about being a woman of TS experience dealing with her white male privilege. Jessica's song made me realize that her white male privilege had negative consequences as well.

However, many voices within the Trans movement are still those with the most access, those that speak the 'King's English,' and some that buy into a unilateral approach.

When I began to reorganize my thoughts about this book I turned to one of the dearest women I knew, Carol Stewart, and asked her what she thought about my title. She let me know that the hairs on the back of her neck stood up a little and she had concerns about the title. I carefully listened to her. I also got some feedback from one of the many trans leaders on the Internet who told me the title was racist. I truly believed in my heart I did not experience white boy privilege because of my early transition. I also believed the title was attesting to that statement. I was wrong. I changed the title.

The objective for the title was not working anymore and I needed to rethink my course.

I did experience privilege because of the shape and color of my skin. I look a certain way and that is why many doors allowed me in. The color of my skin offered me some unearned privilege as well.

However, for 26 years I've been branded with this Scarlet Letter 'T.' This is not to say I am not proud of my TS history, because I most certainly am. It has taken me many decades to get to this internal place. But this is to assert that the 'T' is a small component of all that I am. When I am 'out,' that is all you see, and when I am closeted and just being, that is not all I am. It is a no-win situation.

This book is not just a novelette describing my journey into womanhood. I am not saying that a novelette is not an amazing goal for a book to be. All of us have a story. This is not just queer theory, identity politics, or addiction and recovery. It is more than that. This book is about pain, it's about celebration, it's about taking risks, it's about going crazy, it's about being fabulous and being adventurous. It's about sleaze and decadence and the desire for more. It's about being all-consumed with self, greed, hate and jealousy. It's about healing and loving unconditionally and striving to better oneself and one's environment. This book will entertain, it will inform, it will push your fucking buttons to the limit and challenge you to rethink, review and realize that although we live in the most amazing country, our country has so much work to do in order for all of us to be free. We live in an imperialist time that is damaging our value system, not enhancing it. We have a lot of healing ahead. My hope for you, the reader, is that you are not only entertained, intrigued, mortified, insulted, excited, and emotionally and spiritually challenged by my writing, but that you take what you learn with you and you teach others around you.

DEDICATION

Dedication

This book is dedicated to all trans women of color who have led the way for me and so many others. In New York, the girls from the Gilded Grape, the Barnum Room, the Casa Dario, the girls on the stroll of 9th Avenue, the girls that snapped and screamed and threatened so that so many of us could just be, become, live.

You took me in when I was lost. To the late Kelly, Nicky, Jessy, Mara, Tracey, the La Beija's, Miss Dorian, Marudi, Sugar, Chaka, Muneca, Marsha, Sylvia, Jackie, Sony, Candy, wherever god has taken you, I pray for your spirit. You led the way and made it a safer place for me 'to be.' There is no way to thank you for your pioneering efforts. You were amazing. You made it on the streets without protection of privilege.

To the existing Pink Ladies, Miss Taxi, Carol, Stephanie, Ava, the Housing Work Girls, Rita, Venus, Moshe, the PHP crew, and the Center's GIP clients, you are the divas! You are alive in my heart always. You are the light.

To Arlene, Sheila, Kim, Carla, Vickie, Barbara, Moshe, and even Pauline, continue the work and the world will be a better place.

THIS BOOK IS DEDICATED
TO MY GRANDMOTHER

Special Dedication

My grandmother Esther Joftes Schrager had a desire to put her life story in print. She shared her stories of her family of origin - living with wealth, surviving poverty, the 'Depression,' Russia, her relationship with her deceased husband Benjamin Schrager (*former president of Dr Brown Soda*), her life as the wife of Benjamin Schrager, her travels ... She told these stories over and over with such excitement and pride as if it were the first time she had the opportunity to share them.

Esther had few friends. She was eccentric. She was larger than life, *in her mind*. She was an intellectual snob. On the other hand, when she was around family, she was alive, genuine, real, and down to earth.
I have a lot of friends. I am eccentric. In my mind I am also larger than life. And on the other hand I am always uncomfortable with family of origin, but I am down to earth as well. My grandmother Esther Joftes Schrager and I have a lot in common.

I hated Esther for too many years. I believed she was the reason my mother was dead. She didn't love enough, she didn't give freely of herself enough, she didn't ... I needed to blame someone and, at thirteen, I nominated her. I couldn't blame my immediate family or my grandfather. After all, my grandfather was so heartbroken he died a month after my mother's death. Back then, I didn't understand about my mother's mental illness. I didn't understand my grandmother's ecosystem. I didn't understand.

My grandmother spent her life alone. If it hadn't been for my Aunt Joanne and her family my grandmother would've been totally isolated.
My grandmother was a financially secure woman who lived an unpretentious life. She never bought things to decorate her surroundings, she never traveled after her husband's death, and she never pampered herself. But some close to her say she was basically happy, she was content. I am financially insecure. I have always bought things to decorate my surroundings, I've done a lot of traveling and I have always pampered myself. Some close to me would say I am basically happy and content. But I am always searching.

My grandmother wanted to write, but shortly after my grandfather died she had major troubles with her vision. She never fulfilled this desire.
I never wanted to write. I always attempt to fulfill all my desires.
I am different, but in more ways than one, I am much like my grandmother.
And when I got clean and sober and practiced new principles in my life I learned more about her, me, mental illness, relationships, forgiveness, and acceptance of her and me.
My grandmother, my mother, me ... strange, eccentric beings!

Because of you, dear grandma, your dream will live, through me. You are truly the catalyst for many of my newest experiences. Like writing! This book could be your story with a XXX rating if you were born six decades later, well maybe, but probably not. But this is written in dedication to your belief that good stories should not be wasted only on family!
Rest in peace, Esther. Because a **peace** rests within me.

REAL LIFE
EXPERIENCE

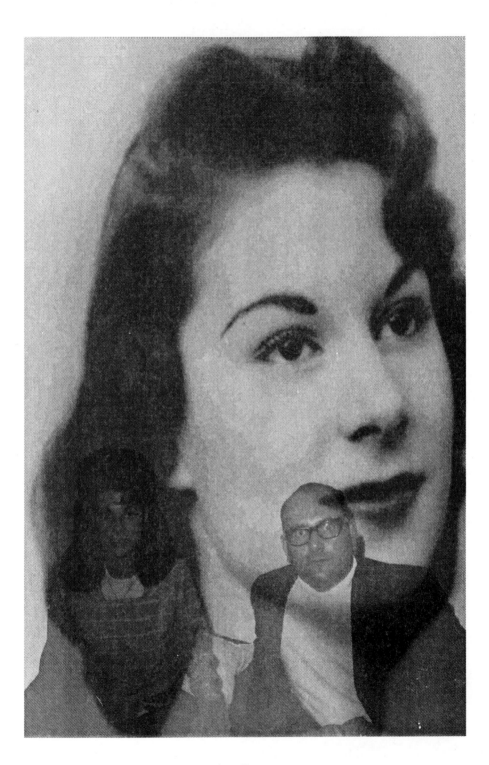

1.
CHILDHOOD

1

Childhood

It was 1960, the year of the rat. I don't recall being born.

I was told I was 5 lbs 2 oz and I still feel a sense of pride for being a slim baby. For some strange reason the doctor told my parents they had a boy. What the hell was he thinking? Oh well, I'll fix that!

My childhood recollections (four years old and on) are wonderful as far as parental visibility is concerned. My desires surrounding gender presentation are another story. I always lived with this feeling of doom. I was scared and shy but had this other side of me that needed to be out there, attention seeking, and in the limelight. It was a contradiction in emotions and a physical incongruity that would carry through to adulthood.

When she was around, my mom was as loving as she could be. My dad did what he was taught to do, and that was to provide room and board for his wife and offspring. My brother was older and still is. We lived in a two-family house in Canarsie, Brooklyn. My Aunt Hannah and Uncle Abe owned the house but we had full run of two floors, backyard, garage and front patio. It seemed like we owned the house. We lived beyond our means and that's how I learned to live my life.

I spent a lot of time in fantasyland. I was sexually curious at a young age and I enjoyed staying in bed pressing my genitalia and dreaming about being slight, delicate and vulnerable.

I would spend a lot of time in the four-by-five pink-tiled psychedelic pink/black/silver wallpapered bathroom playing the rape game. I would use all these towels, one around my head for hair, washcloths over my areolas and one on my groin. I took all of them into the bathtub. I never gave a straight answer to my mom as to why I took so long or why I was leaving behind so many wet towels.

My parents seldom questioned, disciplined or challenged me about my cross gender behavioral patterns. And there were times I had experienced the reality of dressing in clothes that were not deemed appropriate for me, I never got caught until I was in nursery school and I was five years old. There was a large trunk filled with dress-up clothing in my nursery school classroom. You had your pick. I couldn't help yearning to be a bride. So one day, I was. The day I put that white lace onto my body my brother and mom showed up to my classroom. Talk about ruining someone's orgasm! I ran under the table with my sense of shame weighing me down like the table's

4

weight was literally on my under-developed shoulders. I am not sure why I experienced this deep, ingrained sense of inappropriateness, but I did. The teacher kept saying, "Come on out and show your family how pretty you look." I sensed condescension in that old broad's voice and still feel that way today whenever anyone says that I am 'pretty.'

Where do you think we get that sense of right and wrong where gender presentation is concerned? And why, at such a premature age, did I feel that this desire for pink, not the color of the wedding dress but a metaphor for things feminine, was an inappropriate hue for the color of my desire?

That night I collected a bunch of ties from my dad and agreed to use these in my 'dress up' recreational activities. I used the ties in school around my waist and in my hair. I couldn't help myself.

> *The DSM (diagnostic statistical manual compiled by the American Psychiatric Association for the sake of diagnosing and treating psychiatric disorders) would diagnosis this transvestic fetishism and/or gender identity disorder, depending on what further questions the psychiatrist asked and the answers received.*

The shame was embedded in me. Did this sense of shame come subliminally from the DSM, Dr. Seuss, peers, family, or the media? The powerful divide of pink and blue! I still wonder where the transvestic diagnosis is for those who are identified as female at birth when they go towards the blue shade.

All I can say to end this short synopsis of childhood is that I was one lucky transvestic/fetishistic gendered disordered individual. It was the '60s and my mom accepted the drag panache of that era. I had more than enough wigs, wiglets, falsies, eyelashes, various shades of frosted pink and blue eye shadows, and every shade of lipstick to play with. My family and family friends kidded that my dad's wife (my mom) was laid out more on their dresser than she was in the bed. We never goofed about how those body enhancers were entertaining their youngest child right on the other side of that dresser, my bedroom. To Mom and dad, wherever you are, I miss you.

2.
SEXUAL CATEGORICAL
DEFIANCE

SEXUALITY
FANTASY
PROGRESSION
BOUNDERIES
TOO MUCH TOO SOON

2

Sexual Categorical Defiance

Sexuality
Too Much Too Soon

I was always attracted to men, although I had girlfriends as early as kindergarten. Robyn was my first girlfriend. I sensed my mom's annoyance as my parents took me to Robyn's house, fake flowers I wrapped in tin foil in hand and ready to pass on to Miss Robyn. It seemed like it was entertaining to the other parents as I walked into the house and handed Robyn the offerings. I wonder if they would have been as entertained as I tried to put my hand up Robyn's blouse to feel her flat chest during playtime? Robyn was so cute and I wanted to look just like her.

Fantasy

My sex/sexuality was alive and I was always curious. My cousin Denise (my Aunt Hannah and Uncle Abe's granddaughter) and I would play with Barbie dolls for hours. As our play became more elaborate, Ken would always wind up on top of Barbie. Hey, it was the '60s and the missionary position was generation appropriate.

Denise always wanted me to be Ken and I always wanted to be Barbie. Our doll play would end up with Denise and me in my Aunt Hannah's bed masturbating to the scenario. We both dreamt of Ken coming to our rescue. I wonder what my Aunt Hannah would've dreamed about if she had known what these youngsters were doing in her bed?

As I look back I realize my sex/sexuality engulfed my energy. I hated to read. I wanted to fantasize. I didn't like playing sports, although I engaged in punch ball, basketball, football, and softball anyway. Imagine if I'd liked sports? I wasn't good and was always scared I might be hurt. I played because I thought I had to play. I didn't like getting dirty, physically dirty that is, and when I was seven years old I played in a 'puddle of mud' just to appease my concerned parents. I got dirty because I subliminally knew my parents were worried about my cleanliness. I played sports because I wanted to be with the boys, especially Bobby. Bobby was the boy down the block who I had had a crush on since I can't remember. When we were around eleven years old I saw a picture of him naked and I got that deep, heavy, warm feeling inside. Of course, Bobby grabbed the picture away from me as soon as he saw me emotionally melt into and grab at his phallus. Why do you think he showed me the picture in the first place? Things that make you go hmmmmmm!

The juvenescent years should have been filled with trial and error, the experience one feels when one keeps trying and trying and finally gets it right. But I, I hated not being good at something. I didn't have the capacity to work through the difficulties and come out the other side. I sucked my finger until I was eleven years old. I needed a cold sensation against my ear. I needed my time alone, and pressure on my genitals. I needed to just do things, not learn how to do them. I needed to constantly console myself, not challenge myself. I needed fantasy time focusing on what should be and not what was.

I hated following instructions. My brother, father and I would sit and put together models. My brother and father would sit there looking at the directions, carefully placing piece upon piece, handling the glue like they were performing surgery or like they were playing Operation™. My brother and father would paint with the hands and patience of a true artist. Not me! Operation™ was a game I always failed at and so did my paint jobs. I hated directions and I hated to paint. I threw the models together as fast as possible and would feel a sense of defeat because they looked just like the time I spent on them. I couldn't paint because my hands shook. I've joked about being the child with fewer abilities, with challenged abilities, but back then it was no joke. The only time I felt safe and secure was when I played dress up and spent time engaged in sexual fantasy.

Progression

I had to be taken to a speech pathologist to learn where to put my tongue. I've learned since then where to put it, but that is not what I am talking about here. Imagine, even my tongue didn't go where it was supposed to go. It was supposed to relax on the top palate, not on the bottom.

So here I was, a child who liked to play dress up in garb that was not socially acceptable. My hands shook and I wasn't good at coloring or penmanship. I hated sports because I wasn't good. My tongue went where it wanted to and I spent a lot of time fantasizing. No wonder I was troubled.

There was one thing I thought I was perfect at and that was masturbation. I didn't know you were supposed to pull because I pushed. Damn, I wasn't even good at that. But my perception was that I was.

I had a rich, lively sense of sexuality at five years old. I dated girls, but wanted to be one. I was identified as a boy, but was also secretly attracted to boys. I had no patience or tolerance for the learning process and wanted to speed it up. I needed instant gratification. My tongue went the wrong way (I said that already), I had a lisp, my voice sounded queer, and I did not

9

receive much guidance from parental figures on how to tolerate all of this ambiguity. *Hey! Somebody put this kid to sleep!*
I did a lot of comparing myself to my brother and would never come up the winner. For some reason I believed in the winner and loser mentality. So how could I be a winner, you ask. I would get my winning status utilizing outrageous behavior strategies. I was the little actor. Well, my brother even had to steal that from me when he performed in his high school 'Sing'. He was amazing. My brother was smart, talented, sure of himself, witty, presentable, conservative, and extremely handsome. He had good teeth, good hair, he played ball ... However, he was no man's man, either, and my parents must have felt like there was a lack of testosterone between the Blumenstein/Schrager Union. I was unique, outrageous, sensitive, shaky and impatient.

Boundaries
Healthy children learn boundaries. I was very seldom reprimanded and when I was I became upset. I couldn't tolerate (or at least it felt like that) the criticism even if it was constructive. What I do remember is that I would push everything to the limit until somebody around me lost it and then I would cry. This didn't just occur once. This happened a lot. My parents didn't reprimand me or point out when I did something against what was really appropriate for me to do. My dad had money in his desk and I would always take some. My mom smoked Pall Malls and my dad smoked Lucky Strikes and I would steal their cigarettes, much later in childhood, not at this point, but I am just telling the story of boundaries and this fits in, OK?

I was in 3rd grade and I did something in class and all the kids were pointing at me when the teacher asked who did it. I couldn't handle having all those fingers pointing at me and I never wanted to be the center of attention like that again. I didn't want any attention unless I was in control of the situation. I wanted to be in the driver's seat at all times.
When I was ten years old I went and bought a silver metal belt from this 'Head Shop' called Comfortable and my mom was fuming. She felt that I was headed in the direction of smoking dope, and I didn't even know what dope was. How did she know I'd be smoking dope by eleven years old?
Boundaries are something I knew I could place around other people but there were no boundaries for me. My life was controlled except for the tongue, the hands, the sucking of the point finger, mom's clothing, desires, isolated fantasy sex, and the needing of coldness against my ear thing. Besides all that, I was free.

3.
THE EARLY
SEVENTIES

פ"נ מיידל בת ר' דוב

CAROL BLUMENSTEIN

AUG. 11, 1935 — SEPT. 14, 1973

BELOVED WIFE

R MOTHER

3

The Early Seventies

Pu.ber.ty (pyoo-ber-tee) *n.* the stage at which a person's reproductive organs are in the process of becoming mature and he or she becomes capable of producing offspring

Crossing the Threshold into Puberty
Puberty is a time of constant emotional and physical change. You experience a sense of who you are and at the same time don't really know anything about yourself. Internally, hormones are transforming you physically and affecting you emotionally. Your external appearance transforms, which makes you feel like a stranger in a new town. Puberty is a time of new beginnings and strange physical and emotional experiences. It is a time where everything is changing and incongruent. It's a time of growth and evolution. If one is in isolation surrounding these encounters, life can become that much more difficult and unsettling. It seemed my puberty wasn't doing any of this. It remained dormant until I intervened with HRT (hormone replacement therapy).

Theoretical thought

> *As a clinician within the trans communities I have found that many people of trans (transexual, transgender) experience grasp for the ability to discover the legitimacy surrounding the 'trans' experience. We look for biological signs within puberty to prove our gender hypotheses. So many of us want to be validated scientifically since that is where our societal system tends to turn to for legitimate reasoning surrounding biological issues. We grab at anything that states this is not a psychological dysfunction, this is proof as to why I am the way 'I am' and it's not all in my head. Trans-people search for the answers. We search for validity.*
> *The Intersex Society of North America (ISNA, an advocacy group which educates and advocates for the Intersex communities) and the medical community have scientifically proven primary and secondary sexual characteristic malfunctions at birth and throughout puberty due to aberrant hormonal reaction and interaction. Science philosophy is that the intersex condition is a legitimate, medical disorder. The medical communities have*

presented intrusional modus operandi to reconstruct the appropriate pubescent experiences. However, many constituents of ISNA want to challenge the archaic belief system that the intersex condition needs physical intervention in order for the person's identity to be whole. Many within the intersex communities want to allow for genital ambiguity, primary and secondary sex characteristics, to be viewed within a continuum as opposed to being bipolarized as the standard for male or female genitalia. (Extracted from WWW.ISNA.ORG)

Many within the trans community want their identity scientifically legitimized, too. Many want to legitimately justify why one would steer the pubescent experience utilizing hormone replacement therapy at different points of their lives.

Imagine allowing for puberty to be an experience that was directed and celebrated and not an encounter that took over one's life for a year or two? Imagine a trans puberty where secondary characteristics can be changed and celebrated no matter what age! Imagine scientifically legitimizing the trans puberty but not as a psychiatric dysfunction! If we see 'trans' as a psychiatric disorder, its puberty becomes de-legitimized.

So many Trans people grasp at things to prove their personal scientific hypothesis of 'self' in order to possess and legitimize why we steer the pubescent experience at some point in our lives.

I never had acne. My skin was always perfect. While all of my friends began to grow pubes, and large testicles, I had little, pubes and testes that is. While all my friends' penises, those identified as male, began to grow, mine stayed the same. My muscular form did not begin to change, nor would it until I began to lift weights in 1990. I was a fully developed 30-year-old woman by then.

My masculine and feminine pubescence overlapped because of my early intervention and transition. On one hand it confused me, and on the other it legitimized my understanding of self to a greater degree.

Mother's availability

Although my mom had many personal problems, she seemed to be there for me during my pre-pubescent time.

My mother was diagnosed with manic depression and was treated with shock therapy treatments, diazepam (Valium) and talk therapy. Valium is used in short-term treatment as a physical therapeutic release of anxiety and depression. In the 1960s and 70s doctors prescribed this to women to medicate their histrionics, what is now known to us as PMS (Premenstrual

Syndrome). I am not sure when her depression began. My depression began as young as I could remember. I do know that I am very much like my mom when it comes to dealing with life's challenges. My mom was a lovely woman physically and emotionally. She was a friend to everyone, and I felt completely protected by her, although I also felt deserted and alone a lot of the time.

I looked to her for support and I always wanted and needed her love and admiration. I also felt as if I had to protect her from the evils of life. One day, my brother and my mom were arguing and my brother ran downstairs to the finished basement where he had set up his bedroom. My mom sat on the toilet in the bathroom, which was used additionally as her royal seat to put on her make-up, she sat there crying uncontrollably. I wanted to kill my brother for making her cry. My mother seemed to cry a lot. When she was emotional her hands would shake more than usual. Sometimes you would look into her eyes and you would connect with this beautiful woman. And there were other times when it seemed like there was no one there. These were usually the times that she would disappear out of my life for a month or so. I didn't know back then, but she was hospitalized for suicide attempts and depression.

One time, my brother, father and I went to drop her off at the hospital and I lost it emotionally. My mother, my mommy, was leaving me and I couldn't bear being apart from her. My first day of school was a traumatic experience. Going away to camp, and watching her go to a friend's house would resurface her leaving me and going into the hospital. I did not want to let go of her, her support, her love, not even for a moment.

Although I didn't recognize it then, I was a lot like my mom and my brother was a lot like my dad. My brother and I were both much closer to my mom, but my characteristics were much more like hers.

My mom had a best friend named Mickey. She lived five houses down. They would sit forever drinking coffee and smoking their Pall Malls. They would talk, laugh, and Mickey would curse like a sailor. I was jealous of their friendship but saw my mom happy and excited around her friend. I liked seeing her happy and would do things to see her in that state. I was the little performer and would perform for her to make her laugh.

My mom always encouraged me. As I got older (still prepubescent), my mom would always be at Mickey's house and my dad would always be at home on the plastic covered blue and white velvet couch in our living room watching TV. I would spend most of my time alone in fantasyland or with my friends on the block playing or attempting to play boy games. I also spent a lot of time with binoculars playing voyeur and would look into other peoples windows for hours. There was a thrill of watching and waiting for someone to walk by a gaping-curtained window.

When I was 28 years old I spoke to my mother's best friend after not speaking with her since I was eighteen. She told me that my mom had great suspicions about me but did not know what to do.

Most of my childhood I tried to hide my sex/sexuality and my socially incongruent behavior. I am glad my mom recognized it even though nothing was done or was said about it at the time.

Camp
Fear and Shame
I started summer camp at around seven years old. My father's sister's kids (my cousins) went as well. Those boys were rough and tough. My brother and I were the opposite. Our families also rented a bungalow upstate, like every other Jewish family from Brooklyn, and I remember going out into the woods with my cousins. We all had to go to the bathroom and they showed me how to use a leaf for clean up. I felt so uncomfortable with the leaf in addition to being around three boys with our pants down. I am not at all uncomfortable with that anymore.

When I started camp I had to get dressed alone because I couldn't bear the thought of being naked around boys. I was so attracted to the visuals. I never told that part to my mom, but my mother authorized my separate dressing space. A counselor would take me to a facility where I would dress and undress in my own quarters. I sensed embarrassment and annoyance from my counselor because of this.

Negative reinforcement
Although I experienced shame, a feeling of being different, a desire for instant gratification, I wasn't good at sports, and I desired to be Cat Woman, I acted like I was confident. My mother's confidence in me overturned my own negative reinforcement. She instilled in me that I could do no wrong even though my mind disagreed. She always had my back and made sure things went well for me. The negative reinforcement came deep from within and she helped to counterattack my inner voice. Whether it was lack of self, a lack of god, or an inability to believe in me, my mom's confidence carried me through when I couldn't muster it up from within.

It wasn't until I went to sleep-away camp that I confronted my acting out and my internal negativity on a deeper level.

Acting Out
I went to a drama and music sleep-away camp. I sent up a trunk filled with clothes and arrived with two large suitcases. In my bunk, I slept next to the

finest young man, named Ruben. Ruben turned out to be a good friend and I don't think he ever knew how attracted I was to him.

I allowed myself to be more feminine in camp. I was in a bunk filled with boys and I didn't think I belonged. But for some reason I was never really picked on or threatened or made fun of. In fact, it was the other way around. I was a little boisterous and sassy and picked on other kids in my bunk. I did an evil thing. There was a young man in this bunk who was adopted and I hung a sign over his bed. The sign made a mockery of his family status. How could I have been so thoughtless and unkind?

> *I think a lot of the troubles I deal with now are based on karma.*
> *And, as a young child, I tainted my destiny.*

There were three other incidents I need to share in regards to my camp days. We were putting together the play West Side Story and I auditioned for the part of Riff. I didn't get the part and the young person who did received a scholarship into the camp. I called my mother, hysterically demanding she help me. The next day I had the part of Riff. I don't know what my mother said but the camp director reassigned the part. All these kids were upset with me and said that my mother got me the part and I didn't deserve it. I quietly turned to them and said "well, however I got it, I have it now."
Don't you want to smack me across my face and kick me in my stomach right about now? What an obnoxious little f... I was.

That winter of '72 I was invited up to the campgrounds with some of the other kids. What I didn't know was that they had made plans to kick my ass. These were all the kids from the previous summer who were friends with the boy whose part I had got. Ruben, my buddy from my bunk, talked them out of it. I guess I always had some power over the male species using my subtle female ways.

Was I a spoiled brat just because, or was there something defiantly not right in my life gearing me to act out?

I conflate my desire to be center stage – but not my gender incongruency - with pathological ideations. One day we thespians (not lesbians, thespians) were all in the auditorium practicing Pirates of Penzance and a young girl fainted. One of the junior counselors came over and picked her up and carried her to the infirmary. I betcha don't know what I did a week later, right?

My bunk was settling down for the night and I became faint from asthma. I collapsed right there onto the floor. The JC (not the same counselor, besides, he's irrelevant) picked me up and started to carry me to the infirmary. In between my bunk house and the infirmary the JC asked if I was able to walk and, of course, this drama queen in training was not up to it. While in the infirmary I ran around playing with some other kid. A Nazi nurse grabbed me and told me, "I know you are faking. You'd better watch your step." Do you think she meant I was faking because I was acting like a boy or that I was sick with asthma?

The third of this trilogy was my choice to appear in 'female' attire in public with an older group of kids. After my incident in nursery school I still presented as a female character in fantasy play with friends but never came out in full Tammy Faye drag until …

Each bunkhouse had to perform a play once a month. The first month when my bunk got together to plan this I agreed to be the woman on stage. It was exciting and amusing to many of my bunkmates. However, it was exciting and comfortable for me and I didn't want the evening to end. I loved the attention and I felt at home in the gear. The next month my bunk had to come up with a skit and I agreed to play the 'woman' and the guys in the bunk started to get suspicious. It didn't take a rocket scientist to …

Drama

At thirteen years old I had what is called a bar mitzvah. I now call it my Bat Mitzvah (in Judaic culture a boy becomes a man at thirteen and a girl becomes a woman at twelve, and that is all I know about the heritage of bar and bat within Judaic culture). I was brought up to understand that this event was about me getting a lot of money and having a party with family and friends, most of the family I didn't even know.

In fact, when my family started to plan this party a lot of unrealistic/self-induced fantasy self-centered behavior was happening. I wonder if I was caught up in fantasy fulfillment because having this party to display my new status as a man made absolutely no sense to me. I was no closer to being a man than Snow White was to sleeping with six out of the seven dwarfs.

Here are some of the juicy ingredients for this charade.

Within the Judaic culture you are supposed to recite your haftorah, *a reading from the torah,* during the temple preceding the big party. I was in Hebrew school once a week since fourth grade. We were supposed to be learning about our heritage, pride and our culture. I wasn't learning anything except words that were foreign to me. I didn't leave Hebrew school with a sense of god or a sense of god within. I think it was my reluctance to participate in the charade of manhood that kept me from finding a sense of spirituality within the tradition.

I believe that a connection with a higher power (some call god) is as important as bread and water is to one's well-being. Around six months before your bar or bat mitzvah, the young person is supposed to be practicing his or her part of the haftorah with the rabbi of the temple. I went to class around three times and just didn't want to do it.

At that time I started to hang out with a crowd that had more problems then I was used to. In Canarsie in the 1970s we called this group 'Hitters.' The girls wore tight jeans and platform shoes and curled the very front of their hair and smoked cigarettes and chewed a lot of gum and were disrespectful and thought they were cool and skipped class and got in trouble (all in one breath). The boys would wear multi-colored polyester shirts that had pictures beginning on one side of the buttons and pictures ending on the other side. Platforms for men were in style but few boys were wearing them. I mixed and matched the gender garb and was beginning to move from looking like an outrageous cute kid to a more androgynous presentation, even though I thought I was cool looking. I had bought platform shoes and wore tight jeans without a trace of lump in the front.

Up until this age I was always with smart kids, kids that got good grades, kids that didn't care about dressing cool, and were the leaders of the class not the leaders of a gang.

Back to the rabbi and my haftorah:

I was hanging out with a girl named Pamela who I had a mad crush on.

My girlfriend Carrie, who you will read about later in my more 'destructive years,' stated I was with Pamela because she was a loose woman.

I was already smoking cigarettes (since age eleven), and I began to drink a little and smoke pot whenever it was around.

Pamela had a brother who had some rare disease and was deformed. He stayed locked up in a room where no one was allowed to see him. When her brother died, I decided I wanted to be around Pamela and not go to my haftorah lessons anymore. I used this as an excuse to get out of the lessons but sold it to my mother saying I needed to be with Pamela.

The Hebrew school was annoyed that I was missing class and threatened not to work with me anymore. My mother quickly took this fight over and advocated for me. She let the rabbi know that he was a total asshole and that her child was performing a mitzvah by spending time with another grieving child. I loved to see her at work in my behalf. I loved to see her fight my battles. I also knew that I was getting away with something because a big part of me did not want to be with the rabbi or take my haftorah lessons with him. So there was also this feeling I had that I was getting over. As usual my mother quickly came to the rescue and my family hired a private tutor to teach me the haftorah. When there was guidance I was able to succeed but left to my own devices I was lazy and did not want to put effort into anything. Things never came easy for me and I didn't want to work at anything except learning lines for plays or shopping for clothes or redecorating and designing my room.

I performed my haftorah on May 19th 1973 and was told by the cantor that I should consider becoming a cantor.

It turned out that Pamela had a lot of boyfriends. Most of them were older and tougher and one threatened me, which scared me. I had been able to walk through life without being picked on up until then. I mean, I had heard people call me faggot once in a while but never did I feel threatened with violence even though I was always scared of everything. From a young age I hated I mean hated to go into a lunchroom where kids were eating. It scared me to death.

> *When I went back to college at 33 years old and I walked into the*
> *lunchroom, I remembered exactly how I felt*

I stopped hanging out with Pamela. I stopped going to the lunchroom. And then I met a girl at a dance in junior high school, Bildersee, our alma mata; proudly we sing its praise …, through the years I'll always cherish memories of my … OK, I'll stop.

Jackie was her name. She was in ninth grade and I was in seventh. Jackie turned out to be a lesbian and I guess that's why she was attracted to me. I lost my virginity to Jackie, although I had been sexually active since fourth grade.

Jackie was my date at my bar mitzvah. I also had two previous girlfriends from sleep-away camp come to my party as well. I invited too many people I was not close to just so the dais was attractive. I had around 23 friends in all. My parents should have made me eliminate some of these acquaintances, but they didn't. Again, there were few boundaries and I rode the wave that I wanted.

One of the girls that I dated in sleep-away camp wrote me a nasty letter telling me she had had a miserable time at my party and I had treated her like shit. I felt so bad, specifically because she was right. Again, the law of karma would rear its face in my not so distant future.

I treated girls like toys when I was young. In fourth grade, if you refused me a hand job I wouldn't go out with you. If you were flat-chested, I got bored with feeling you up (and in my late teens that is how I was treated by the men I dated).

My mom designed her dress for my bar mitzvah. She wore this long white gown made out of taffeta and satin. It had a silver embroidered cummerbund and there was embroidery on the sleeves as well. We went shopping for my

21

outfit and, since I couldn't wear my mom's dress, I chose a blue velvet tuxedo number with three-inch platform shoes.

The party was a big hit and I was as self-centered as could be. I remember my brother was playing my mom's favorite song on the trumpet, 'Sunrise Sunset,' and I had to interrupt her and ask her something so that her attention would come back to me. I remember when she came up to light a candle on my cake, a tradition that people do at these shindigs. She came up and lit the cake and gave me that look, that look that said I love you so much, you are my child, my world ... at that time I didn't realize I would only see that look in her eyes one more time.

That night, my father fell asleep in the middle of the party. He drank too much and missed what he had paid for.

Right before the evening events there was a photographer at my house taking pictures of the family. At one point the photographer was in the living room. He set my mom up in one of our plastic covered, blue velvet chairs that matched the blue drapes and blue velvet lamp shades. He sat her in that chair alone and she got hysterical. She said she did not want a picture of herself alone. She had a family to take a picture with. I looked at her. Her eyes were red and sad and at that moment I felt as alone as her.

Death

It was September 4th 1973. I had just returned home from sleep-away camp. It was a beautiful morning but I had my first fight with my mom since returning home. I was wondering what was up with her as I left to take a swim in Mickey's pool. Being a smartass I said some stupid things to Mickey about my mom's attitude. I went back home, took a shower and went off to get a haircut for the beginning of the school year. I hated the beginning of a new term in school and I hated the end of the summer.

I was sitting in the chair getting my hair cut when a police officer walked in and asked for me. He came over and I got nervous. He asked me if I knew where my father was and I immediately responded with a sarcastic reply. The officer rubbed me on my head and said nothing. I can still feel his hand as he brushed his sympathy through my newly cut strands. I goofed around with the stylist and went on my way. I arrived at my house early in the afternoon and in ran Mickey like she had seen a ghost. She ran past me and screamed for my brother. My brother ran upstairs and came outside in front of our house. "Carol OD'd again," she asserted and they both had this horrific look on their faces. What did "OD" mean? I had no idea. I can't remember who explained it or what happened next or when my dad came into the scenario but I do remember being thrown into the car and driven to Brookdale Hospital. In that instant my whole life was being turned around. I didn't even have the chance to be with her a week and here she was lying in a hospital bed with tubes coming out of her. I was embarrassed because she had no clothes on and I wasn't sure which way to look or what to do. There, lying there, was my mom and I wanted to wake her up and tell her, "I am so sorry for this morning's argument and I'll do anything to change this. I'll be good. I'll stop smoking. I won't be attracted to boys. I'll be conservative like my brother, anything, just let's go home." The next few days were a horror. My mother was in a coma. I had just spent the summer away from home and now I was home without a home. I recall absolutely nothing about those days except going to the hospital and sitting by her bed. One afternoon, we walked into her room and she woke up for an instant. She looked at me and mouthed "I love you" and went right back into the coma. On Friday, September 14th in the early afternoon, we got the dreaded call and rushed to the hospital. She was dead.

Not only did my mother die that day but my soul, my spirit, my belief in me went right with her.

> *As my life's journey went on I became more and more like my mom and my inability to forgive that part of me that is fear-based, or suicidal, or depressed haunts me in my ability to succeed or feel good about any accomplishment in my life.*

You see, my mom was my anchor and when that was lifted I drifted, no rhyme intended.

I was left with a broken family, a brother who went off in his own direction and a father who shut down as his coping mechanism. I hadn't even had the opportunity to show her how much I loved her or how much she meant to me. I was still in my self-centered phase of development. I had all these internal secrets, and puberty was not working for me. She didn't stay around long enough for us to really get to know each other.

Humiliation

This was the beginning of life's humiliation. Without my mom to protect me from the world, the world would now begin its course of real experiences and I did not have the necessary tools to deal with it.

I fell apart as soon as my mother died and the grieving process began. I wept on the way home from the hospital and, as my father went to his room and my brother went to the basement, I felt lost. I did not hold anything back and what happened was that I quickly got rid of all the initial pain. My dad called upon my brother and me to come into his room and I was totally compliant. My brother had his own agenda. I did not understand the dynamics between my brother and my father at the time so I kept getting pissed at my brother. My brother was seventeen and had already established

23

an adult relationship with my parents. My brother had loved our mother dearly and had a great rapport with her. I, on the other hand, wasn't there yet and had not really had conversations with either parent. I wanted so much to make everything right in the house at that moment. I wanted to be a caretaker. I wanted all of us together. I tried, but it failed.

We buried my mom in the white dress she had designed for my bar/bat mitzvah. I wept on the way to the funeral. I wept as I said goodbye to her in her casket and played with her wiglet. I wept as my grandfather aged ten years in that one moment as he kissed his middle daughter on her keppelah for the last time, and I wept as I saw my grandmother not shed a tear. I wept at the cemetery. At the cemetery, the line of cars seemed like a mile long. My mother was loved by so many. And by the time I got home there were no more '*wepts*' in me. My mom was loved by many. Too bad she didn't know quite how to love herself.

At home my brother went downstairs with his friends and sat silent. My dad was in the living room with family, and I was in the bedroom with my friends in all my glory. I was now the center of attention and I loved it. I had done enough crying and now I was laughing with all my friends around me. One of my friends, Michael, came up to me and said the stupidest thing. He said, "Well, you said you hated her anyway. I didn't think you would be so upset." That statement hit me like a dull kitchen knife to the heart; it pushed but didn't pierce. How could he say such a thing and how could I feel such a thing that I would say that to a friend?

> *People have told me I have made some idiotic remarks and that was just the beginning of a life full of 'how I wish I could take that back' kind of statements.*

At that moment my dad came into the room and told me to keep it down. He then told me later to look around the room because I would never see these people again in a week or two. He told me that family would probably not be available as they would go back to their own lives and routines. When a parent kills him or herself, usually loved ones around feel a sense of guilt. I felt humiliation. It was a reflection on me and who I was. I was Carol's kid and if Carol was so messed up then so I should be. All of a sudden I was branded and I was not sure how to deal with this internal humiliation.

Excuses

My mother's death became the basis for illegitimate excuses in my life. I went to the Student Guidance Counselor and said I couldn't go to the gym because my mother had died and I was depressed. I don't even remember if they gave me another class or I just had free time during that period. I used

24

her death as an excuse not to have to face the gym and the boys' locker room. So I smoked pot during Health Ed instead. I wore the black ribbon that Jewish mourners wear. I wore it for six weeks in school so as to get the attention I was missing from my mom, from my peers. Everything that happened to me during the next few months had the excuse "You see my mom is dead and I am all messed up."

I was in eighth grade and started to hang with some of the students who were into school. This was not by choice, so it must have been Divine Intervention. In seventh grade I was slowly slipping into the Hitter crowd. In eighth grade I spent more time with kids in my class - a class consisting of over-achievers. My concentration was not good, and the pot smoking did not help either, but I wanted some stability and focus. I don't remember having any relationship with my brother that year. And my dad just didn't know what to do.

I hated myself for using my mother's death as an excuse but there was truth in the justification. One night I went out with Jackie, my unknown to both of us lesbian girlfriend, and got drunk off my ass at someone's house. I started to cry and scream for my mom. I was putting it on and screaming "mommy come back", why did you have to kill yourself. By that time Jackie was the only one I confided in that my mother didn't only die from a cerebral hemorrhage. I was getting more and more into the screaming and the attention and then I wound up at home with my mother's younger sister, my dearest Aunt Joanne, and my dad. I was throwing up all over the place. That night, I think, I was the closest to my dad that I would ever be and it surrounded our inability to both control our liquor. He held me that night as I slept in his room with him. Although my dad was a part of my life until I was 33, I don't think we were ever that close or connected like that again.

Excuses became my middle name and I didn't apply myself to anything for almost two years. The only thing I did was audition for High School of the Performing Arts in the early ninth grade, and I didn't use any excuse with that. In fact, I had just gotten over chicken pox for the second time when I had to audition for the school. I barely made it through eighth grade. My grades slowly dropped and I could see the disappointment in my dad's face every time he received my report card. Thank god for my brother. Although my dad and brother did not get along, my brother did well in school and that made my father proud. But my father was 'support challenged,'

> *When my brother turned to my father for some bereavement support my dad said, "There is nothing you can do, she is dead, just get over it."*

Life just was not the same and there was nothing anyone of us could do about it.

The Ponderosa

Shortly after my mother's death my favorite cousins were spending time at this dude ranch called Sunnycroft Ponderosa, which was in Walkhill, NY. They thought it would be a good idea for my dad and me to come too. My brother didn't want to go. My cousin Denise and her parents would be up there every weekend, and the escapades of that family could be a whole chapter. Douglas, Denise's brother, like my brother, would not come up either. Douglas was gorgeous, and so were his parents. Marsha and Sheldon, Douglas and Denise's parents, had just had another baby, named Darren. So it was Denise, Marsha, Darren and Sheldon.

I immediately fell in love with the dude ranch and wanted to go back as soon as I could. My cousins would go every weekend and then, gradually, my dad and I would go too. I think my dad liked it because he was getting laid and he didn't have to supervise me. I was busy having fun. During the week I was spending a little more time at my cousin's house since Denise was just one year older than me and I was in desperate need of a family. One day when I was at their house, Denise brought up the fact that she knew my mom killed herself. I felt so invaded by her bringing this up and it was difficult for me to be around her after that without feeling vengeful.

The Ponderosa gave me the opportunity to get away from Canarsie and get away from my life. I started to spend more time at the stables with the wranglers and the hacks. But I did not blend in. I was in RedneckVille, where men were men and women weren't. The hotel would give me a room to sleep by the barn, so it made me feel like I was one of the workers. Slowly, I was trusted with a beginner's ride and I would lead the ride out on the tour of the land. I was smoking cigarettes and drinking and smoking pot and thought I was all grown up. The Ponderosa was a gift and a detriment to my future. My school week focused on being upstate and not on school or my academic future. The Ponderosa also gave me the time not to have to figure out a relationship with my dad. He just gave me money and I went off. I had no adult supervision up there and I began to realize more and more how different I was from other guys.

I had experienced very little physical bashing because of my femininity until I went to the Ponderosa. One day I came out of my room to go to work in the barn and this guy ran out naked screaming at me, saying "I know you want this, you f..ing fag, come and get it." I was best friends with his girlfriend, a chambermaid. I didn't know why he was picking on me and I was all excited to see him naked in front of me. It seemed like he knew something about me that I wasn't discussing, or he was all upset about his girlfriend's relationship with me. Or he saw something in me that kicked up something in him. All I knew was that he hurt my feelings and I couldn't stop looking at him.

I fell in love with my first man at the Ponderosa. He was tall, dark and handsome and his name was Eddy. He must have been around 23 years old. We used to smoke pot all the time together. Every day he would say, "One day I am going to get you so high I am going to make you suck my dick." Every time we were together I would say, "Oh my god, I am so high," but Eddy never crossed that line. He used to call me Guzano, which means 'worm' in Spanish. When I was eighteen years old I went back to the Ponderosa as Roe and knocked on his door. He said, "Do I know you?" and I told him it was Guzana.

ADDICTION

4.
SEXUAL
CATEGORICAL
DEFIANCE AND
ADDICTION

4

Sexual Categorical Defiance and Addiction

Adolescence and my succeeding Puberty

I started to enjoy not being in my skin by using substances that took me outside of myself. I repeatedly reached out to and for alcohol, pot, sex and food.

When I graduated ninth grade my dad married this woman by the name of Gail. He decided to buy a four-bedroom, three-storey house in Wantagh, Long Island. We were paying $100 a month rent for our apartment in Canarsie. We were leaving this house, this house that had seen the death of my Uncle Abe upstairs, the death of my mom downstairs, the death of a childhood full of hamsters, cats, birds and dogs. This house was the only house I had ever known, but it was a house I was ready to leave. There was no more security within these four walls.

> *My mom's last letter to me and my brother in sleep-away camp the summer of '73, "My darling ... now I know what they mean, a house is not a home without my children. These four and a half rooms are just a house ... have fun, miss you very much ... all my love, mommy."*

For the past one and a half years this house had been just a house, haunted with secrets, lies, confusion, remorse and loneliness. My mom's clothes were gone so I didn't have access to the 'real' me. My mom was gone, so I didn't have access to the support I needed. This house was no longer a home. I had little parental guidance, and I spent most of my weekends up in Monticello, New York with Denise, Darren, Marsha and her new boyfriend Bobby. Sheldon and Marsha split and got into new relationships. Marsha played house with Bobby, a head wrangler from Sunnycroft, and Sheldon later met a wonderful woman by the name of Claire. It seemed to work out for all.

My father was getting married and we were supposed to be leaving this tortured past behind. I didn't realize it then, but we were leaving my Aunt Hannah all alone. She had put up with my family for seventeen years. She had family here and now we were leaving her. That apartment with use of the basement could have easily gone for $400 in 1973. We lived well because we paid so little rent. Now my dad bought a house, was taking on a mortgage and high taxes, and had his business lease a Cadillac for him and his new partner. From the outside we looked like we were doing great. I wasn't the only addict in the family.

My father was around 41 years old and probably was desperate to get a parental figure for his children and a body in his bed. Gail was his choice. Gail had long brown hair and sculptured, perfectly polished nails. Gail was a jeweler. She had a son who was eleven years old. In external appearance Gail was the opposite of my mother. Although I thought my mom to be gorgeous, my mom was a cross between Carol Lawrence, Dolly Parton, Ru Paul and Tammy Faye Baker. She was always dolled up. Gail wore hardly any makeup and she wore her own hair. She came from a different era. My dad was seeking a new life and it was totally the opposite of what he had had with my mom. I remember telling my dad that if this is what would make him happy then I was all for it. And on some level I was. But I knew deep down in my heart that my life with this family would never happen again, and because my family of origin ended on such a tragic note I played a part in making sure there was no 'family' left for me to be a part of.

I was accepted into the High School of the Performing Arts (PA) and was excited to go to school in New York City. I was excited to have the opportunity to redecorate another room in another house and I was stoned most of the time on pot so I was excited about spending more time alone sexually dreaming about Michael Mazza, Bobby Savader, and Michael Rabinowitz, or '*cock a doodle do, any c..k will do.*'

As soon as these two families merged there were many fights and uncomfortable situations. The dynamics of these two groups of people coming together did not work. My brother was identified as the troublemaker because I would complain to my brother and he would complain to Gail and my dad, and nothing would ever get settled. My dad wanted Gail to be our new mom and, for sure, my brother was not allowing this trollop to ever take his mother's place. I just needed someone desperately to nurture me and this woman was not going to play the role of nurturer. She was going to be real with me. She let me know that she didn't think I had any talent, which on some level was true. She let me know that I was in her way when I was in her way. She also showed me how not to be a stepmother. One weekend at the end of the summer, right before my brother was going off to college, there was a big blow out. My brother got real nasty with Gail and my father turned to us and said, "Don't you dare talk to your mother that way." My brother was infuriated and started screaming, "This whore ain't my mother," and Gail jumped in and started to say, "Let me tell you some things you don't know about your mother." I hated the confrontations and I wanted it all to end. I was also curious about what she had to say since I wasn't sure who my mother actually was. Why did she kill herself? My mother, that is, not Gail, darnit!

I felt bad for Gail's son, my dog was unhappy, and all I wanted was to get high and fantasize.

I met a kid next door. I was the city kid moving to the suburbs and I played it up like I had it together. My cousin Marsha (Denise's mom) gave me a humungous bag of what was thought to be marijuana and I sold it to my neighbor for five dollars. My neighbor and some of his friends got arrested with the bag of pot in the schoolyard and they sent the cops to my house. I had just moved in and was already causing trouble in the neighborhood. On a deep level I considered myself tainted goods. My mom killed herself, I was differently gendered, I was attracted to boys but slept with girls, and I already had a drug problem.

The pot turned out to be oregano, everyone was relieved, this boy next door thought I was trying to get one over on him, and there went the new friendship. I was branded **T** for trouble in Wantagh, Long Island. I think it was a saving grace that I did not stay friends with him or attend high school out there. I think the jocks, the hicks, the racists and the sexist attitude would have eaten me up alive in Wantagh High. Even though I was, high that is!

High School Humility

Starting high school was exciting and scary. I stood outside the school on 47th Street between 6th and 7th Avenue in Manhattan. I had to take the Long Island Rail Road (LIRR) to Penn Station 34th Street and then take the train to 47th and 50th Street, Rockefeller Center. Up until this time I had always walked to school and now I was commuting. There was all this sexual and frightening energy on the LIRR and the MTA. There was always some man either flashing me or playing with himself or trying to talk to me on those commuter trains. It was all so sexually and physically crowded. I was not sure why men were publicly coming on to me or why all of this was so frightening and exciting at the same time. But I had to play it cool. I had to get from point A to point B without anyone knowing I didn't quite belong. In order to attend this high school you had to be a resident of NY, which I now was not any longer. We kept my Brooklyn address and what would get lost, besides myself, was the continuous communication between the school and my legal guardian, my dad. In Bildersee Junior High School my talents stood out. Here, in this high school, it was all about talented young hopefuls. I was just one of many. Without the ability to nurture myself, keep trying, and be the best that I could be it was a setup for failure. By this time in life I was so confused and unsure of myself. I was using pot often, I was so attracted to men and felt I had to hide this, and I was so uncomfortable presenting myself the way I was because I was not developing like the rest of the boys around me. I was not a young man, I was not a young girl, I did not believe in myself, I was not happy at home, I did not know how to apply myself, I did not feel encouraged, and I did not feel loved. In '70s Freddie Prince had just graduated, Isaac Mizrahi was a freshman, and I was taking classes with Gina Belafonte. These kids had real talent. It seemed like they were going places or coming from something. I should've been excited surrounded by all this life but I was scared, lonely, needed to be the center of attention, and I was not. I connected with a group of kids and started dating this girl Caroline. She was beautiful with long blonde hair and the most exquisite bedroom eyes. The first Halloween while I was attending PA I was invited to a party in Queens. I got ready at Caroline's house and went to the party as Caroline. I remember her father looking at me in disgust as I was taking his daughter out to a party dressed up as his daughter. Did he know something I was not ready to face or talk about? We got to the party and all the guys were playing with me and rubbing against me and laughing and paying attention to me. I was in heaven. At one point one of the girls wanted to try on my wig and I was indignant about her taking it off my head. I was Caroline for the night and refused to relinquish the identity. Caroline's hair didn't come off and neither did mine.

I spent one and a half years at PA and this is where my true sexual identity began to surface. There was a redhead who was identified as female in the school who looked just like David Bowie. In fact, that was her whole idea. One day we were standing around in a circle and someone said that this person was a transexual. I asked them what a transexual was and they gave me the medical description. All at once my life, my identity, my soul, my core, finally had a definition. And right in front of me there was someone who was experiencing the same exact things that I must've been experiencing. But for some reason this person seemed much more at ease with him/herself then I did.

> *I didn't figure it out until much later while doing the social justice work that I do that this had a lot more to do with the patriarch system which I will discuss in later chapters.*

That summer, after the first year of high school, I began implementing this journey to 'self.' I came back to school the fall of '76 looking androgynous and, slowly, towards winter break I broke the rules surrounding 'gender appropriateness' and demanded the students and teachers call me first Rhonda and then Roe. Shortly thereafter I was called into the Director's office and was told I couldn't come to school dressed the way I was dressed.

I was told I had been accepted into this school as a boy and couldn't come dressed as a girl. I argued that I had been accepted because of my talents not my gender, but they didn't budge and I didn't really care anymore anyway. Although it was disheartening I was not concentrating on school, I was failing my classes, and my talent and chutzpah seemed depleted within this milieu anyway.

Addiction and the Street Scene
"The Freaks Come Out at Night ... The Freaks Come Out at Night."
The summer before I was asked to leave school, a mild way to state institutional transphobia, discrimination, ignorance and intolerance, I was spending more and more time away from my home in Long Island and staying with friends and school chums in New York, Brooklyn, Queens and New Jersey. I wanted to go out 'dressed' as much as possible and the only way I could do this was if I was at somebody else's house.

> *Now I know you must be asking yourself, "What the hell? Did this kid go out naked before deciding to go out dressed? What the hell is wrong here?" So when I say 'dressed,' I mean dressed in clothing that celebrated that part of me that was 'Roe.'*

I picked the name Roe, instead of Rhonda, because one of my brother's girlfriends was named Roe and I thought she was the coolest. (I am using this jargon because this is the seventies, man, and, like, man, she was cool). I would find myself going from house to house and becoming more and more transient. There was this girl I went to school with whose father was killed in the 1975 fire at the Blue Angel, a trendy New York City nightclub. I didn't know until later that this club catered to drag queens and their admirers. This girl and her mom would let me get dressed up at their house and then I would get on the train and go to the city, New York City that is ... Times Square. I think they got a kick out of me. I am not sure what the correlation was, if any, to me getting dolled up and her dad, but I know getting dressed there was a positive experience.

For some reason my fear did not keep me from going out alone, going out dressed as Roe, traveling on public transportation, etc. I just did it. Some days I would find myself on the Long Island Railroad going back to my dad's house, to 1599 Roland Avenue in Wantagh, NY, and I would change in the bathroom of the train. I would go in looking lovely and come out this ambiguous, androgynous kid. I wonder what the neighbors, my train buddies, would think?

I very seldom got harassed and I never got beat up. Go figure!

I became more familiar and comfortable with the streets. As I searched through doorways of queer-identified bars and hidden alleyways, within my mind I began to lose myself and find myself, if that makes any sense.

I had already experienced gay culture but knew I didn't fit in perfectly within that milieu. I hung out at the Broadway Bar in Brooklyn and spent some time in some Latino/a venues, The Hollywood and the Ipanema. And, as I showed up for life, I needed more substances to keep me warm and safe.

Father's Ignorance

I used my father's house as a stopping ground, an unfriendly hotel, a place to slow down when things were getting too speedy. I knew my father had bought this house so that he could have a family again. He was looking for a mother for his children without thinking about the work he needed to participate in, in order for this to transpire. One of his children had already gone away to college and his other child had no foundation to family responsibility. I had no boundaries. I had no specific responsibilities. I was using drugs. I was lost in a socially constructed gender war and no one knew. I was lost in sexual fantasy and instant gratification, and I was not even attending school in Long Island, so I was not building a foundation there. His new wife was not really interested in making a family with my brother or me, and until I dated a man with children I did not realize what part I played in messing this marriage up.

My dog Chebe was so unhappy in that house, and I knew that because all he did was pee in the house. One weekend I was away and they put Chebe to sleep. Chebe was my mother's dog, even though my mother had never wanted him. They put Chebe to sleep and that was the last straw, so I thought. I didn't take into consideration that I was not taking on any of the responsibilities of the dog. I was just on my own taking care of my needs and no one else in this family mattered. But I was furious about what they did to Chebe.

It was getting more difficult to hide my transgression of gender and one weekend I came home with nail polish on and was yelled at. I said I was in a play in New York and no one questioned it. One weekend I came home and they had gone through my dresser. They had found pot, needles and crab medicine. I was enraged they had intruded upon my privacy, not being used to a family crossing that boundary. I had to explain all three. I said I was holding the needles and pot for a friend. I was a great liar. I had had a lot of practice. And about the crabs, well, I couldn't say I got it from Red Lobster! The next week I came home with a book by the late Harry Benjamin titled 'A Transsexual Phenomenon,' I told my dad that I wanted to start hormone therapy, and he said if I did that I would have to move out. I had already started, so that night I left.

Carrie and Ellen

I left that house in Long Island and met up with two friends from Canarsie, Ellen and Carrie. Ellen was our leader. She had spent time in Spaffa Correctional facility. Spaffa was a detention home for youth. She owned her false sense of 'power'. She possessed charisma, chutzpah, and a great deal of potential. Ellen didn't know how much latent talent she possessed so she never used her abilities in a vocational arena. Ellen had balls. She was the first woman I ever met who had balls. Well, she didn't literally have balls. I've met many women after her who literally did have balls, including myself (little ones, and sometimes undescended).

Carrie, her younger sister, was my age. Carrie had a lot of inherent desires and talents but few possibilities. Carrie and I dated when we were eight years old and, again, at eleven. Little did we know we were involved in a lesbian affair at such an early age. Carrie and Ellen were very interesting women. They were streetwise, cunning, and a lot of fun. Ellen definitely had charm and Carrie was a smartass. They were both cute, pale, and could move on the dance floor. What more could someone want from life? Of course, I was jealous. I was half a girl. I only dreamt of being totally female. Oh god, please make me Barbie! They were my mentors into the lost-world. They will always own a place in my heart. We went through the worst of our adolescence together.

Ellen was involved with a man named David. Ellen, Carrie and I had no steady place to live. We would sometimes return home for food or shelter, but most of the time we would wander the streets of New York. I had just left PA and Carrie was leaving this alternative high school. And Ellen, well, school was not her forte. David was a big man and that was school enough for her. David dealt pot on 'the deuce'. He was one of many drug dealers on that street in the '70s. 42nd Street was seedy and colorful. This was where homeless youth connected to the wheelers and dealers, the prostitutes and their pimps, the insurgent, the freaks, the anomalous, the lost and the found. There were songs that stated what 'the deuce' was like. 'The deuce' attracted freaks, thieves, hookers and addicts. You know, what society deems scum of the earth. These were people who had no shade on who they were. They were just what they were, without camouflage! This is where Ellen met her sweetheart David, Carrie met her boyfriends, and I found my future.

David, Ellen, Carrie and I were this new family. David was our man. He watched out for us. Our first home besides the Port Authority was north of 42nd Street.

Transient Hotel Life
43rd Street Dump, the Strand Hotel

A man came to the window with a knife one night while David was hard at work selling beat pot on 'the deuce'. Ellen was in the shower, and I was on the toilet. He started to bang on the glass. Ellen and I ran out of the room and down the hall. Nobody in the hotel was particularly interested in our account of this incident. For months after that incident I needed someone to be with while I sat on the toilet, and if there was a window, I just couldn't relax. Imagine trying to talk someone into sitting with you while you were performing peristalsis?

Another night, David, Ellen, Carrie and I were all asleep in one bed. We were hit over the head and robbed by the intruders. They stole our future rent money, which consisted of unsold half marijuana, half oregano baggies. The next day we had to pack up our belongings into fresh, green, giant garbage bags and head uptown like the Jeffersons, except we were moving to a bigger dump on the Westside, nowhere near the 'deluxe apartment in the sky.' We moved to the Landseer Hotel, where I met my future mentors within the 'drag' community.

The Landseer Hotel

The Landseer Hotel was filled with more diversity. This hotel didn't just house pimps. It housed pimps, prostitutes, drag queens, eccentric artists, welfare recipients, and those with many axis I and II diagnoses. The drag queens were fabulous. They were bad, black and gorgeous. You did not fuck with these queens. They had style, flair and could read you to filth (they could tell you off and cut you down literally with their tongues). We had a friend by the name of Kathy living in this hotel. Kathy was an extremely overweight, beautiful white chick who swore she 'wuz black.' She lived with Hah 'Huzband' who dated one of the queens on the side. This was low-life Peyton Place.

> *My mother used to sit in front of the television set watching Peyton Place while smoking a pack of Pall Malls in the late 1960s. She would sit there and cry and I would stand in the corner and giggle. And now I was living Peyton Place and I was the one crying, but not on a couch, I didn't have one.*

Life in low-life Peyton Place was never dull. Our days and nights consisted of, but were not limited to, being chased by people with guns, hiding from police, taking the train back to Brooklyn, sneaking into Carrie and Ellen's mom's house to steal food, hanging out on 'the deuce', and hustling money for rent. We would, *well not me,* beat up on other kids on the train because others would make fun of me because of my femininity. We would hustle quarters on the street to get into clubs or to eat.

Ellen and I shared some other things as well. While living at the Landseer Ellen would deviate from her relationship with David. Ellen and I would pick up guys at clubs and we would fornicate right in front of each other, well, side by side, well, in the same abandoned building. Ellen and I also got beat up because of it, together. One night, after David had given us both a beating for sleeping around, we slept in Central Park. One and a half white girls (*society still considered me androgynous*) lost in midtown together! One and a half white girls lost!

Back to the Landseer Hotel…

I remember one mighty big pimp being really friendly with me. David and Ellen would tell me to be careful because many pimps snatch kids up and you would never see them again. (What a homey, secure feeling the Landseer afforded me!)

I remember when I first saw Kelly and Vicky, two amazing, nasty and arrogant queens. They would strut through the hotel with such attitude. I wanted to be just like them, confident and powerful. They demanded so much attention. When I first met Kelly I had already heard so much about her. She was the DRAG QUEEN who was stealing Kathy's husband. Kathy's husband would tell us that he just hung out with her for the money and they were just friends. Then, as real as daylight, I saw her. She had a 'doorag' on her head, a lime green tube top, tight jeans, and come-fuck me pumps. She was bigger than life. What a figure! She had breasts! Real breasts, silicone or not, they were hers. I was amazed. Her girlfriends were real fem as well. I was in awe. Kelly read me. "You a woman honey. You'll be in them soon enough." Did she know I was transexual? Didn't she know that was a compliment? Was she trying to be friendly? Her friend came up and on to me. *"No, he won't,"* Vicky asserted. "I like me a young white boy," she hollered. You should come visit me." So I did. I was scared to death but I wanted, I needed, to be close to them, no, to be them, to be 'me.' I went to their room where Vicky was undressing. Her whole body was constructed with padding. It was a puzzle. She was an artist the way she put herself together. *My mother would do the same thing* so Vicky, my mother, Dolly Parton, and Tammy Faye weren't that different. Vicky started to come on to me when Kelly said, "Leave the sister alone, Vicky. She's just like us."

Vicky was vibrant, funny, caddy, comical and alive. Around a month after I met the Black Charlie's Angels they found Vicky splattered in the back of the hotel. They say she jumped off the roof, but Kelly said she was pushed.

All I know is this was another introduction to the rest of my life.

I began to hang out in Kelly's room all the time after that event and at first Kelly appreciated the company, even if it was with someone from a different cultural experience and mindset. But soon enough Kelly got tired of me hanging around and borrowing her clothes. She saw me becoming a burden. I adopted Kelly as my mentor. She honored the role for a moment.

There were some interesting escapades between Kelly, Kathy, her husband and Ellen. Ellen slept with Kelly once. Ellen needed to prove something about her femininity and Kelly wanted to have one over on David, Ellen's man. Are you confused? Well, so were we. I think all of us at the Landseer Hotel were befuddled. Not about Ellen, non-trans female sleeping with Kelly, drag-queen, or non-trans-heavy-female Kathy's husband, Latino-non-trans male who likes non-trans-heavy-women and black-drag-queens Kelly, but about the complexities of life and oppression.

This hotel was filled with sexual transients. We were truly the melting pot. Sex was a ploy, a business, a way of life, a powerful mechanism to be utilized for fun or authority. It was fun and exciting, simple and complex.

David, Ellen's man, would ask me to perform fellatio on him. I was still identified as an effeminate boy perceived as passive. This was acceptable to David. But David would never ask Kelly, a gorgeous, sexy queen to fool around. He was turned off by her. Gender, sex and sexuality really threw many people for a loop. Yet it was one of the devices we were all strongly connected to.

> *When someone is attractive and they have the power to turn others on, it pushes buttons. Especially if you are excited by something or someone that you feel should not have that type of power over you.*

David did not want to experience any excitement over Kelly. Kelly was a hard-ass black woman from the south who had a penis. I had a penis but David could get turned on by me. And David was straight and Kelly was gorgeous and I looked ridiculous.

> *There were definite gender issues but no such thing as color barriers within the hotel. We got together and nurtured each other in a way that I'd never experienced before.*

41

Hormones began to change me physically and my transition changed my relationships with Carrie, Ellen, David and the other straight, hip, 42nd Street men I interacted with. There was one man in particular named David. He was Ellen's boyfriend's friend. A lot of these guys were named David – big David, little David, David with crabs, Big Man David ... All Davids accepted me as an effeminate white boy, but not as a neo-queen/trans-woman. David used to tell me he liked me. Which one? Take your pick. He was straight. But he said he liked me. Which one? Take your pick. When I started to live full time he told me that I shouldn't. He told me that I was going to turn out to be just like the other drag queens and I looked silly in make-up. Queens were on the bottom of this social hierarchy. All of this was confusing to me. Here were these straight men who liked me. I really felt more feminine and wanted to express that side of me. But when I finally allowed my deepest emotions to surface, I wasn't 'liked' anymore.

What do you think his sexuality was and how do you think this affected me, and what the hell does all this mean?

5.
FANTASY-SEX
.....Prerequisites Geared Towards My Ph.D

the Club Scene...
BROADWAY
Virginity Lost at
the Hollywood Continental Baths
I'm Coming Out
the Gilded Grape

5

Fantasy-Sex ... prerequisites geared towards my Ph.D.

The Club Scenes ...

Note:
> Before we move along in transition, let's take a step back and review the cultural environment that assisted in the developmental stages of transition. Contextually one might understand the foundation set for the future.

Broadway
I went to a club called The Broadway in Brooklyn and the Hollywood in Manhattan. The Broadway was my initiation into Queer Culture. It was a thrilling time. I consider the **Broadway** and the **Hollywood** the freshman years of my informal education. They were the foundation for the next ten years of my existence. I'm a little confused about age and time period. From fourteen to eighteen years of age so much transpired that it tends to amalgamate. I am somewhat jumbled about that time in my life. Therefore, when this book becomes a best seller, any of you who survived this era and knew me, please do not attack my inconsequential inconsistencies, ALL RIGHT?
However, I will NEVER fail to remember the emotions that transpired within those years as well as the decadent existence that I inhabited.

I'll never forget - I promise not to keep repeating 'I'll never forget' - New Year's Eve at the Broadway in Brooklyn. It had to be 1974 or '75. Two things transpired; I met my first drag queen and I engaged in my first public sexual act, not with the drag queen. That would be incestuous.
The drag queen's name was Candy. She was the 'talk' of the Broadway. Everyone knew who she was because she was frighteningly beautiful and just as unapproachable. I saw Candy and I was in awe of her. She brought more reality to my existence.

> *I think non-trans people are always in awe of the transgender people who seem to be 'pulling it off.' Also, I think we dehumanize the beautiful people in our society. And that is what I did with Candy.*

46

I dehumanized her. Her being a drag queen was inconceivable. Before Candy, I had never heard of, or seen, a drag queen besides the one in the mirror. I was thrilled by the feelings of seeing her. I would watch Candy's every move within the disco. However, I wouldn't dare approach her. She was royalty and I was a peasant.

> *I ran into Candy in the early 1990s on 14th Street in Manhattan. This is right around the corner from the LGBT Community Services Center in Manhattan. Imagine this? Candy was one block away from where the LGBT communities appear collectively and here was Candy, twenty years later, isolated, on the street, and beaten down. Candy's appearance brought to light the stormy life of a drag queen. We were never close friends. In fact, we never formally met at the Broadway. I was an admirer from afar. I was a drag queen wannabe. In the 1970s Candy was a vision of loveliness. In the 1990s I observed how life handles many drag queens and I became more and more enraged. In fact, as I write, I could throw this computer to the ground. However, I wouldn't be able to finish this story and get to meet all those people I haven't met yet or do the book circuit, or tell this story ... So I will contain for the sake of your future. Candy was a Role Model. Candy was someone who showed me from afar that there was a reality to all of my fantasies. To see her destruction broke my heart. She was the beginning as to what the rest of my life was going to look like. It isn't fair. She deserved better.*

One of my other tales, and I have many, much like my grandmother, involved New Year's Eve at the Broadway. We will call this 'The blow-job.' It was performed on me by a good-looking, redheaded, young femme/butch queen. I ran into this man 25 years later in 12-Step rooms, and how awkward was that?

In the Broadway I masqueraded as a butch queen (top/aggressor), all the while wanting to be just like Candy. I met this guy and he met me, under the table. I sat there sipping on my little rum and coke and he hid under the table sipping on my little ... I watched Candy and he ate some.

> *Ru Paul, the infamous drag queen, said it best, "We are born naked, then the rest of our life is drag." Pretending to be male was drag, and the rest of my life would be a magnitude of drag. Professional, sexual, social, informal and formal drag are tools I use to interact within the world. Life, to me, is a costume ball. This is not fantasy.*

47

> This is my reality. I appreciate performing life. Within this performance, I live. When I identified as a boy, people would call me a girl. When I transitioned from what others perceive as male to female, people were upset with my neoteric female identity. I think we all masquerade emotionally as well as physically. It's called living. The 'club-scene' was not actually living, but it was a significant avenue for someone interested in drag, theatre, pretend, fantasy and escape.
>
> As soon as I walked, or hustled, into my first disco, I knew that this was where I belonged. The 'disco' allowed me the freedom from me, my life, the tragedy of my family, the loss of my mother, my gender identity, and it also rid me of many responsibilities. This was a 'Freedom' that I would pay a substantial price for, and sometimes life was just that, a drag.

Virginity Lost at the Hollywood

I knew the appeals of sex and sexuality from a young age. I experienced many sexual encounters as a young boy, a very young boy. I'm not speaking about intercourse, I am talking about the art of fondling, masturbation, getting hand-jobs and having fellatio performed on me. I was thirteen years old and had already lost my perceived-male virginity, being a top, not a good one, but a top nonetheless. Now I was going to lose my virginity to a male, a Latino male, an older Latino male. It was time to pay up for being allowed into the Hollywood. Ellen coaxed me into going home with the Bartender.

I don't recall the Bartender's name and I've lost sight of many names of men that I conquered, I mean slept with, I mean…. The Bartender took me to the South Bronx. That was the onset of this scary event. No, I'm not South Bronx-phobic.

It was unfamiliar territory. It was a terrifying ordeal trying to find my way home from the South Bronx, if one can call a fleabag hotel in NYC a home. We utilized what is generically called poppers/amyl nitrate. He entered me and relinquished me from my second, but not final, virginity. This sexual experience was much the same as my first loss of virginity. This was nondescript. My first was with Jackie. Jackie was a wonderful girl but sex with her was nondescript as well. It had nothing to do with her. She was a hot little dyke in the making. It had everything to do with me, my self-centeredness, my inability to see beyond me, and my gender identity confusion. I entered Jackie and had an orgasm instantaneously. It seemed that this man entered me, finished, and I left. Can we say déjà vu?

Leaving the South Bronx was the true experience. I'm surprised that I wasn't an article within the NY Post: **Androgynous Person Murdered in**

the South Bronx, traces of nondescript Latino sperm surrounding Androgynous Person's anus.

I learned at an early age that sex could be a tool to get what you needed in life. Ellen, Carrie and I were allowed to enter the Hollywood many times for free after that sexual escapade. The only question I had was why did I have to do it?

Back to the Hollywood and my escapades!

But first, some more views about the ambiance of the club.

I know I'm objectifying and merely sexualizing them, but the Hollywood was filled with hot, straight-looking Latino men. As the homophobic adage asserts, I was happier than a 'Fag in Boys Town' and I was also twice as intimidated. This was a mixed club with the majority being heterosexual. But my presentation was 'little-boy drag,' and my femininity would always surface. I was fourteen or fifteen years old, I had no identification and I was partying the night away with my girl friends in this adult disco. We were way underage. The bouncers let us in anyway. It pays to know the right people.

Whatever I looked like was irrelevant to what was in store for me. I was on my first of many runs. This was a run from life and from me. This was a run from my father and his wife who had no control over me and didn't seem to own their responsibility towards me anyway. It sounds like a victim role, doesn't it? Well, at fifteen years old, it was. I partied and soul-searched with liquor, weed, the bump, and the hustle. I was a very nervous young person. I was insecure, confused, lost, bewildered, sad, and excited. The nightlife was frightening and invigorating. I can never forget the feelings the Hollywood stirred in me. It was sexuality and superficiality. It was the inception of a complicating, uncomplicated existence. It was a place I lost my boyhood and unearthed my femaleness. It was a place I got lost.

Continental Baths

I recall, I didn't say 'I'll never forget,' going to the Continental Baths. The Continental Baths was a club/bathhouse mostly catering to gay men. You'd walk in and smell the sensuality, the forbidden fruits, and the spermazoa! Men were everywhere. Latin men, Black men, White men, were everywhere. The Continental Baths had lockers to keep your clothes in and rooms where male hustlers spent the night. Imagine a club with lockers for your clothes. The Men went to the lockers. I hung out with the fag hags, *women who love to date gay men.* I was frightened by all this sensuality yet I was dying to partake in the festivities of the locker room and the hustle boys. But all I got were the fag hags to connect with. Somehow, for some reason, I just didn't fit in. Although the majority who frequented the

Continental Baths were gay men, there were many straight male hustlers and women who would participate in the festivities. Bette Midler was a tremendous hit at the Continental Baths in the early 1970s, but I wasn't. I wonder why?

How did I get involved in the club scene? I did not fall into this arena on my own cognition. I was led by other deviant night prowlers. We entered the battle 'together.'

The Gilded Grape/I'm Coming Out ...

Diana Ross wasn't the only one ...

I'll never forget (since I am so good at not forgetting, can somebody please tell me where I left my car keys?) the first time I appeared in public dressed. Dressed in female attire, that is. I had been dressed in public before, but this was not nursery school, play with juvenescent friends, Halloween, a sleep-away camp show, or a high school party. This was real life!

This was *Harry Benjamin's International Gender Dysphoria Association HBIGDA guidelines for transexuals, which states you must dress and live in the opposite sex for a certain period of time before you can be considered for hormone therapy HT or sex reassignment surgery SRS. This was the [sic]* 'real-life test' (1990, HBIGDA Standards of Care).

I had some transitory thoughts. Will I be murdered as I was coming out, I mean really coming out, and I mean every day, not just on the weekend kind of thing? After all, this was not just 'dress up' going from any friend's house to a club, I was serious. I was living in New York and this was Times Square and I got a taste of how my friends on 'the deuce' were going to react.

'Coming Out Balls' within the elite culture are thrown all the time but I was never invited. This was 'My Official Coming Out' soiree. This was not for the privileged young women who get to meet and greet eligible bachelors. I was not a privileged anything in anybody's eyes. I had the opportunity to meet tricks, rapists and thugs.

> *There were a few genuinely nice men on 8th Avenue I am sure, but this part of the city was drenched with perversion, although my objective here is not to judge tricks and thugs.*

Within the elite courting practice young women are presented to their male counterparts. I was accosted. Young available women date young gentlemen. There were no age restrictions on 8th Avenue. Young religious girls keep themselves occupied with other important activities until they are ready for marriage and copulation, while young religious boys, not all so don't quote me on this, visit 8th Avenue. My Coming Out, my courting system, my corner of this aristocratic initiation was a stroll down 8th Avenue to an infamous drag club called the Gilded Grape. In the sociologically focused volume 'Honey, Honey Miss Thang,' Detra, a black femme queen speaks about strolling the streets in a white see-through dress, high-heels and being perceived as a model. That was her description.

For me, Coming Out was filled with fear, trepidation, excitement, exploration and freedom. And what was the price? My courting system, my arena to be courted, and my prerogative to 'meet and greet' were devoid of deference.

> *Many people of transgender experience are perceived as deviant, sick, or are not identified in the way that is most respectful to who we are.*
>
> *Author of Honey, Honey Miss Thang, Leon Pettiway, attempts to explain the coming out process for the femme, the TS, the street queen. He made an effort to be supportive but doesn't get the whole gender experience. He connects it wholly to gayness. Coming out as gay is a different experience taking into consideration basic demographics, examples being age, race, economic status ... Coming out as trans and physically, emotionally and spiritually celebrating that identity, everything in your life, your mindset, is revolutionized. This is not about an orientation that doesn't fit neatly within our heterosexist culture. It challenges societal construct, our legal system, bathroom culture, vocational space, academic arenas, church, state ... It challenges and reconstructs all power within western civilization. And it affects all basic belief systems including, but not limited to, how many leaves Adam and Eve are allowed to display.*

Coming Out on 8th Avenue and going into the Gilded Grape had nothing to do with my questioning my sexual orientation. It had to do with my gender expression. That might be gayness to some folk, but it was not my ideation. Leon Pettiway and the rest of our culture have a different meaning and sometimes denounce this experience.

Walking down 8th Avenue and into a fleabag hole in the wall was my justification, my nourishment, and my connection to self-acceptance. And no matter what I lost as I walked into that environment, the road to owning 'me' was worth every cent.

So what were my options or my expectations as I came out?

I strutted and shook on those black stiletto heels that I borrowed from Ellen's closet. I styled a pink wraparound skirt and a lime green tube top stuffed with David's dirty socks. 8th Avenue was the most frightening, unsafe, slimy avenue imaginable. I was white, from lower middle class Canarsie Brooklyn, and I was naïve. 8th Avenue was scary for any young person of any color or background. Here I was, a baby drag queen, alone, strutting, and stuttering down the block. Men were honking and whistling. It was invigorating, frightening and demeaning. 8th Avenue was where all the prostitutes hung out. I wasn't a prostitute. My personal safety was on the line but I did not genuinely recognize that. The heels slowed me down and that made it feel like I was walking in a dream. I thought to myself, if I have to run for safety it feels like I would not live to tell the tale. I made it to the Gilded Grape, New York City's Tranny Capital of the world in the '70s, and now there were other safety issues I had to contend with.

The Gilded Grape was a Drag/TS/TV/Hustlers club. The crowd was an eclectic bunch. Remember the thugs, rapists and tricks? This made up a percentage of the population entering the Gilded Grape. There were trans girls, girls of trans experience, cross dressers, street punks looking for extra money, drug dealers, businessmen in female attire, transexuals from all over the country, illegal aliens, kids dressed up as adults, and runaways. I had to quickly figure out where I belonged in this enigma.

I was underage, I was of no color, I was not cool, I was awkward, and I needed desperately to connect with someone to feel safe.

The manager of the Gilded Grape was a man named Chickey. Chickey was an older white man with the same personality type as Archie Bunker without the racist state of mind. Chickey quickly became my link and additionally became a father image. He looked and acted like my biological father, yet he was accepting of my gender status.

> *Remember, when I came out to my father and told him I was TS and was going to start hormone therapy, he said "over his dead body." I handed my father Harry Benjamin's book "Transsexual Phenomenon." He told me if I was going to do this I would have to leave home. That night I left. Hey, don't yell at me in that stern, patronizing judgmental tone and assert, "What do you expect?" And don't remind me that I have already told you this. There's a strategy behind saying it again!*

Chickey, I would quickly learn, would let some of the girls into the club for free if they performed fellatio on him. So, being a starving baby tranny girl, I would do it (nothing like blowing a man that reminds you of your father).

The Gilded Grape crowd was predominantly African-American, Jamaican, South African, Nigerian, Latino/a, Puerto Rican, Cubana, Mexicana, Dominicana, Panamanian, street-wise, transexuals, drag queens, drag kings, hustlers, and prostitutes. The tricks, *Johns and tranny-chasers,* were predominantly white. However, the bangy-boys were Latino and represented the many cultural groups I just described. The crowd was filled with tranny thugs, drug addicts, performers, wannabes, immigrants and our followers. The club was also filled with atmosphere, acceptance, community, safety, and a sense of family, as well as hate, remorse, hustle, desire, escape, and revenge. The music was loud with a mixture of disco, show tunes, salsa, and melodramatic sex vigilant reverberation. It was a small place right on the corner of 45th Street and 8th Avenue. It was not unusual for someone to be stabbed on the corner or in front of the Camelot Inn, an apartment building right next door on 45th Street that housed the infamous queens Marudi and Jeaenette. Marudi and Jeanette were the crème de la crème of the tranny population in NYC in 1976.

The Gilded Grape was an enthralling place for many reasons. Besides the decadence, cat fighting, shady aura, sense of glamour, drugs and sex, you felt accepted even if you were 'read to filth' about your neo-gender presentation (told by others that you looked ridiculous). There was a sense of 'authenticity and sincerity' within these walls and there was no other place to go for a person of TG/TS/TV experience to receive that.
Within the Gilded Grape I had the opportunity to meet people who would guide me and support my 'evolution' from 'unearned false privileged spoiled white boy' to 'tranny trash.' Granted, this sub-culture had many illegal activities festering within its walls. This club challenged the nomenclature, focusing on a deviant underworld with jaded morals and values. However, the category 'deviance' seemed to dissipate and become the 'norm' once you utilized substances and/or physically connected and surrendered yourself to the culture of the space.

> *Right wing religious groups, 'save the nuclear family' organizations, Born Agains et al, might use this and assert that this deprivation of morals is the work of Satan and this populace must be saved. Coming from the population's perspectives, we were. See, everyone is fulfilled.*

I was living in the Baron Hotel, a rooming house for the elite on 51st Street between 8th and 9th Avenue at the time of my Official Coming Out phase. I was a week behind in my $30 a week rent. I met this woman by the name of Mickey through a man I had met in the Gilded Grape the night before. He took me to Mickey and Sly's house to have dinner. I had sores on my face from malnutrition and a 'bad-beauty-school-orange-in-color' perm, yet for some reason my 'spirit' was intact. I was in awe of Mickey. I used my talents, my vibrant personality, to have her rapidly grow to be in awe of me as well. I moved in with Mickey and Sly that night. Mickey helped me move the garbage bag of clothing and my TV set to a small back room in their apartment on 10th Avenue and 55th Street.

Pettiway, E. Leon <u>Honey, Honey Miss Thang: Being Black, Gay, and on the streets</u>. Temple University Press 1996

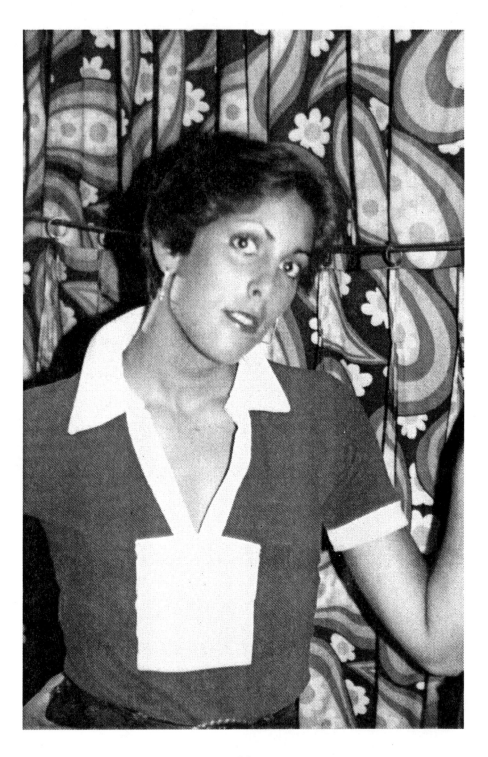

6.
SWEET SIXTEEN

WORKING GIRL/MARY MAGDALENE
AND THE CHALLENGE OF FUNCTIONING ON THE STROLL

LOSING MY SPIRT
GAINING MY SPIRT

THE LONG WINTER
CONEY ISLAND AND DR. WOLLMAN

JIMMY TREETOP......
THE MODEL MAKER
THE PEDOPHILE
THE TRICK
UNCLE JIMMY

6

Sweet Sixteen

Working Girl/Mary Magdalene and the challenge of functioning on the 'Stroll'

All I kept thinking about was the book Go Ask Alice.

These episodes with Mickey, my newfound mentor and friend, would fit the section in Go Ask Alice that states, "Another day, another blowjob." But I couldn't even begin to give my first one.

> The scene took place on 47th Street and 10th Avenue. Mickey and I were standing on the corner, but we weren't 'watching all the girls go by.' We were looking provocatively at passing cars.

Mickey kept going in and out of cars and I was just standing there. This was extremely humiliating. Mickey was what urban youth call nowadays 'da bomb.' In the '70s, within the people of color ball communities, she was 'OVAH.' And that she was. She was short and curvaceous. She had almond-slanted eyes with full, dark, purple painted lips that clashed wonderfully with her Delancey Street, orange leather, knee length, 'shaped to the body' coat. Her long in the back, straight and banged in the front, jet black hair was shiny, her red nails were painted to perfection, and her sexual aura was captivating. I was caught up in my jealousy, my rage, my overwhelming fear, and the sad reality that I couldn't compete with her ethnic beauty and sexuality.

After all, just last year I was still making out with girls in high school, presenting as an androgynous creature, and being identified by society and those girls I was kissing as a boy. Just last year I had my own room in this lavish house in Wantagh, Long Island and now I was living in the back of this tenement. Just last year I was having my dinner served to me by a woman who hated my guts, and now I was struggling to buy a cooked meal out of a Smilers Delicatessen. Just last year I had had dreams and aspirations and a false confidence about myself that could break down the thickest of walls, and now I was struggling to exist.

I remember her shouting, "Roe, you gotta chase them a little. Don't just stand there like a stupid white boy. Lure them to you."

Every time Mickey got back from turning a date we would laugh and dance like two kids without a care in the world. I would sing my show tunes when she returned and when she would get another date I'd be scared to death. It was winter and very cold. That year will always feel like an eternity. As I have stated before, '76 and '77 shaped the rest of my life. People talk about the loss of their youth. I view it as the loss of my soul, my sole compassion, myself. I also view it as the price I had to pay 'to be.'

Let's get back to 10th Avenue, shall we?
Mickey turned her third trick and I was still standing there. I was long and skinny, all five feet ten inches of me. The one thing I did have going for me at that time were my eyes and what was left of my spirit. They were the biggest, roundest, saddest eyes you could ever encounter. And my spirit, well, I was a youth and I was living my dream no matter how nightmarish it seemed to outsiders. The Tuinals, the combination of amobarbital and secobarbital I would pop, would make my eyes dangle even lower on the far end of my long skinny face. Who would believe that I was considered Tyrone Power's look-alike just three years ago?
Anyway, Mickey got into another trick's car. I believe it was one of her regulars. She had so many men coming back for her professional cock sucking, and I was left alone once again. When all of a sudden, oh my god, there was someone stopping for me. He pulled up right in front of me to the southeast side of 47th Street and 10th Avenue; he stopped, and down came the window. I'm not sure if it was electric or not (the lock on the door certainly was and I would find out about that later).

I strutted up to the car with the fear and trepidation of a new school kid reporting to their teacher. "You wanna go out?" I hardly asked! He said yes. I then stressed, "$10 for a blowjob, OK?" "Sure," he said. Oh my god, I couldn't believe it. I was going to make $10. In my short life I hadn't worked that hard and never really earned a living.

When I was eleven years old I had a paper route that lasted two weeks and my mother would drive me in the car to deliver the papers. However, I had always had money. My parents had never confronted me with the reality that I would take money out of both their wallets every week and would sometimes remove coins from my dad's coin collection that was set in a blue felt, hard-covered book. No boundaries were planted for me to respect. I needed money, so I took it. Not a lot, but I truly earned none of it. After all, some children might rationalize, well I do all my chores therefore I've earned this. Not me! I didn't do many chores around the house. Before my mother died I was a spoiled brat. She knew I was a spoiled brat. I think she let me get away with it because of her being sick. Probably, in her own way, this is how she would nurture me by not calling on my idiosyncrasies, like not making me be responsible. Well this is a mind read and I will never know what she was thinking or feeling.

I do know that I was about to make $10. Part of me wished that Mickey were there to see someone stop for me. Ha, Ha, Mickey. See? Someone wants me! Oh well, if Mickey were there she would probably be getting into the car and not me. I couldn't stop thinking how nice the car was. It had a white leather interior and was quite roomy. I couldn't believe this big black man wanted me to suck his dick. I was honored and scared to death at the same time. Mickey had instructed me on where to take the tricks so that the space could double as a lookout area for each other. I couldn't wait to see her face on that hideaway hill across from the Sanitation Department on 56th Street right off the West Side Highway. I couldn't wait to drive into that space in this humongous white Cadillac.

This wasn't reality. It didn't feel like a crime. I didn't feel like a prostitute. It felt like I was playing an extremely scary game, but I was in way over my head. The car, and the man driving, did not feel safe but I got in and drove off with him anyway. It was cold and snowy, and I needed to break luck. We got to the hill, which was located on the south end of West 56th Street, but Mickey was nowhere in sight.

Before I go any further I have to describe me, Roe!

I was wearing a $12 fur that was either given to me by my brother's girlfriend or that I bought in a thrift shop in the West Village. I had some type of kerchief wrapped around my dried-frizzy hair. I was a young person playing dress-up, but not doing a very good job at that. I had on a brassiere filled with hard rubber pads. Besides the fact that I was not qualified to enter any beauty contest, I knew that much less about sucking dick. I mean I had done it before, perform fellatio and dressing up, but had always hated it, fellatio that is. Oh well, doesn't everybody hate to do what they have to do for a living? I was going to get paid for doing something I hate and am not good at. America, what a wonderful country!

I took into account a few things Mickey had said. "Roe, get the money first and always remember to peek at the trick while you're blowing him, just in case he has a knife to cut your head off."

This was a little more challenging compared to stealing money from my dad's plastic change holder originating from the Carvel Ice Cream Parlor.

"Mister," I said, "could I have the $10 first before we do it." For a split second I thought I could jump out of the car right after he gave me the money so I wouldn't have to do it. This man would kill me. I'll have to give him his money's worth. He then asserted, "How about I give you $20 so I could fuck ya too?" Oh dear, I thought, I couldn't do that. I have a penis and he doesn't know.

> *It's dark and cold and snowing and two years ago I was accepted into Performing Arts High School and my life was so totally different. I was one of 50 out of 1,000 applicants. I was the only one that year accepted from Bildersee Junior High School in Canarsie. I was special, I had talent, I was unique, and now what am I?*

I told the man, "Just $10 would be fine," as my voice cracked and my hands shook as I put my palm out to him. He said OK and went into the middle compartment in the front seat of the car. A second of relief turned into an eternity of horror. He pulled out a knife. Don't ask what kind, how long or sharp, it was a knife. In my childhood, knives were used for dinner and that's all I knew.

> *The only time I saw someone use a knife as a weapon was when my mother took this young black boy who was being chased by a group of ignorant Canarsie white boys into our house. They had beaten this boy up and my mother chased the group away and took this boy into our house to clean him up. All I thought about was how brave my mother was to stop those boys and how interesting it was to have this young black boy in our home. My mother was a natural at nurturing. She left this boy with me for two minutes to go get something and the kid pulled a knife out from where our lunch dishes were drying. All I thought about was I wish he would leave our house because I was scared. I was scared for me. My mother came back in the room, saw the boy with the knife and told him that the knife would only cause him more pain. She told him not to fall into the same violence that was perpetrated onto him. It wouldn't help him, she said, it would only make things worse. And with that, she took the knife back. I couldn't believe her courage. I was dumbfounded.*

I was paralyzed back then, and I was paralyzed again in this car. Oh how I wished my mommy was there to take this knife away from this bigger, blacker man. He immediately told me to take off all my clothes. "I'm gonna fuck this white thing," he said. "Take your clothes off." Besides the fact that I was humiliated by the whole scenario I now had to tell him that I wasn't all girl and he couldn't fuck me, so I thought! I'm a boy, I declared. I was far from a boy, but there was no other way to explain it. "Oh yeah? Well I'll fuck you in your ass." Oh no, I thought. You need to prepare for that type of interaction. There was a whole ritual I would engage in, in order to support me from having bodily accidents.

This was not up for discussion. I submitted to his instruction. I took off my clothes and he threw me into the back seat. All I kept thinking about while he was pounding me was I hope I don't make a mess. He'll kill me. Oh well, we don't always have our prayers answered the way we want. My nerves were flowing and so were my excretions. He reached climax and I was aspiring to leave with or without my $10. "Now suck my dick," he said. This was not my day. How could I do this with all that doodoo on his penis. I screeched, "Oh please, don't make me do that," as he shoved it down my throat. After the whole messy incident was completed I was told to clean up the back seat with the blouse that I was wearing. The tears were frozen in my mind. The physical as well as the emotional distress was competing heavily with the nausea that I was feeling. I knew if I threw up it would just be something extra I would have to attend to so I kept swallowing it. This white car was a mess and this white, lower-middle class youth was horrified. He told me to exit his car and, as fast as I could, I flung the door open and threw myself to the ground. He drove up the hill without me, but with some of my clothes. At the top of the hill he threw out some of my outerwear. I still had on my brassiere, pads, ripped panties and a kerchief. I ran up the hill to collect my stuff and my composure. I couldn't believe that this had just happened. I could not believe that I was just tortured this way. I couldn't believe that I just had a knife to my neck and I had to perform all those horrible deeds. I had reached the top of the hill when I unexpectedly saw three sanitation men standing across the street talking. I was frightened but my urgency to reconnect in some way to other humans was overriding my fear. I ran to them hoping that they would help me make what just happened go away. I was desperately eager to feel a sense of connection in some way that would lighten what I was feeling right now. I ran to them in the freezing cold, no clothes on except underwear and a handkerchief covering my falsies. I ran to them with my last glimpse of pride and hope. They seemed honestly concerned when I reached close range. "I've been raped and thrown out of a car." I did not say that I had picked him up on a corner or that I was transexual. They seemed disturbed and interested in helping me. And along came a wind and flung the handkerchief off my padded bra. They looked at my padded chest and looked at each other and began to laugh. "You're a man," one of them asserted. I screamed "I'm sixteen years old and I've just been raped." They did not care. So I ran as I owned their words and laughter deep into my heart, my veins, and my blood. As I ran through the streets in the snow and the cold, the sadness and disgrace ran right along with me. I kept tumbling upon pieces of my clothing. When I came upon 10th Avenue the cars could not stop honking, people could not stop pointing.

> *I retrieved back somewhere in my mind in third grade when I was called out by the whole class for doing something wrong. I hated being pointed at back then, and I hated being pointed at at this moment as well.*

I made it home where Mickey, Sly, and I lived. I ran up the stairs with tatted fur in hand. "Where were you?" Mickey said. "I was raped by this guy and ..."I went through the story in five minutes.
Sly and Mickey began to laugh and I started to laugh as well. This was just one of the many initiations into transgender street life.

There are pros and cons to the laughter and to this story. The laughter assisted me in not taking what happened to me so seriously. If Sly and Mickey would've hovered over me I might have fallen into more self-pity. However, I believed in my heart that this was what came with the territory of being transexual. Therefore, I believed that this was somehow what I deserved. I will always remember that night and I will always have the emotional and physical scars to remind me. That night, I contracted syphilis and this will show up on every blood test I take for the rest of my days.

Forget Go Ask Alice! Just go ask many men and women of transexual experience about transitioning early in life and having to contend with the way in which our society engages these sexual minorities, especially when their family of origin, peers, church, temple, and academic environment choose not to. You need less to comprehend the self-objectification of the young trans woman. What you need to do is ask yourself why must this be the alternative for a transitioning youth.

Losing Many Virginities
Vir-gin-I-ty
The state, or condition of being pure, fresh, or unused.

Do you think specific body parts, genitalia, canals, openings, protrusions, should be considered virgin-like if they haven't been poked as of yet? If you agree, can we say that a person who has a vagina, an anus, and a mouth can still be considered a virgin if they have not performed fellatio on their partner, even though they have engaged in sexual anal and vaginal intercourse? For the sake of this discussion one would believe this identity to be an honorary factor, since many want and need to hold onto that virginal status, be it due to religious, spiritual, peer or family pressure.

At the ripe age of sixteen there was nothing left of me to identify that was virginal, or was there?

Let's look at my virginal History.

Perceived Male

I lost my virginity to Robyn in kindergarten (my hand to … breast). I lost my virginity to Sherry, 4th grade (my penis to … mouth). I lost my virginity to Jackie, 7th grade (my penis to … vagina). I lost my virginity to Rob, my cousin's boyfriend, 8th grade (my penis to … penis). I lost my virginity to butch/femme queen at the Broadway, 9th grade (my penis to … mouth). I lost my virginity to the Hollywood Bartender in NYC, 10th grade (his penis to my anus).

Perceived Queen

I lost my virginity to a trick at sixteen years old (his penis to my back vagina and my mouth).

> *Try your luck. Guess. Am I through? Am I all virgin'd out in your eyes? Is this considered used goods, yesterday's newspaper, tainted corpus, brand it with an 'S'? Nothing else can happen to this body? Well, hang on dahl, there's more come in 1977 and in 1983 when genitals are realigned!*

Losing my spirit/gaining my spirit

> *You walk around urban areas and you cannot count the homeless. In many sections of urban cities there is always a homeless person in sight. Sometimes I feel so helpless. I see them and I remember. I see them and I know that that could be me at any stage in my life. They frighten me. I get angry and disgusted at them, and at me for getting angry and disgusted. I get furious with our society.*
>
> *A component of the work I am involved with includes advocating for people without homes and it is quite difficult to triumph over this societal quandary. It is even more difficult to get them into adequate housing facilities. I don't think the issue of homelessness was as audible in 1976 as it is now. I don't remember seeing many programs or outreach workers.*
>
> *Maybe with all the harm, desperation, pain and suffering that HIV/AIDS has caused, it has also brought about some good. Maybe*

AIDS, particularly the advocates and activists surrounding the pandemic, have taught the privileged that they must reach out to the disenfranchised. Or maybe AIDS has made so many of us so angry that we all realized we need to reach out to the disenfranchised ourselves in ways in which they will be served more appropriately? Maybe not! Maybe there have been programs available to help the homeless forever. In Social Work school I read the history of how the health care workers aided the disenfranchised and the impoverished, indigenous populations. I just never saw or knew there was help out there when I was on the streets.

Sometimes, being lost in the night, in the darkness of the streets, has a negative effect on your disposition. No, really! When you are young and filled with piss and vinegar, few circumstances stop you and make you think. Youth is somehow correlated with immortality. However, when you realize your true mortality and your situation is not pretty, it's frightening. There were a few incidences in my youth where I woke up and truly felt beaten. Before my mother died I always felt a sense of security. No matter what happened or what depression or difficulties emerged, I always knew someone was there on my side. This degenerated with the loss of my mother, then it was regained, and then … my spirit began to meet its limits.

Remember that song 'Street Life'? That song used to kick my ass. I'd be out and dressed in a disco and the DJ would play 'Street Life,' or 'I'll always love my mother,' and for that moment I would become conscious; hey I'm not in school, I have no parental guidance, my $30 a week rent is due, or I need to break luck, *make some money*, or what's for dinner, lunch, breakfast … and all of a sudden, I was defeated.

That was the end of 'spirit,' I falsely deliberated. Or was it?

Many Rockers have complained that Disco sucked. Yet many of the recordings in the 1970s would stir many emotions for me. Music would get me out of myself. However, it would also take me to spaces within my psyche I didn't have control of going. Some disco songs would make me realize how fucked up I really was. And we're talking teenage years here. Like many young people, life was dramatic. However, I was truly a 'Drama Queen' with a small amount of breathing space. And this was no camp, queer slang for theatrics! My life was not a joke.

Father Ritter, one of the founders of Covenant House, spoke about the lost youth. Homelessness and street life is no joke when you are an adult, let alone a youth.

I truly believe there is a trade-off in life for everything. I defied gender constrictions at an early age. My decision to transition from a more masculine disguise to a feminine, more authentic identity, no matter how compulsive my decision, was a trade off. In order to experience myself as a young woman I gave up young male privilege. This release of privilege was sometimes devastating. Some right-wingers might assert, you lie with the devil, you get burnt! And for many years I bought into that falsifier.

Does your spirit ever truly die? Does your soul see you through the most difficult trying times? My transition from young white boy with a false sense of privilege in the 1970s to young tranny-girl with no or little privilege was a real smack in the face. My spirit and soul seemed to be uplifted and smashed on a daily basis. Hello Poverty, Hello Discrimination, Goodbye Exemption!

Some would say not only did I lose my spirit, but I lost my mind. And I would say, 'I lost my spirit and I secured a new one.'

FOOT PRINTS

Last night I dreamed I was walking

Along the beach with the Lord.

Many scenes from my life flashed across the sky.

In each scene I noticed footprints in the sand.

Sometimes there were two sets of footprints.

Other times there were one set of footprints.

This bothered me because I noticed that

During the low periods of my life when I was

Suffering from anguish, sorrow, or defeat,

I could see only one set of footprints,

So I said to the Lord, You promised me,

Lord, that if I followed You,

You would walk with me always.

But I noticed that during the most trying periods

Of my life there have only been

One set of prints in the sand.

Why, When I have needed You most,

You have not been there for me?

The Lord replied,

The times when you have seen only one set of footprints

Is when I carried you.

By Mary Stevenson

The Long Winter

Second Edition 11/2002
As I write, I feel the wind blow from the coastal breeze coming in through my terrace door in Hollywood, California. As I write, I sit at my desk typing on my $2,000 computer that I just purchased that I can't afford to pay off yet. As I write, I think about the decision to own a computer. After all, I am now in my early forties, slowly saying goodbye to turning heads and honking cars. As I write, I am hoping to land a new job, in a new town and live the next few years of my journey towards peace of mind, a deeper spirituality, and a reduced amount of anger.

First Edition 7/1997
As I write, I feel the cold going through my now warped, nurtured and estrogen-replaced veins. As I write, I sit at my metal desk in my comfy, secure apartment working on my $3,000 computer that was paid for by my nurturing, loving and ever supportive fiancé. As I write, I think about the decision to own a computer. I was a college graduate summa cum laude. I was in my late thirties and I was so proud of myself and how much work I knew I had, and have, in store for me in my newfound future. How I wish my parents were alive to share this feeling with me.

This must have transpired in January of '76.
As I write, I think about that cold, lonely, desperate winter of '76. There were many, but this was one I'll never forget. Did someone hear elephant reverberation?

Mickey, my streetwalking mentor, was in jail on a prostitution case. This meant that I would have to attempt, once again, to try to make some money by standing on a corner and hopefully flagging some other lonely person down who would pay me to perform lousy fellatio on their limp, sequestered, horny, sex organ. I think it was around another holiday season because I felt immensely alone. Holidays do that to the best of us.

They did that to me especially since the expiration of my mom. My parents used to spoil my brother and me rotten. It was somehow like she, my mom, knew she wasn't going to be around for very long so she had to give us all this loving for the short period of time that she stayed close to us. So when the winters felt dark, without her, her spoiling, her kind words, and her confidence, I felt alone.

I was on 47th Street and 10th Avenue once again. My experience with this street was not healthy! In fact, it was infuriating and vile! It was dark, cold, scary and mortifying. First of all, I wasn't attractive as a neo-tranny. My ability to perform was questionable. I didn't care for the hours this labor entailed and the benefits sucked. It must've been an hour that I was standing there on this dark, lonely corner with the innocence of the snow hitting the impurity of my Maybelline-mascara'd eyelashes dripping and soaking into my defeated eyes and spirit. No one stopped. No one struck their horn, which ate away at what was left of my ego. On the one hand, I didn't want anyone to stop because if someone did I would have to get in his car.

When I was young I was told never to talk to strangers, let alone get in their cars.

However, no one ever told me not to put my mouth on their private parts for currency! If a car stopped I would have to get in, and if they didn't stop, I was a failure as a woman. Go figure!

Please, I really don't want any nasty letters from feminists asserting that this is totally an unacceptable description of how young women should be represented in our society.

I was sixteen years old. I was lost and I was confused. And I was being exploited, not merely self-exploiting. In this society we exploit tranny women, tranny girls. We don't celebrate them at all. Oh, how I dreaded a car stopping for me and oh ,how I dreaded if they didn't.

Those of you unfamiliar to New York in midtown in the 1970s need to know this:

In 1976, 47th Street and 10th Avenue, Hell's Kitchen, was barren and scary. And in 1976 I wasn't the acculturated, diverse, semi-attractive woman I am now. I was lost and in pain. I had balls of steel, still intact, and extremely low self-esteem. I had microscopic hope within my hopelessness. I left the desolate, indigent, isolated street and walked towards the Gilded Grape. The Gilded Grape was my falsified safety net for me and many 'genderly' different people. I sauntered towards my safety net experiencing the heaviest sense of leaded loneliness in the pit of my stomach. Why I didn't run in front of a car I have no idea. The blackness of my heart ran down my face from the mixture of snow frost, frost eye shadow, and mascara.

As I got to the entrance I realized I didn't have the admission fee to enter the dungeon of the 'friends of the friendless.' Spirit, you ask, where was my spirit? Did I experience my spirit diminishing before my now blurry with warm salt, cold air, and dripping mascara'd eyes? Maybe it's true that higher power is always around and when one door shuts another one opens. 'Billy,' a more mature woman of the night, paid my way in, took me to the bathroom, and cleaned me up with her ever-so-faithful Woolworth's bought cover stick. Losing my spirit to the long lonely winter? Well, not tonight!

Coney Island and Dr Wollman

My initiation into HRT (hormone replacement therapy) was through a sweet little old doctor in Coney Island. Dr Wollman agreed to see me in 1976, even before my sixteenth birthday. I did not tell the truth about my age. I had just met with a friend in high school and heard of the word transexualism. I've told this story before. I think I got his name and number from the 'David Bowie look-alike,' the person in school who was born identified as female but was challenging the incongruent identity.

I took the train and bus to his office where we sat down and spoke for fifteen minutes. I was already a proficient liar and was able to sell myself as an adult. He gave me a bottle of hormones, Provera. But I never went back for more.

> *The utilization of Provera has been in conjunction with another estrogen called Premarin.*
>
> *Provera and Premarin have been used to mimic the non trans woman's cycle. You would take 21 days of Premarin and ten days of Provera. It is interesting how HRT models the cycle when so many women deal with PMS and how that has been such a negative and challenging emotional experience for women all over the world. Why would doctors want to mimic that cycle when there are so many negative side effects to this hormonal experience? You would think that HRT would be studied in a way that would not only assist a woman physically after menopause, but would also progress so that one wouldn't go through as many emotional changes as one has gone through when the body didn't need this estrogen replacement therapy.*

I never went back to Dr Wollman, but did meet my next mentor of HRT, Jimmy Treetop.

Jimmy Treetop ... The Model Maker/The Pedophile/The Trick/Uncle Jimmy

These next few paragraphs are going to be a challenge to you. I ask that you sit with an open mind as I struggle with these realities surrounding this man named Jimmy.

As I write this, I find myself in a quandary, not really understanding the depth of the harm this man had done to so many youngsters and not being able to negate how he saved so many of us at the same time. On one hand,

70

Jimmy gave us wings in addition to wetting and supplementing these wings with a sticky coating.

So, here's Jimmy.

Jimmy Treetop did not, did not live on top of a tree. He had a walk-up apartment in a pre-war building on the west side of the street in New York City's Hells Kitchen between 47th and 48th. His building was right over a laundromat and a bodega. The area was predominantly Latino/a.

> *I am not sure why no one ever turned this man in, as folks had to have seen very young children – Do you hear me? – children, boys and girls, a numerous amount of their own ninos/as going in and out of this man's house on a daily basis. This was not a junior or high school setting. This was an old man's apartment.*

Jimmy lived on the third floor. His door had six locks on it. You walked into the tenement and it was one of those apartments one would usually see on the lower east side, where the bathtub was also utilized as a kitchen table once you threw a piece of wood over it. Jimmy had a police lock that I am sure he did not purchase directly from the police. This was a one-bedroom flat without a living room. It was a train track designed apartment; kitchen, tiny hall with bathroom on right and the 'back room,' as the bedroom.

> *Forget the movie 'If These Walls Could Talk,' because if Jimmy's walls could talk, those walls would shut up and listen!*

I met Jimmy Treetop when I was sixteen years old. I looked up to him. Many of us yearned for his attention. He was a photographer and possessed miracle medicine. The word on the street about Jimmy was that his hormones transformed you into the lovely, vivacious, well-rounded (and I don't mean eclectic) woman that you were supposed to be. Jimmy pushed, I mean dealt, I mean sold hormones, intramuscular hormones. These were supposed to be the most powerful hormones imaginable. And at sixteen one didn't really do research or totally comprehend the ramifications of using an injectable substance that one knew little about. You just saw the results of those that were administering this substance under the supervision of this pedophile. I watched the girls from the Gilded Grape transform before my eyes. The first time I got a shot from Jimmy it was purely professional, as professional as it could be when you go buy something injectable from someone's apartment with a napkin tightly taped around an already-filled syringe.

You walked into this man's house; he was around six feet, five inches tall. He greeted you with his kindly Lurch mystique. The house smelled of '*old white man.*' He had a grey Santa Clause beard, his clothes were old, and his energy was that of a distrusting relative, welcoming but uncomfortable. Jimmy immediately walked you through the apartment to 'the room.' You can tell that this is where he was in most control, excited, and proud. There was no place to sit in this room so one immediately had to sit on the bed that took up the whole space except for the dresser that opened up right onto the bed. The bed was covered with satin. One wall was completely covered with a mirror. The lighting was that of a club scene. with lots of reds and blues to hide flaws. The room was cold, very cold. as if one could feel, taste and smell the loss of youth and death of innocence. Yet one could also feel the celebration of gender reconstruction, freedom, hope, life, energy, and excitement as well. The room was filled with all of this in addition to a certain odor that one would only find in a peep show, gay movie theater or bathhouse. On the other side of the mirrored wall were pictures of Jimmy's prize possessions, pictures of trans women who could stand next to or knock over any non trans-female model appearing in Vogue or Cosmopolitan.

I gave Jimmy my $15, the price of the injection. He told me in a warm, pleasant voice, unruffled, with a distrusting edge and tone, to take down my pants and panties. The syringe was filled to the top with an oil-based substance and red liquid, which he identified as vitamin B12, like I cared or knew what that was. I lay face down on his silk sheet, not knowing how many asses had been exposed to this man, or if there was some sperm ejaculated right on the spot that my nostrils were now sniffing, or how many dreams began here, or how much innocence lost here, or god knows what had happened in that room where so many lost and found souls began right at that very spot where my face and ass were lying. The injection took a while to seep through the opening of the needle and into my muscle. I sensed his eyes on me and his voice was softer as I lay there under his power. He pulled the long needle out of my ass cheek, which seemed to last a few minutes, and he started rubbing. He rubbed and laughed and rubbed and laughed and rubbed and enjoyed rubbing a little too long. I got up and was dizzy from his odor, the air conditioning, the odor of the sheets and the new pain I had in the muscle of my left butt cheek. The next day I was nauseous all day, my nipples were sore and I was on my way. I went back every week whenever I could afford it, and whenever I couldn't …

Jimmy, the model maker
Remember those pictures I told you about that hung over Jimmy's bed on the opposite side of the wall-to-wall mirror? Those were '*Jimmy Treetop*

Creations,' and that is what this indigent population identified ourselves as. We were the new breed of queens, transexuals, locas, and we all aspired to be a picture on Jimmy Treetop's wall. Only the most beautiful received the honor of appearing on this *pedo's* wall. Jimmy's hormones made me blossom, they made me sick. My hips went from 34 inches to 40 inches in the first year of taking them. My nipples grew from pink to brown, from soft and small to hard and nickel shaped. My long face rounded out and my hair shone. What was this price I had paid for this newfound femininity? I never made it to his wall but I quickly became a young woman who didn't have problems 'passing' in society as the young woman that I was. Many days I would not have money for an injection, so my pay was Jimmy's used up cock in my mouth and a hormone shot in my ass. My pay was having this man exploit and devour more of my youth as he fed me my new found drug. And I was not the only one, nor was I one of his favorites. His favorites were the illegal, gorgeous young Latinas from Mexico, Honduras, Santa Domingo, and legal in immigration terms, but illegal as far as age is concerned, hot Latinas from Puerto Rico. His favorites were those who clung to him because they were lost in a city that did not give a flying fuck about them anyway. His favorites were those who could take feminizing hormones but could still perform by getting an erection. I know this might sound sick, but I was jealous I wasn't a favorite.

Jimmy's favorites were within the cultural milieu that Jimmy was living in. Someone should have stopped Jimmy from terrorizing this disenfranchised community, and thank god nobody stopped Jimmy, because without him many might never had experienced the life we began to lead.

Jimmy, the pedophile

Jimmy was a grown man, an adult. He must have been in his late thirties, early forties. He <u>believed</u> that we were his creations. He walked through life with power, entering all tranny clubs without fear of arrest or being prosecuted for his illegal sexual interactions with minors. And this was not all. Jimmy not only sold and injected illegal hormones into the backsides of minors, Jimmy sold Tuinals, Seconals, Quaaludes and pot. You were told not to drink alcohol whenever you got an injection because it 'would eat away at the estrogen.' But you could smoke as much pot as you wanted and your usual injection at Jimmy's house began with a pass of the peace pipe. There were a few clubs that catered to trannies in the seventies and everyone knew the escapades of Jimmy and his 'room.' Why didn't any of the adults running these establishments intervene? Jimmy met the 'girls' at the Gilded Grape, a.k.a. GG Knickerbocker, the Barnum Room, the Grape Vine, the Casa Dario, as well as the Hay Market (predominantly white male engaging hustle bar with young queens hanging around), Blues (gay male black bar with younger femme queens hanging out), Peter Rabbits (a club downtown on the west side highway for the more faggy street queens). Why did these places let us in their establishments to begin with? Why did they let us turn tricks (pick up men for money), why did they let us drink, and why did they exploit us in a way that benefited their pockets, their business and, of course, their sexual interactions?

There was no questioning this ethical dilemma. Back then anything 'trans' was seen as something or someone who could be exploited for personal and financial gain, no matter if that tranny was twelve years old or 50. There were no laws as to how we would treat these people, and people treated this population any way they wanted.

Jimmy, the trick

In reality, Jimmy was also at the mercy of the power tranny youth possessed. The true 'beauties' (the ones that Jimmy would live for) treated him like every other trick that they had. It didn't matter that they hung proudly on his wall or that they had access to all the goodies a tranny junkie needed. He was just another trick. What Jimmy did was create some monsters. They were drop dead gorgeous refugees who now had the power and prestige of the false 'American Dream.' They had a man who lived for them and they were worshipped by many a tranny and tranny wannabe. Jimmy, with all his power, was also Jimmy, Jimmy, the trick.

Uncle Jimmy

I will always be grateful to Jimmy. Jimmy was the uncle I never had. Jimmy was the uncle who recognized my femininity and celebrated it with me. Jimmy made me feel excited when he got a good snapshot of me. He would honor my newfound self-expression and he would delight in my growing process.

> *When you think about a person who is a pedophile, one immediately wants to lash out at this individual. We should throw these people into prison until they are rehabilitated. I am not condoning any of Jimmy's actions. Jimmy should have never been allowed to treat me and others medically, physically or psychologically the way he did. But when does our society own some of the responsibility? How can we point our finger at Jimmy when we do not look at what part we played and continually play in this? In October of 2002, a young Latina transgender was murdered in California by a group of kids who found out she had a penis. The media called her a 'he' and some papers in the United States stated that it made sense to 'lose it' with a person like this. They understood murdering a man who*

was making believe he was a woman. Does any of this make any sense?

Developing

I developed into the woman I had always wanted to be, well almost. I did not consider myself that pretty.

I was striking, but not pretty. But I was extremely feminine and very sexual looking. I learned to hone my sexuality as I got older. But I wore this newfound sexuality a little too provocatively and I always bordered on inappropriate when it came to dress and sensuality.

My Aunt Hannah, in whose house I grew up, owned a printing company on Chambers Street in NYC. I went down there one day and my cousin Douglas, remember the gorgeous child of Marsha and Sheldon, was working with my aunt. He was very complimentary on my newfound femininity and never made me feel bad. I walked into my aunt's office with short shorts, I mean short dungaree shorts, and a see-through danskin which totally exposed my budding breasts. She lost it and started to scold me. "How dare you come to my office dressed so inappropriately? You are disgusting." Her words went right through me as I tried to defend myself internally from her insults. I never saw her again until a month before she died. She gave me a check that day in her office and she wrote me out a $25 check the day I saw her in her dying bed. I did not ask her for money the last time and I have always felt so guilty taking that $25 from her bedside. She died and left my cousin Sheldon, his daughter Denise, sons Douglas and Darren financially comfortable. Even though I felt guilty about the $25, I have always felt cheated that I didn't receive any of that financial comfort from her, *as if I deserved it.*

> *How I wish she could've seen the rest of my years when I finally learned how to present myself in a way that was appropriate. She might have been proud.*

So this youngster developed all right! I passed myself around so that everyone had an opportunity to experience my development. My mentors were street whores, the impoverished and the extreme. Midtown taught me my dress code and I followed suit. Developing included, but was not limited to, physical appearance, emotional status, culture, and an internal belief system.

Dress code: I had to dress provocatively for many reasons. I needed for all to see my budding femininity. Without tight clothes no one could celebrate my neo-curves.

Emotional status: HRT changed my moods drastically and affected my nervous system. I was already shaky and estrogen had a negative effect on what I would later have diagnosed as Essential Tremor. The pills I was already 'addicted' to did not help either.

7.
17 AND ENTERING
AN OFFICALLY AUTHORIZED...

The EMBASSY
Home to Long Island
Lynda, the Passing FANCY
Dr. Wesser the messer

Goodbye to "Tessy"...
the nose is messy

Dr. Schiffman

7

17 and Entering an Officially Authorized ...

The Embassy

Sly, Mickey's old man [see Chapter 6, working girl], went to jail for an old case he had. Sly had just spent the last year working on his DJ skills. Mickey supplied Sly with record after record and money after money for records after records. Sly was not a criminal and the judicial system was taking a man from his family for something that happened too many years ago. No one totally understood why Mickey was with Sly anyway, and now it didn't matter. Mickey and I couldn't afford the monthly rent without Sly's Veteran's check. The lease was in Sly's name. There were many Jehovah's Witnesses living in the building who prayed on a daily basis for Mickey and me. They prayed that we would move out of the building. The odds were against us and we were thrown out two weeks after Sly went to prison. Mickey and I carted our stuff up to a hotel on 72nd Street right off Broadway called the Embassy.

> *The Embassy is now called the Embassy Towers. It is a lavish co-op Apartment Complex. When we moved there it was a hotel catering to pimps, prostitutes, welfare recipients, sexual deviants, artsy folks, and the aged. We fit right in. How interesting that all these hotel rooms that housed these diverse groups are now $1,500 Studio Apartments.*
> *Where did all the colorful residents go? We didn't all move to Hollywood!*

We paid a weekly rent and that was easier to manage, even though it turned out to be more in the long run. We had one bed, which Mickey and I shared. We had a lot of fun but we began to get on each other's nerves. Mickey became more sexually promiscuous. I mean she began to sleep with other men for fun and love and not for money. And I was always looking to score, get shtupped, as well.

We were right by Central Park and would hang out by the fountain every weekend. Back then queens blended in and if we were spooked, read, clocked, identified as trans-women, nothing would really happen. Mickey and I wore very sexual and provocative clothing. Mickey was officially free from marriage and I was new to my femininity. She was my mentor and I followed her lead. One summer day we went to the park and there was a guy there with a camera who took a liking to us. He wanted to take our picture. Being the shy, refined and well-groomed women that we were, we quickly did anything he asked. He said, "Hey go in the water and jump up and down." We obliged. This was the '70s and the lake at Central Park was polluted with homeless feces, garbage, spit, urine and who knows what else. Here were a 29-year-old, five foot, five inch Latina and a seventeen-year-old five foot, ten inch white girl in see-through leotards jumping up and down in this bacteria infested water. Never got to see the film developed!

Without a main man around Mickey and I began to let things fall apart. The Embassy establishment employees were not the friendliest to the trans-women in the building. Some would secretly flirt behind their colleagues' backs, but most were pretty rude.

Our toilet broke after an argument during which I threw something at Mickey in the bathroom but hit the toilet instead. We never got it fixed. We just used the toilet and would not flush it. Get back here. I know this is disgusting but it's the truth.

One day we were in a cab fighting and screaming and Mickey jumped out of the cab and scratched my arm. Being the type of person who needed to get even I waited patiently for the right moment. That afternoon Mickey took a shower. I put nose plugs on and started to shovel out the stuffed-up toilet. The old fumes and smoke began to seep towards the shower as I shoveled the feces into a pail. All of a sudden I heard gagging and choking and Mickey ran out of the shower, out of the hotel room, and into the hall butt naked, little peepee swinging in the air. I won! We told that story so many times to our friends, because after the fact the whole scenario was hysterical. Life with the Bradys it was not.

Many things transpired in 1977. I took my first horrible acid trip and it was the year there was a major blackout in New York City. Both times I found myself walking the streets of New York City, headed to a dark and desolate hotel room.

During this acid trip I walked from the Gilded Grape on 45th Street to my hotel on 72nd. I was scared to death and everything around me was disgusting, scary, unsafe and isolating. When I got to the hotel I sat in my bed for 24 hours, scared to death and miserable from the trip. I soon took acid again. Doesn't that make sense?

The night of the blackout I had to take the stairs of the hotel to the 23rd floor and began trembling from the fright. There was looting on the streets and I didn't know what I was going to find as I walked up those dark stairs. I could never get used to this unsafe environment I was now living in. In a desperate plea for help I called my dad in Long Island and begged him to let me come back home. He agreed. The next day I told Mickey. I packed up and I left her in that hotel room alone to fend for herself. Our relationship would never be the same after that.

Our relationship became estranged. Later Mickey went home to her family and went back to school. She became academically sharp. She was studying to be a paralegal. In the early 1990s I heard about Mickey's HIV status. I invited her to a round-table discussion when I began to work as a coordinator of an HIV/AIDS Intervention Program. I kept trying to connect with and support her but she wanted nothing to do with me. In fact, I heard through the grapevine (no pun intended) that she hated my guts. I didn't understand. But as I write this, maybe there was some underlying fury for me leaving her alone in 1977. This is not an excuse, but I was seventeen, just about to turn eighteen, and I couldn't take the lifestyle or what came with it anymore. I needed a solid foundation. I needed some safety.

Home to Long Island

The furniture from my old house on East 85th Street Brooklyn was still there in the house in Long Island. Some things were still familiar to me. A lot went down in the almost two years I was in New York City. My dad, his wife, and son were the same, but I was a totally different person, besides the obvious, *smartass!*

They used my Brooklyn living room furniture in the second floor living space, which was not lived in. No one used that room. It was a reminder to me that the era of my true family of origin was gone. Most of the time my dad, his wife, and her son, would hang out in the den. My 'living room' just sat there like a reminder that there was no Blumenstein family anymore.

At first my dad wanted me to dress like a boy. I told him no matter what I dressed like I would still be a girl. He and his wife felt I would confuse her son. Her son was eleven years old and had an eating disorder. But, as usual, I was considered the child with all the problems.

I immediately called the son over to the two of them and said, "Is this confusing? You met me as a boy but I am really a girl and now I want you to call me Roe. Is that confusing to you?" He said no and it was settled.

It was hard being back in his house, a house in Long Island, a house where there was no love. My being there must've caused so much tension between him and his new wife. But the ability to lie my head down on a pillow and feel safe was worth every fight those two would get into. How I had missed three meals a day, not worrying about rent,

not worrying about knives or guns, or being raped, or turning a trick, or
...

Those two short years on the streets laid my neo-intrapsychic foundation for many years to come.

Lynda, the 'passing' fancy

I went to the city every weekend. I hung out and partied and then I would go home and rest up all week for my weekend excursions. Life was tedious.

One night at the Gilded Grape I was in the bathroom with Miss Billy and Miss Cricket, and this very lovely, pale-skinned lady. There were very few pretty white faces at the Gilded Grape. There were many high-yellow-skinned beauties, but few women who looked like my old neighborhood. They were looking at pictures of a wedding and discussing how 'real' the maid of honor was. I then realized that Lynda was the light-skinned beauty and was like me. We would quickly become friends, as with Mickey, even though there was a big discrepancy with our ages as well. Lynda was fifteen years my senior and became my big sister right away.

In meeting Lynda I saw a whole new world of how a woman like me was allowed to live. Lynda had this great apartment right in the suburbs of the Bronx. Her apartment was flashy and mod, her lifestyle was demure and sophisticated, and her belief in herself was strong and vibrant. Lynda was a great cook, a fantastic obsessive house cleaner, she could sew, and she could fix anything around the house. Lynda had talent and drive and she was also a working girl. Lynda was a dominatrix and had a real attitude with her clientele. She had clients who picked her up and drove her around shopping. She had clients to bathe and feed her. She had clients to do all sorts of things. She was sophisticated, but she also had an edge. She had many boyfriends and she was even legally married. Lynda showed me all these new opportunities. She was also a nurturer. She believed that I had a lot going for me and she helped me dream again. She was a drug dealer and it was so simple to cop now that she was around. Her drugs and her energy enhanced my dreaming capabilities.

Lynda turned me on to so many new things. I was in awe of her talents. She took me under her wing and there was no turning back.

When Lynda was 23 she was living with her soon-to-be husband and she got castrated. Lynda had the silkiest skin I had ever seen and she had so few hairs on her legs she could actually just tweeze them. She believed it was due to castration. We made the decision that I would have the same procedure done to me. I was seventeen and this was illegal. Lynda set up an appointment for me to meet the 'tranny' doctor on east 86th Street and Park.

Dr. Wesser the messer
Goodbye to 'tessie,' the nose is messy

There was a line to get into his office. Everybody there was TS, TV, a queen, a porno star, Latina, and/or their admirers. It was a zoo and I was scared to death. I went up to the window to sign in. I was trembling. The woman behind the window gave me some paperwork to fill out. They didn't ask for proof of age and I didn't offer it. The 'girls' in the room were snapping on each other, folks were laughing and carrying on. I felt so awkward and out of place. It was mostly Latinas and they were all pumped up with silicone in their asses and cheeks. Many had big breasts. And many were well put together, their bodies dripping with labeled accessories. These women looked like a cross between chipmunks and Fredericks of Hollywood models. Remember, it was the late '70s and these girls started in the '60s where lots of hair, eyelashes and big cheeks were the rage. I was plain, with tight jeans and a simple blouse. I was shy and awkward. The nurse called out 'Roe Blumenstein' and I had to get up and walk all the way across the room in front of these judgmental sassy bitches.

I met with Dr. Wesser and he was so friendly and calming it helped me calm down. I told him I wanted to get castrated and also wanted my nose done, (fixed, made smaller). He agreed and said it would cost a certain amount of money. I told him I didn't have a lot of money and his fee immediately went down. He told me that he would do my castration for $500 and my nose for $400, since I could still use my dad's health insurance for the hospital stay. He said he would write it up as a deviated septum – which I still have!

I don't know how I managed it but I got my dad to give me his health insurance information and give me $1,000 from my bank account. I set up the appointments.

Lynda would get one of her clients to take me to the doctor for the castration. It would be done right in his office and I would leave right after. The nose was to be done a month later in the hospital and I would stay overnight.

Lynda was going to make sure everything was all right for me. I later found out that she had been left alone after her first surgery so she wanted to make sure I would be in good hands and not have to experience the emotional trauma alone. (It can be an emotional rollercoaster when all of a sudden your body stops producing hormones.)

She wanted to make sure I wasn't alone. Her client Gus picked us up right on time and took us downtown to meet with the chopper, I mean the doctor. I never gave this any thought. I knew that the only way to make sure I didn't begin to look like a man was to remove the testosterone from my body. I didn't think about future childbearing issues, I didn't think about complications, and I didn't think about how my father was going to react to what I was about to do. I just knew that this was what had to be done because Lynda was living proof that without those things in-between one's legs a woman like us had more chances in life to blend in. I was extremely passable as Roe, but I was also seventeen. As I got older that might have changed, maybe. My dad was a big, hairy gorilla and my brother was pretty hairy as well. I had no facial hair except a peach fuzz mustache (which I still enjoying ripping off every six weeks! Shush, don't tell anybody).

When we got to Dr. Wesser's office he told me to take off my pants. He took a needle and shot it in the middle of what's now my labia majora. That needle made me see stars. I could feel the blood dripping down my crotch towards my backside. The room was too bright and the feeling was surreal. I would feel a tug and then another tug and I would hear a snip and then another snip. I felt something being tied but there was no pain. He said, "OK kid. Hey, wanna say goodbye to these babies?" and I was immediately nauseous. How did he know I was still a kid and why did I have my tubes tied so early in life? I was bandaged and told to get dressed. I couldn't believe it was over that quickly. I also couldn't believe I was expected to dress myself. I got a script for 'Tuiys' (Tuinals, yummy) and some antibiotics. We drove home, Lynda grinning in the front seat asserting her baby was now a grown woman. Hey, the song wasn't I left my heart in San Francisco, it was I left my balls on 86th Street.

As soon as we got to Lynda's house I popped my Tuiys. She put me in bed and cooked me a great dinner. She remembered how she was starving and alone and wanted to make it up to herself by taking the best care of me. The Tuiys knocked me right out and I never ate her delicious steak dinner. So much for her healing herself and so much for my dinner! The next day I saw stars and we weren't watching Star Search. I stayed in bed for two days. Lynda played nursemaid, and I am not talking about the enemas she used to give her clients. She brought over a bedpan for me and took care for me. At that time she had started dating a man who turned her world around as well as her body. I could tell her nursemaid attitude was wearing thin and it was time for me to get out of her house and out of her bed so she could roll around with her little Italian stallion. I called my boyfriend and he told me to come over. I left Lynda's house less than a week after the surgery. If you can call a clip, snip, drip, flip procedure a surgery.

I got to my boyfriend's house and we immediately made love. I got the hardest erection I ever got. I would never get erections. Besides, I would never use that part of my body with any relationship since my transition. I would always hide it, but this time I couldn't. I was so embarrassed. I also felt my stitches pull and tear. What was I thinking? We broke up shortly after due to my embarrassment. He was fine. I wasn't. I left his house Monday morning to head back to Long Island.

Monday night my dad came home from a hard day's work and found me in bed. He came into my room and asked me what was up. I said, "Dad, I had the first part of my operation." "What the fuck are you talking about?" he sternly asserted. I said, "I got castrated." My dad lost his temper from that moment and the louder he got the smaller I felt. "You fucken' freak. How dare you do this and lie here in my house? What the fuck is wrong with you, you fucken freak? How dare you? I can't believe you did this." I couldn't believe he wasn't congratulating me for doing what I needed to do and 'taking the road less traveled.' Didn't he understand that now I would be even 'lovelier' and stay 'passable?' Didn't he understand that this was a great thing and he should be proud of me for having the balls to get rid of them? I sat up and slowly said, "You are too late for saying this, it is already done. Now I need to sleep. Please leave my room." He left and I felt so bad that he didn't understand. After all, he wasn't going through what I had to deal with? They weren't his nuts that had been cracked, they were mine!

The next month I went to the doctor and got my new nose. After a week with bandages Lynda took me to the doctor to have the cast removed. I walked out of the office where Lynda was but she wasn't smiling. What do you want for $400, a good nose job?
Two weeks passed and my nose looked a little crooked. One day, I was in the mirror looking at it and I tried to push it over a little, when all of a sudden I heard a crack and my nose moved a little more to the right. Nothing like sneezing and wiping your right cheek!

Dr Schiffman
Dr Schiffman was a doctor I met when I was sixteen. He was not nearly as nurturing as Wesser the Messer. His bedside manner was abrupt. And he would make comments attesting to the need for his services. He did a lot of silicone injections which would 'camouflage masculine characteristics' – his words. In the '70s loose silicone was still legal (even though it has been considered illegal and then legal in some states, many plastic surgeons use it to camouflage 'wasting syndrome' for people dealing with HIV/AIDS).
One day I was in his office and he had an Asian doctor there as well. He began to discuss my face with this doctor. He said, "Now look how long this face is. I can make this face appear shorter by shooting some silicone into the chin and in the cheeks." He did not even ask me if I wanted any in my chin. One always felt like a freak of nature and an experiment when going to Schiffman's office. And one would always go there. One, meaning me!

Schiffman made sure of it. I wonder if he did that intentionally so that we would always come back trying hard to appear more feminine? He would tell me that I was extremely feminine for what I was. Do you think that was a compliment?

8.
LEGAL AND LOOSE

51 Street and Ninth
the 51 Club
the Thief
Death of an Aunt

Sex, drugs and disco
Suicide I
My brief College Experience

the 220 Club, the Pink Ladies
Miss 220, Self Obession
the Healing Pill Q
Fire Island; 42nd with a beach
the jealousies

the CLUB SCENE continues...
G.G. Knickerbocker
G. Barnums, Hello Christoper
MISSed GAY NEW YORK
Miss 220 Revival

8

Legal and Loose

51 Street and Ninth

Right before my eighteenth birthday I went home to my father's house, after breaking night, and found a note in my room. It said, "Roe, here is your bank book and your stocks. I moved into an apartment in Aunt Helen's building ... Dad." I couldn't believe this letter. I didn't know who to turn to, where to turn, or how to negotiate my feelings. I thought I was home and safe but I actually wasn't. Nothing at that moment made sense. I once again felt abandoned by another parent. On one level I was ecstatic that I had a bank account with $11,000, and on the other I felt more lost than I ever had in my whole life.

You see, when you are a runaway or throwaway and you are on the streets, you understand the predicament that you are in. Your mind has already negotiated and accepted your homelessness status. But when you are hanging out days at a time whoring around and take a train to Long Island expecting housing normalcy and it's not there, you are thrown off. My dad had, once again, disappointed me.

> *For most of my young adult life I would secretly battle my feelings about disappointing him, not considering he was failing me as well.*

I was very nice to Gail when I saw her soon after I read the note. She came home and found me in the house. She changed the locks immediately, as I found out the next day when I stopped by to get more stuff. I never saw most of my stuff after that. All of my family's possessions from childhood were left in that house. My dad took with him two lamps and some pictures. My dad had given Gail one of my mother's only two pieces of jewelry. Gail was not a total disgusting piece of shit. She gave my dad back my mother's Moses pendant.

My bank account was in Canarsie, Brooklyn. As I walked into the bank I started to feel like I was getting bigger and bigger. I knew as soon as I met with a teller I was going to have to explain why this bank account had a boy's name and I wasn't a boy but I was the owner of this account. There would be endless times I would have to go through this and each time made me feel worse. It would've been great if it could be explained matter of factly and all who were involved would react in a positive way. On the other hand if I had felt positive about the whole 'T' experience it would not matter how others reacted.

I found an apartment on 51st Street right in Hell's Kitchen area. The rent was $425 a month. My friend Mickey and her boyfriend lived across the street. I was so attracted to Mickey and her boyfriend. They were the hustle king and queen and all I was, was a queen without the … Mickey was gorge, *beautiful*, had a perfect black woman's ass, *Mickey was white,* and the best bedroom eyes. Mickey had her own demons, as did her boyfriend, but they wouldn't be revealed to me until much later.

The 51 Club
The 51 Club was a bar/disco just down the block from my house. It cost five dollars to get in. It was an after-hours bar that opened right after all other clubs were closing. Get it, after-hours!
I first went to the 51 Club when I was sixteen years old. And now I lived right down the block. How convenient!
The 51 Club was a place to hang out and dance the hustle, latin hustle of course, no doofy white hustle for me.
The 51 Club was a place where working girls and boys, and I don't mean cashiers or waitresses, would go to party after a tough night of hustling. Some of us would go to the 51 Club to hustle, dance, and some of us would go to drink and party after a night of hustling.
The 51 Club had rooms in the back on the left where people could go and have a relaxing private conversation, hmmm.

When I was just sixteen I was sitting in one of these rooms with my newfound hormone induced body. I was sitting in the room with a few folks, one of whom was the infamous Carol Durelle. Carol was this gorgeous African-American woman who was from the Jewel Box Revue. She was famous back then, but I didn't know it. We were talking about money and prestige and I wanted so much to join in the discussion. I blurted out, "When I turn eighteen I get $11,000." I was so proud. Carol, an absolute adult, quickly turned around and let me know that I was a peasant. Carol explained to us about her stocks and property and every other thing she had. Carol must've been at least in her mid to late twenties. Didn't she understand her responsibility to nurture this youth? Or was I supposed to learn the reality of being shot down at that moment?
Another incident was when I finally began to grow breasts. I stopped wearing falsies. I went to the 51 Club with one of my only three outfits on, my lime green tube top and my wraparound pink skirt. But this time I just wore the tube top. As I was being thrown around the dance floor my tube

top fell down. Of course it did, I had no breasts to speak about to hold it up. This guy named Lefty was on the sideline screaming, "The little girl finally got knots. Look at her. How cute." A quality of sarcasm within his broken English announcement that left me, not Lefty, mortified. Lefty would degrade me once more in the future. There was another incident with this damn green tube top. When I first came 'Out' I was on the Gilded Grape dance floor doing the hustle. I was such a hustler! I had Ellen's boyfriend's socks for breasts in this tube top and one went flying out, tumbling onto the dance floor. I think I would've been less appalled if the socks were clean and David didn't have athlete foot concerns.

The thief
When I got my apartment I wanted everything that belonged to me. My mom had had two pieces of jewelry that she wore all the time. She had her Moses pendant from her father-in-law and she had a charm bracelet representing substantial happenings in her life: engagement, babies, marriage, etc. Mickey, my mother's friend, had my mom's charm bracelet in her house. I don't know why. Mickey hated my father's new wife and I remember Mickey making sure some of my mom's things didn't end up with that bitch. Shortly after I got my apartment I went to Mickey and asked her for my mom's bracelet. She gave it to me. My mom kept this in a clear plastic box. Along with my mom's bracelet I had a few pocket watches and my birth ring. I don't think Mickey wanted to give me the bracelet but knew she had to. Mickey was not happy to see me as Roe and just wanted me out of her house and away from her and her daughter.

I remember one night at the 51 Club Lefty and his girl had a fight. He had no place to stay. I offered him my apartment to crash in. I had an air-conditioner in only one room. It was a hot summer night. We dragged the mattress into the living room and this is where we slept. Lefty and I fooled around a little but nothing about him or his appeal is worth discussing. The next day I woke up to find him gone and so was my jewelry. Another part of my mom was immediately gone, taken away, and I was left devastated. To add insult to injury I saw Lefty that night on the block where one of the clubs we frequented was. I threatened him and told him how I felt. He immediately threatened me back and put fear in my heart. I tried to get him 86'd from the club but I didn't have that much juice in the bar industry yet. I wasn't accepting of this injustice and I prayed for revenge. Keep in mind the law of karma? Well, who knows what happened to Lefty.

Death of an aunt

I've discussed going to see my aunt at her sick bed. I had been living on my own for approximately three months now. Life was great as far as lack of responsibilities was concerned. I lived high. I partied high. Every day, I got high! I slept around. I danced. I got dressed up in that white, trashy disco flavor sort of way. I didn't have to hustle (sleep with strangers for money), but I practiced, continuously, the hustle, every night! I felt one above others, although on another level I was not that vicious or full of myself. I got a call from my dad. He told me my aunt, my dear Aunt Hannah, was dead. I knew I would have to go to the funeral and was secretly excited to go, pay my respects, see my cousins, and have them see me. My dad informed me the funeral had been the week before. "How come you didn't call me?" I asked. He said he had tried to call but there had been no answer. One more time my dad, in his roundabout way, let me know how ashamed he was of me. I felt like he could've tried again. This was the aunt that I had lived with my whole entire early childhood. Although she had thrown me out of her office two years prior, I knew she loved me. My dad instilled more shame into me, although I know he didn't intentionally do that. What would family think about me? I didn't show up to the funeral. I wanted to see Denise, Douglas, Marsha, Sheldon and his new girlfriend Claire, and that was my chance. Did I want to go to show off the new Roe or did I want to go to connect to some semblance of normalcy, normalcy that was totally devoid of this lifestyle; clubs, drugs, nightlife, thievery, no responsibility, the city streets ...

I've lost a lot of people since then. But losing my aunt and not being able to appropriately mourn added to the ways in which I would be traumatized by family death. Hey, would someone go get me a tissue and a harp!

Sex/Drugs And disco
Sex/Drugs And disco

Life at this time consisted of important rituals and concerns. The responsibility I had to my colleagues, peers and fellow cohorts was overwhelming. I needed a specific outfit to wear each night. Not having a tremendous income it was taxing trying to come up with a fab outfit each and every night. I needed something that could travel, since I might not go home for a few days. I needed something that would bring attention to my elongated skeleton. I needed something that would get me drugs and get me laid. This was a highly stressful position and I was grateful to the downers and the uppers to help me through these trying times. There was a girl by the name of Taxi, [see Pink Ladies], who was the queen, well, queen of queens, in NYC. She could make a rope look like a fashion statement. She had the amazing talent of taking nothing and making it look like something. In reality she had nothing, but she definitely looked like she had everything. I guess that was the point. It didn't matter what you had, what you were, your morals, values, education or spirituality. None of that mattered in the discos. It just mattered what you looked like (this kind of reminds me of where I live now in Los Angeles).

My responsibilities to life and my fellow hombres was that I looked a certain way (I never looked the way I wanted anyway, so I guess I wasn't a success). I needed to be available sexually and I needed to take the right amount of substances so that I could function, i.e. dance the hustle, give good head, get laid, and make it home and go back out the next evening. These were some trying times, and at eighteen years old I don't think it was fair that I had to juggle so much responsibility.

Suicide I

> *This first suicide attempt is vague. I don't remember what occurred that made me react so impulsively. However, the things I do remember I will share with you. These issues I bring up are important for many reasons. They symbolize and reinstate the power of addiction and how it plays out in a person's life in addition to how it directly affects the family system. These issues touch upon internal racism and sexism that one must work on on a daily basis to heal from it as well as to help others heal who are affected by its ignorance. This also touches upon how societal transphobia plays out in one's (a person of TS experience) life.*

My first suicide attempt took place in my dad's apartment in Midwood, Brooklyn. I moved back to his house after running out of my bat/bar mitzvah money. I think I spent all the money in six months. I am not totally sure of the time frame. My dad had a one-bedroom and I was living in the living room. Or should I say existing, or taking up space in that apartment. I used a lot of uppers. I snorted coke when people offered it to me, and took Tuinals often. I needed to control my emotions and these drugs helped. You see, life on the streets, the death of my mom, my irresponsible behaviors and actions to myself, my family, my inability to focus, my transexual identity, the issues a youngster faces who is trans, and a world full of misunderstanding, ignorance and hatred towards the trans experience led me down this path. I am not a victim, but at this point in my life I needed direction. I needed therapy, support, guidance, and lots of loving. Drugs did all that and more. That was the positive side effect of drugs. They kept me going and they kept my overwhelming sadness dormant. However, sometimes the drugs just didn't work and this is when the suicide attempts would emerge.

> *I am telling this part of my story for these reasons. My priority is that it might help the reader who is depressed and does not see the light. Somehow I am hoping this book gets into your hands and mind and you will see that there is 'a light at the end of the tunnel.' I aspire to see that your impulsivity does not have to be exploited and you can ride the depression through. Exactly what I now do and what I should've known at the ages of 19, 23, 26, as well as many other times.*

It was nighttime and I made a decision. I was going to take all my pills because there was no hope. I knew I wanted to die a pretty corpse so I made myself up. I put on my best bra and panties. I heard somewhere that if one has injected silicone anywhere in their body that it would shift when you die. So I put this bra on so that I would keep the new bozangas in place. I wrote a note to my dad, my poor dad. (How dare I do this to him again. He had lived through this with his wife and now his youngest kid was going to put him through this torture.)

I told him I was sorry but my life was wrong. I couldn't get past what had happened to me with my mom, trans stuff, and my self-hate. I didn't realize it then but my depression had a lot to do with my drug intake and how the drugs magnified everything.

> *I believe I will die with a depressive personality but it is manageable if it is not magnified by substances.*

I wrote this note and left it next to my bed. I took the pills with a glass of milk because milk is good for your bones. No, you asshole!

I took it because I didn't want to throw up all those pills. You ask, "What was she thinking?" Did I think I was going to die before anyone found me? Was I screaming out for help? Did I need more attention like the fainting spell at summer camp?

I did think I was going to die and I wanted to die. I didn't have the luxury of a car like my mom, so I had to stay home (they found my mom in her car in Seaview Park).

How selfish to leave the remains of me for my dad to pick up!

In my own defense I think it had to do with the drugs and the lifestyle, not just that I was totally self-centered and didn't care about my dad. I don't think I thought it through. And I don't think many people who attempt suicide think it through. We just want the pain to end. We just want it to stop.

I woke up in my dad's arms being carried into Kings County Hospital. I was screaming obscenities. I was saying racist things. And no, I wasn't reliving the drama I displayed in summer camp eight years prior! I was distraught, but deep in my mind I felt like as soon as they found out my trans identity, I wouldn't even be allowed to stay there. My dad dropped me off and I was locked up for 72 hours. It seemed as though they didn't want to deal with me. On some level it seemed like they couldn't wait to get rid of me. Was this me talking to me or was I onto something? I called my dad pleading for help and I could hear his pain and confusion but his inability to get real with me as well. We both agreed I needed to go to college when I got home. Home? Home! Somehow there was no more 'home,' and I wouldn't see a home for quite some time. Maybe never!

> *In my work as a clinician, when I engage people who attempt suicide, their treatment plan is: 1. Out of the hospital after 72 hours; 2. Into college; and 3.Let's not discuss it.*
> *Yeah, that will work!*

I started classes in September of '79.

My brief college experience

Although I transgressed gender boundaries, at sixteen years old most of my time was spent in clubs, on the streets, and not within an academic arena. And now I was back in school with my paperwork changed to Roe. It was simple. I don't remember how I did it, I just did it. I registered at Kings Borough Community College right on the coast of Brooklyn's Manhattan Beach. It was a lovely campus. But I wasn't.

I believed myself not to be attractive especially in the real world and that was very upsetting to me. There was a different look and dress code and I didn't have the internal or external tools to compete. I was scared to speak up in class. I was scared to go to the lunchroom. I was scared. I was scared of the lunchroom as a child and now I was just as terrified as an adult. One day I had to give a speech and I was humiliated.

Not only did it have to do with the statistics that state there's a high percentage of our population that fears public speaking. It also had to do with the fact that I was trans and I was told my voice had to always sound a certain way so no one would detect that I was trans. Not being able to be myself was a lot to carry in addition to trying to excel in an environment that I was not familiar with. In addition, I had just attempted suicide and had no outlet as to why this (school) was the answer to the depression. In addition, I was an addict but no one was diagnosing me as such, simply because they were too concerned with my transexual identity.

So here I am in school taking up space, I mean thinking about recreational leadership as a major. I stayed in school for one semester and barely got by. I did meet a bunch of nice potheads with whom I cut classes. I also realized as a female I was ugly and could not stand next to any of the women who had beautiful hair, nails, teeth, etc.

Where's a counselor when you need one?

The 220 Club

During my long, arduous tenure at Kings Borough Community College I needed a break on the weekends to get loose and let go of all the tension I was building up within my weekday responsibilities. All that pot smoking in-between classes was getting to me. I would frequent a club called the 220 Club, which was on 220 West Houston in NYC's West Village/Little Italy/Flat Iron district.

> *The paradox of life is that this once after-hours, drug infested disco is now a place for 12-step meetings.*

I would go out to the 220 Club, especially if I didn't meet the man of my dreams at an earlier event or if I didn't reach that drug induced plateau. The 220 opened at 4 a.m. and closed between ten and noon every day. There were three floors filled with an eclectic group.

The 220 Club's manager was named Sal (Sally, may s/he rest in peace). Sal offered me a job as the front desk cashier during my winter break from school. I never went back for another semester in school and I sat at that front desk for two and a half years.

The eclectic crew at the 220 consisted of:

Sal, the manager, who was gay. I say 'was' because he is dead now. Are you still gay when you are dead?

He was also a transgendered individual. Sally was a doll. Sally was an effeminate man around five feet nine inches. He was a little chunky, had the sweetest eyes and a caring demeanor. He was very supportive of the tranny girls.

Kelly was the owner of the 220 and owned another club in the West Village named Kellys. Kelly was a short, dykey woman who seldom said hello to the staff of the 220 unless she was toasted (drunk).

Mona (another gay guy) worked behind the first floor bar. He was the main bartender. He was a loud, boisterous, hateful queen who was funny as shit.

97

The bouncers/doormen consisted of hot Latino, African-American and Italian popis who loved the girls, trans or not. Get them drunk enough and they would even fool around with some of the guys. Most of them had records, and I don't mean solos on an album. The second floor bartender's name was Hector. Hector began his profession at the 220 dating Sally but they broke up shortly thereafter. Hector was a gorgeous Latino/a popi who was a dear friend.

On the third floor there was Marvin and Jessie. Marvin was an older gay white man who lived not far from me in Brooklyn. He was my drive to and from work every night. Marvin was heavyset, with a dry humor, and very smart.

Jessie (may she rest in peace) was the sweetest Latina queen anyone could ever want to know. Jessie was a big girl, I mean a big girl. Jessie had the prettiest face and the most endearing smile.

Then there were the waitress staff. This job was pretty transient. But the main waitress/coat check, sometimes bartenderesses, were Billy, Leslie, and my friend Lynda. Billy and Leslie were queens at night and physically female challenged during the day. Lynda we've already discussed.

The patrons of the 220 Club consisted of, but were not limited to, the drag communities, working girls and boys, the bar communities, drug dealers, trans women, party animals, addicts and alcoholics, the mafia, and tourists. We were one big happy family. This group protected me as well as financially took care of me. It was an extremely exciting time in my life. Within the trans/drag/gay communities I became a part of, I truly lucked out with jobs, an opportunity to have some power within the bar scene, financial security, and responsibility to a new family that accepted me 'as is.'

I made a small salary but I also had opportunities to increase my income here and there. Most of the girls I knew had to sleep with strangers to survive.

Unfortunately, that was the cultural milieu for trans women back then, and to this day as well.

At least this was the case for the trannies who were transitioning young, or were women of color. I lucked out with this job, although I still had to sleep with strangers, but it was by choice. Working for an after-hours joint was great in the summer. It was also great if you were an addict, which I was, but didn't identify as such. Most of us were addicts but we didn't identify as that. Even when Lynda went into the hospital because of her IVDU issues we all looked at her as having a problem and did not look at ourselves. Sally was a big cokehead, Kelly was an alcoholic and coke fiend, Mona was a drunk, Jessie was a big druggy ... and I, you ask? I took lots of anything and everything and used crème de cacao with milk to wash it all down.

To get into the 220 cost someone seven dollars, but if you had a Quaalude you got in for one dollar without a drink ticket. I loved my Quaaludes and Tuinals and Black Beauties and Puerto Rican, *oops!* I mean I had a great time at the 220 Club. I forgot which was a pill and which was a man, I was swallowing so many.

I fell in love, and got my heart broken by two men I met while working at the 220. No matter what went on in my life during these two and a half years, the 220 Club was the place to turn for solace, for support, for recognition, for fun, for drugs, for atmosphere, for romance … This was the hub within my eco-system. Sally, Marvin, Lynda and the rest of the gang were my family. The bouncers became my older brothers. The front desk became a shrine to a self-centered wannabe – me. Sally was always my confidant, and Lynda was my older sister, my seamstress, the power behind my 'wannabe star' status. I received many gifts and experienced many tragedies during the 220 days.

And we will touch upon them as you read on, so read on, dammit!

The pink ladies

Remember Mickey (Mary Magdalene) and Taxi (fashion model with a 25 cent piece)? Mickey, Taxi, Pamela and I were the Pink Ladies of the New Gilded Grape a.k.a. GG Barnum Room. We formed this club to build camaraderie, get some media attention, and have fun as the new girls in town. By this time Mickey was 30 years old, and that was over-the-hill for the club scene. However, Mickey turned heads and there was no taking that away from her. Taxi and I were the youngest. Two African-American women (Taxi was half French as well), one Latina, and a Jew. We were the Benetton commercial before Benetton thought of becoming culturally diverse. That was how I lived my life. We came together across race, across socio-economic status, across age. Together we were invincible. The Pink Ladies lasted about an hour, club standard time.

But our friendships would interconnect on and off for the next 20 years.

Miss 220

All I remember about this first after-hours' beauty contest was that I was in it and came in second or third. Imagine an after-hours joint having a beauty contest? To tell you the truth, the previous Miss 220s were extremely lovely, some cut-throat, crazed, and drug addicted, but lovely.

There was Jackie La Frenchie (may she rest in peace). Jackie was a short Latina powerhouse who skipped town (the west coast) after cutting someone. She had that two-toned hairdo where it was bleach blonde in the front, feathered and very Farrah Fawcett-like, and dark brown and bra length in the back. Yes, I did say she cut someone, didn't I? As a kid she was dangerous, and maybe she had to be. After all, she grew up in a tough neighborhood and she was a femme Latino, now Latina. She was short and she probably had to defend herself from all the hate.

I am not condoning slashing anyone's throat, I am just making our society, and you, the reader, look at what part we play in all the violence.

Jackie had no problem passing as Jackie. She was completely femme. But she was also known for throwing the guys that she dated over and plunging them like the bitch they thought she was. She was a tough, but sensitive, woman and had many sides to her personality. She was always cool with me. When Jackie performed on stage she would sing live and impersonate Tina Turner.

Another Miss 220 was 'Tishe' Sherve, a.k.a. Brian Belovitch. Brian was lovely as 'Tishe' and spent fifteen years of his life as 'Tishe.' As 'Tishe,' Brian looked like a big Jewish bombshell. She had these humongous breasts and these big, brown, almond eyes. S/he was a true thespian and her aura would hit a room two blocks before s/he got there, and so would hir breasts.

When Tishe had two years clean and sober in the early 1990s s/he went back to being Brian. It took a lot of guts and I give him all the respect he deserves. He just has issues with the trans community and I guess it has a lot to do with his soul searching.
When Brian was 'Tishe' he was my second sponsor in 12-step programs.

Then there was Pamela (one of the pink ladies). Pamela was, in essence, always a lady (although she made sure her men kissed the pillow like Jackie did). When I first entered the Gilded Grape in 1976 there was a guy by the name of Tido who took a liking to me. He liked me so much he took me by the West Side Highway, bent me over, fucked me, and then wouldn't even pay my way back into the Gilded Grape.

Well, I guess I could understand. After all, it was a five-dollar cover.

It turned out that Pam and Tido were an item. I went to the Gilded Grape one night and was told that Pam was looking for me. Here was this exotic black woman coming my way. I can't tell you my heart was pumping Kool-Aid. It was pumping terror. She was loving and respectful and said I deserved better than a punk like Tido. Now that's a fucking lady, eh?

Another face on the wall of the 220 Club was Blondie, a.k.a. Muneca. Blondie was a hot Latina who could hustle her ass off on the dance floor. She looked just like Blondie (Deborah Harry) and I think that is where she got her name, Blondie that is. She was sexy and cute and a little chubby, and sweet and …

Jessy was one of the Miss 220s as well. I think she won the year I was in my first Miss 220 contest. Bitch!

Another, Hollywood, Princess Ava Hollywood, that is. She was a queen to be remembered. Ava was a year older than me and we both came 'Out' around the same time. Ava got her nose done and there was no talking to her after that. People fed her ego. And she was lovely, with this thick, curly dark red mane and these piercing blue/green eyes. She immediately became a hit at Studio 54. She would come over to my side of town, I guess when she wanted to slum it or to turn a trick or cop Tuiys (Tuinals). One day, Ava and I were on the dance floor, a space I frequented 90 per cent of the time in the late 70s. She had a brand new Louis Vuitton. I couldn't afford a Luigie Vuten but I had a fake one that Lynda designed. Ava acted like she was the queen of the world and she would pull anyone who was around into her fantasy and onto the dance floor. As we were dancing and posing I said, "Hey, Ava, let's throw our Louis' on the floor and kick them around because we can." She kicked her $200 bag all over the dance floor and I kicked my Woolworth's original around as well.

This was the line-up of most of the girls hanging on the walls of the first floor of the 220 Club. These reigning queens were in full black and white photographs staring at me every night. I think that might have been one of the reasons I made a shrine of me (from my Jimmy Treetop Collection) at the front desk. I was so darn jealous that I was not a black and white Miss sleaze after-hours 220 princess. I was just a runner-up.

Self-obsession
Make me a star, make me beautiful, have everyone take notice, please! What do you mean I am still the exact same way?

I worked at the front desk of the 220 Club with a light shining on my face. I sat at that cashier's station posed and lit, in more ways than one. I went out all the time and spent the night looking for one of those lights to shine on me. I would dance and stare and pose and fantasize. Although it seemed a long time ago when I was in Performing Arts (PA) High School, the training was worth it. I did win the Best Actress Award at the GG Knickerbocker Club 'Academy Awards Night.'

> *Self-obsession is a component of the disease of addiction. And one might say this book is still a way to allow that part of me to shine and stand out.*

However, the logic behind the writing of this book has less to do with self-obsession and more to do with my desire for you to see the world through my understanding of cultural norms.

The healing pill Q

I don't care what anyone says, I thank god every day for Quaaludes. They made life lovely. My make-up always looked better when I had Quaaludes in my system. It was so much more exciting to pick up a stray and go to a hotel or his house or sneak him into my dad's place, when I was on Quaaludes. Ludes (Quaaludes) were my life, ludes gave me life, ludes gave me freedom from pain, ludes offered great sex, ludes were my god. It was the late '70s and lemons/714s (ludes) were all over the place. I never got a script for them but I bought them from everyone and took them everywhere.

Remember don't leave home without it? That began with ludes before the credit card company got that for its marketing strategy.

Fire Island; 42nd with a beach

In the summer, a lot of the bar scene would go to Cherry Grove in Fire Island. Fire Island was a large gay hangout. There was a definite class separation on Fire Island. The Pines was where the ritzy she-she gay boys and lesbians went. There were gorgeous houses and it was very uppity. I never went to the Pines.

Who needed to? Cherry Grove was where it was hopping. Although it was considered gay territory, all different kinds of people hung out on the island. The best part was that many bar people would hang out there on Mondays and Tuesdays and there were always rooms available. There were hustlers and their drugs, sex workers and their drugs, bar people and their drugs. It was just like 42nd Street except there were beaches and pools. Every day, every night, was a party. Every day and night there was some type of sexual activity available for anyone, no matter what they looked like, how they dressed or how they identified. Because I was female and young I got all the meat I needed for a balanced diet. It didn't matter that I was what one might consider a 'queen.' Although that might be the title others gave me, I never identified as such. Not that I thought I was better or more real. Who am I kidding? Of course I thought I was the realest thing since white bread. I couldn't help it. I identified as Roe, I lived at home with my dad. Although my life was one big party, one big fantasy lacking in substance, I thought I was normal. It didn't matter that I had this appendage that was too long to be a clit. I felt I was who I was and nobody was going to take that away from me.

Although many people were able to take that feeling away from me during my life, and I would always be devastated when they exercised that power.

Anyway, many of the older gay men had issues with us young femme 'girls' hanging around having their trade after they've paid for it. I didn't care who was who or who was with who, when I wanted or needed and I lusted, I went for it. Now, mind you, I was not this outgoing person, I was shy, especially with men. But I was shy and high and needed to lie under one of them on any given moment. I heard about men lying around in the bushes and sex happening everywhere but I was not involved in those sexually exploratory adventures. My sexual experiences were very different from those of my butch queen brothers. Although we all were having sex, it was a different cultural encounter.

Jealousies

As the '70s came to a close and the '80s started to take over, my desire to be beautiful became more overwhelming. I needed to be. Be the one. Be the one that you wanted. I needed to be high, I needed to be special. I needed. The club scene was only telling me one thing. And that was 'to be beautiful was where it was at' and life was not worth anything if you were not beautiful.

I was hanging out with a bunch of 'Latina queens' in my late teens and I remember one of them discussing me. "Roe ain't much to look at but she is definitely 'real.'" That wasn't good enough for me. I would enter Balls in Harlem but never win. I thought they were racist, even though the other women, Raquel, Marudi, Tiny, the La Beigas ... were all much prettier than I. There were very few white girls who would or could compete, especially in Harlem. There were few white girls who were cool enough to even be involved. I was a Latina/African-American girl trapped in a white girl's body. Although I wasn't considered a 'Diva,' I was popular. I was popular because I held a job and was responsible. I was popular because I was fun and down and I loved to party. I was popular because I was a regular girl.

In retrospect, I never learned that I was enough and that was why I always needed to be in the center of things. The drugs kept me going and life revolved around me when I was high. I could never get too high, but I did get too low too many times.

The Club scene continues ...
G.G. Knickerbocker
G.G. Barnums

How much fun could one girl have? Life was just not fair. I had all the time to go to these places and receive some cordial treatment because of my association with the 220 Club. Bar people took care of bar people. And I was Bar People, so I would frequent all these raunchy beer and cigarette infested places daily.

I worked in the Barnum Room as a coat-check girl. The Barnum Room opened in the late '70s. It took the place of the Peppermint Lounge, which was located on 45th Street between 6th and 7th Avenue. It was right around the corner from my old school. Down the block there was a restaurant where all the thugs hung out. I was always scared to go there but because I worked in the bars and I was friends with some of the thuggets, the women who hung out in the restaurant, I would never get jumped or ripped off. The Barnum Room was as hip as Studio 54, Zenon's and the Limelight. But the Barnum Room catered to a more eclectic, shall we say common and perverse, clientele.

Trans women and non-trans women who were working girls working out of the Barnum Room would sometimes take their tricks past the restaurant on 45th and Sixth and then their boyfriends would come out and rip the johns off or beat them up. This was the cultural norm in my life. My girlfriend Mickey, who lived across the street from me when I lived on 51st Street, hung out at this restaurant more and more. She began to get more involved in illegal activities and would be arrested here and there. Life was changing and some folks seemed to be sinking. I mean, I worked at an illegal club, I sold drugs, I stole from the cashier box, I slept with other people's boyfriends or husbands, but I never meant to hurt anybody. And I was not a junkie by my definition. I am not saying I was better or worse than anyone else, I am saying I was surrounded by thieves, whores, drug dealers, homelessness, sexually promiscuous folks, the mafia, queens, and violence. This was the cultural milieu, and I was a component of this cohort.

Missed Gay New York

It was 1980 and the Barnum Room was having a Miss Gay NY contest. Although it was called Miss Gay NY, no one within the pageant identified as gay except for one female impersonator. On several degrees none of this gay/trans interaction made a lot of sense. If trans was a celebrated identity as trans, the gay/trans connection would be a terrific relationship. However, gay was the 'term' the control group back then used, and it seemed to de-legitimize those of us who were TS living in this 'world' who did not identify as gay. But we didn't even know it. Who cared as long as we had the opportunity to be on stage, have some drugs in our system, and a platform from which to shine?.

The more things change, the more they stay the same, as you will see in Appendix I and II.

I entered the contest not even thinking the word 'gay' had anything to do with me or the contest. Drugs were great for taking away the thought process. And gay just meant that women who were not TS could not participate. My understanding made perfect sense to me.

I was so unsure of myself but full of false pride. I constantly yearned for acknowledgement. On the one hand I was going to win and on the other I was desperately embarrassed by 'me.' I went for it anyway. Besides, I had Lynda behind me pushing me like a big sister. Out of thirty girls they picked twenty as semi-finalists, and I was one. The late Sugar Belane and the late Mara Devau were two as well. Sugar was already in her thirties. She was an amazing redheaded Tina Louise, showgirl look-alike. Mara was a Cubana princess with a face that was sculptured much like a Greek Goddess. They were both Latina.

It was talent night and the room was filled with over 300 people. I performed 'Lay Down/Candles in the Rain' by Melanie. I started the song on the floor. I had on a white danskin and tights. I had my hair snatched tightly back with long, black beaded braids hanging to my waist. I had dark black eye shadow circling round my almond hazel eyes (are you getting excited?).

The song started off, "Little sisters of the sun ...". Melanie is talking until all of a sudden she says, "Let your white bird (Me) smile up," and talks about Mayor Baba living again and how this was a time to rejoice. As the drums rolled and got louder I stood up with my back to the audience and I had chains and handcuffs on my arms. My heart was pounding, my emotions were rolling. My arms went straight up in the air, my head and braids flipped back, the light was shining right on my face, and the crowd went wild.

They started to calm down and the song began. The song seemed surreal, very Woodstock, a little hokey and pinkish, until all of a sudden I pulled out a knife and stabbed myself. The white leotard and tights became drenched in blood and people began to scream. I was in heaven and after my performance I saw the amazing Mara Devau and sweet ass Sugar Belane backstage, sweating. They let me know they were impressed. To have them give me that feedback, I was already a winner. I was totally honored.

> *I had the opportunity to perform this piece in 'They Lived it Out,' a show I produced and directed in honor of those TG/TS folks who died from HIV/AIDS, Addiction, Suicide and Murder. It was aired on the A&E Special 'A Transgender Revolution.'*

I was named one of ten finalists that night and next was the swimsuit/gown/question competition. I felt like I should wear something really revealing as far as a swimsuit was concerned. In 1980 I was small-breasted. I didn't want to wear pantyhose because I wanted to show how 'real' I was. I guess I should've listened to Lynda. It turned out that my one-piece revealing bathing suit made me look cheap and not 'real.' I lost points for that. Then there was the ballgown competition. Lynda lent me this all white lace beaded gown that was tighter than a small condom on a large-sized penis. The gown was so tight my escort had to lift me up onto the stage. I had just permed my hair and it looked like I had just permed my hair at a beauty school. In the gown you were asked a question. I was asked what I thought of male designers. At that moment I thought, who gave a flying … what I thought of male designers? I pondered.

I had to respond. And no amount of drugs would calm down my shaky squeaky voice. As I was answering the question I didn't take into account that the judges were comprised mainly of men, gay men. I responded. I said that I thought nothing of male designers. I felt they couldn't possibly know how to design clothes for women. I looked up in the balcony and saw Lynda's face. I was a total disappointment.

> *How come, no matter what I achieve in life, I am always able to connect with those disappointing experiences and feel them immediately?*

Thirty minutes later the male judges were announcing the winners.

Fourth runner-up went to the female impersonator.

Third runner-up, 'Roe.' That was me. As everyone congratulated me, I was fuming. Sugar was first runner-up and Mara was the reigning champion and I don't remember who was second. They all deserved it but I just couldn't take being third. I was so upset I grabbed all my stuff, got Lynda, and went to storm out of the club. At the front door of the club Jimmy Treetop stood. As I passed by he congratulated me and I told him to fuck off.

Does anybody think I needed a psychiatrist? If yes, push 1, if no, push 2.

Hello Christopher

I blasted the club and all it stood for. I got over it as soon as I met my next exciting piece.

I was sitting at the cashier desk at the 220 Club. I was staring into the light and fantasizing about life. A bartender/manager from One Potato Two Potato, a gay bar on Christopher Street, and his entourage walked in. The policy was all bar people came in for free. The manager was a silly queen and I thought he was annoying. Sometimes he would walk in and ignore the fish (me*)* at the door. Within his group there was this amazingly handsome Latino man. It was a long night and I was feeling out of it until that moment. I immediately got nervous and rumbled through my bag for a Quaalude. As the night went on and he sat by the bar I sat there staring into the light (my lamp) hoping this guy would look my way and see this amazing beauty at the door (me). He did and we soon began talking. That morning I went with him to the bar he was working at and we kept talking and flirting. I needed uppers and some coke to stay up as well as more Quaaludes to stay cool and loose. He got them for me. What a gentleman!

That night we stayed at Mona's (the bartenderess from the 220) house in the city. He made me scream in more ways than one (the Latino man, not Mona). He had never been with a woman like me before and that made me feel all the more special. This man won my heart that night.
We soon began a long relationship that interconnected us with our immediate families. The first time he met my dad we were in the shower together at my dad's house. My dad came home earlier than I expected. I told Robert (the new Latin man in my life) to hide in the shower since my dad was banging on the door asking when I would be done. Robert refused and we both walked out of the bathroom with towels wrapped around us. "Dad, er, this is, er, Robert," I explained. My dad called me into his room and told me to get that spick out of his house. I said, "Dad, I am going to marry this man so you better get used to him." And at that point in my life I truly thought this was the man for me. After all, he was gorgeous and a great lay, I was 20 years old already, he had a bouncer job, and he had never dated women like me before. He was perfect. Besides, his mother adored me and I loved having in-laws. Dating Robert kicked up all my insecurities. The more I thought I loved him (actually it was his anteater dick I loved), the more I lost self. Our relationship was filled with drugs and sex and nothing else. Isn't that enough?

Miss 220 revival

After losing the battle at Miss Gay NY I constantly complained it was fixed. The 220 Club decided to have all the previous Miss 220s compete against each other for Queen de la Queen, or Crème de la Crème. All previous Miss 220s and their runner-ups competed (all that were not incarcerated or dead entered the contest).

Once again I did my 'Lay Down' number. Lynda had just got out of the hospital. She was in there for a month due to her own battle with drugs. So she wasn't much help in putting my outfits together. I called upon Mara and she lent me this lime green chiffon, see-through quilted gown. Sally was the MC of the contest. I had taken around seven Quaaludes and did line after line of coke. All of the contestants participated in all of the events of the contest. It came to the question component of the evening: "Roe, what is your wildest fantasy?"

Well, this was more like it.

Immediately I asserted, "Sleeping with ten men and wearing them all out."

The crowd went wild and I was crowned the queen of the queens.

Imagine that response for a Miss America Pageant? Maybe they should've asked that kind of question to Vanessa?

Now do you think that this pageant was fixed? I mean, after all I was the only employee besides Jessy in the contest. And I was the only one ranting and raving about not winning Miss Gay NY. Do you think my mom was around once again to give me what I needed? And do you think I cared if it was fixed or not?

Shortly thereafter Jimmy Treetop did a whole photo shoot with me and my new crown. I had a crown of rhinestones, a black and white photo on the 220's first floor wall, a boyfriend, a job, lots of drugs, a roof over my head ... who could ask for anything more? Ba-dap-bap!

9.

THE CLUB SCENE CONTINUES...

THE GRAPE VINE AKA CASA DARIO
LA ESCUELITA, CRISCO DISCO
BEAUTY AND THE BEAST
THERE'S A DOCTOR IN THE HOUSE
STRANGE SENSE OF SELF, SUICIDE II
THE TRIP TO COLORADO

111

9

The Club Scene continues …

The Grape Vine AKA Casa Dario

The Barnum Room was shut down due to complaints from the Neighboring Business Association. As with many trans-identified clubs, they lost their liquor license and to quote legendary Miss Sherry, "Folks didn't look as good when you're sober." No liquor, no trannies, no following.

The club changed owners and moved to 46th Street between 6th and 7th Avenue. The front bar was hosted by Miss Edie Lane. One year later they found Miss Lane, and I'm not talking about Lois, murdered, stabbed to death in her apartment on the Upper East Side. It was said that Edie picked up a man and didn't tell him she was a 'sex-change.'

Edie had just come back from surgery in Colorado. It seemed like that was the place to go in the early '80s, for surgery that is. Everyone was talking about Dr. Biber's work in ole Trinidad, Colorado.

Edie's murder was upsetting. But it was the norm to hear about or see people stabbed. Clubs were filled with partygoers and sometimes the parties just got out of hand. It didn't matter. Many of us were in the scene for entertainment, insanity and adventure. And crime and trauma came with the territory.

The club scene also afforded many a striving thespian a stage to present their art, be it DJ skills, dressing, dancing, hustling pool, or lip-synching on stage. I was very much involved with the performance circle of the club scene. I impersonated Cher, Laura Brannigan, Blondie … I sang songs that were rock, disco, and extremely melodramatic. I learned to perform in silent. That is the art of Lip-synching and Pantomime. I loved the stage, I loved the attention. I loved the art. But I didn't love the violence and the murder of many a spirit.

I never performed clean or sober. In fact, life was one big drug run on stage and off. I was what you call a functional addict. That is, I got my ass to work, I was pretty responsible. And I showed up for friends when they needed me.

There were many performers who really had their act together. I would never turn the mike on and speak with the audience. I only went on and turned off.

The tranny clubs were going downhill and my art was moving with the venue. The Grape Vine was a tremendous let down from the amazing Barnum Room.

No one verbally stated it back then but this is what it was like when clubs catered to this specific sexual minority group. They were closed down due to heavy violence and prostitution. One might assert that the trans communities brought this upon themselves.
I say, what part does society play? A qualified researcher should look at the high rate of drug use and illegal activity within these racially and sexually oppressed and marginalized communities and come up with some hypothesis as to why this happens within these specific groups.

Chickey, my foster dad, died while working at the Barnum Room. Besides him, I got really friendly with his oldest daughter. She was a cashier at the Barnum Room. Chickey took a risk by having his daughter work within an environment such as the Barnum. This either attested to Chickey's beliefs in the rights for all people to congregate, socialize and celebrate variant identities, or it just says Chickey was off his rocker for having his daughter spend time in an environment where he participated in extramarital sexual activity (may he rest in peace)!

La Escuelita
Crisco Disco
La Escuelita was a Spanish club on 8th Avenue right by the Port Authority.
This club still exists two decades later.
La Esquelita used drag queens, non-op trannies and femme queens within their entertainment but they were not allowed to be clients of the club. Many a drag queen was turned away from entering the establishment. They could come to entertain, but not be entertained. That was back then and is not the regulation today.
And the Crisco Disco was a rival after-hours that catered to a much more mainstream eclectic group of druggies and party animals. At first, I was able to get into both bars free because of my bar status.
But in August of 1982 my boyfriend Robert who was a bouncer at the door of the 220 Club with me, broke my heart. He was tripping on acid and he stabbed a guy at the front door. I only dated the nicest of people. I couldn't believe they fired him the next day. Right after that, in September, Robert was taking me to the A train to send me back to Brooklyn (he lived in Richmond Hills, Queens) and he told me it was over. I got on the train, got home and immediately did the only logical thing to do. I had a mural of me painted by a set designer and I chopped it to pieces. That would teach Robert for breaking my heart. For the next month I kept falling asleep at the

door of the 220 Club. It was not from exhaustion it was from drug overload. I was fired in October of 1982.

My bar status immediately disappeared. Fall of 1982 I lost my future huzzzzzband, I lost my job, I lost my bar status. What's a girl to do? So, impulsively I decided it was time to speed up my trip to Colorado and Dr Beiber.

Beauty and the beast

It was late September, early October. The seasons were changing. There also seemed to be this strange energy in the world (I am not talking globally yet). You could sense death in the air. You also sensed something strange happening within the queer club culture. People started to come down with illnesses and people began to die quickly. I don't think I knew about 'the gay cancer' until 1984, but we were seeing the beginnings of this pandemic even before 1983. So the nightlife continued. The party never stopped. Drugs were in abundance. Many people began to smoke cocaine rather than snort it. I wasn't familiar with IVDU (Intravenous Drug Use) back then except for the injection of hormone therapy. I never thought about injecting drugs. It was so much simpler to just pop something and wait patiently. Besides, my essential tremor kept me from using my hands in a way that was beneficial to my drug intake. I did smoke cocaine, which was called freebasing. I hated cocaine. It made me shaky and more paranoid and I did it as much as possible (makes sense?). The 'Beast' was on my back. The 'Beast' was in the air and all that we breathed. The 'Beast' was waiting patiently to terrorize what was a big part of the beauty of this nightlife. The 'Beast' had already begun to attack. I was fighting internally with many things that drugs just didn't seem to resolve. The 'Beast' was not only on my back or in my mind, the 'Beast' was in the air and something was happening to not only my world, but to the world at large. Drastic measures had to be taken. I needed another goal. I needed something to look forward to. I lost my bar status so I needed some other status. Again, surgery seemed like the right answer.

There's a Dr. in his house

In order to have the procedure called 'the sex change operation,, like anybody had the power besides me and my own god to change my sex, I was told I must get two letters of recommendation from a professional, and they were not talking about a working girl or a performer.

I had already achieved what some surgeon was going to get credit for. I had already challenged the idea of how the world was going to perceive or identify me. But within our culture the credit is given to the miracle workers, a.k.a. the surgeons.

114

Since the inception of the Internet this medium has been used internationally for sharing information, with transexuals identifying surgeons all over the world. This has given people more opportunities to be educated and/or to educate. Sy Simms asserts, "An educated consumer is our best customer."

Many trans people around the world study their options. They research the various procedures surrounding genital modification, hormone replacement therapy, political ramifications of being a person on the trans continuum, etc. There are amazing websites, see www.annelawrence.com,FTMInternational's website or www.lorencameron.com, showing how one's genitals will look after they have been modified by different doctors. There are doctors in Detroit, Colorado, Pennsylvania, California, Nebraska, Oregon, England, Texas, New York, Japan, Belgium, the Netherlands, and more. Trans people have options depending upon their socioeconomic status and, for some, on their HIV status.

The way I made my decision upon which doctor to go to was simple. Edie Lane (before she was murdered, of course) went to Colorado to have her surgery performed. I asked Edie to step into the Casa Dario's bathroom and get up on the sink. She obliged. "Open your legs, please," I said. Bam, no dick, that's where I am going. I sent a letter to the doctor. They told me what I needed to do. I refused to see a psychiatrist. I thought, how the fuck is someone who doesn't know me going to tell me what I can and cannot do with my body. I did not realize some of the benefits of meeting with a professional. All I thought about was that I am not going to see anybody and that was that. I met a lawyer in the Casa Dario who forged two letters for me and they were sent off to little old Trinidad. There were only a few concerns. I had saved up $5,000 from working at the door of the 220 Club for two and a half years. The surgery was going to cost $6,500 and the airfare was around $250. Where was I going to get this money without a job?

Strange sense of self
Suicide II

No matter what went on in my life, if I wanted something I would get it. Nothing ever stopped me from achieving my goals. But here I did not see the forest from the trees, I didn't see the light, I did not have hope. But I was determined anyway. I began to sell more of my pills that I continued to get from my doctors. I began to sell Jimmy Treetop hormone shots at the Casa Dario to the girls who wanted them. I didn't really turn tricks. I was working for a Madam as her receptionist because I was just too sleazy to go to the hotels that the clients were staying at. Also, that wasn't my shtick. Again, I could sleep around with any mutt but sleeping with an old geezer for money was not my idea of a fun evening. I didn't care if I didn't have all the money, I was going to set the date for this surgery. January 13 was the day and I began to identify as a 'sex-change.'

> *Again, this is not my language. It was the language of the time and the cultural norm to identify this way*

One night Lynda and I went to the Crisco Disco after a night of whoring around at the Casa Dario. I wore a red Kansii International turtleneck sweater and mini skirt set. Kansaii was the rage in the early '80s. I met this nondescript man at the Crisco Disco that night who would send me for another traumatic, depressive, internalized transphobic spin.

But let's take a step back for a second to really understand the dynamics of this warped brain and the context to which I am about to refer.
The Crisco Disco was a club filled with mostly gay constituents. The club catered to gays as well as their hustlers, fag hags, and straight folks without hang-ups, or too drugged to realize they were not the majority... This was not a Green Acres, folks. This was a place where people truly understood and lived the nightlife that catered to people like me and those constituents who wanted to party hard. I met this guy on the dance floor. I was always in dire need of attention, love or a stiff ... you know the rest. The guy asked me if I was a queen. I immediately defended my seat on the gender scale and stated proudly that I was a sex-change.
I thought this was going to score me some brownie points and maybe a date in the near future. He said that he could be my friend but that he could never date someone like me. I immediately went to my hopeless energy to ask for this energy to take me where I rightfully belonged. I couldn't believe my ears. All my life, I had hoped that crossing that track to my ultimate journey would free me from the ties that bound me to the status I was given at birth. I truly believed that being a sex-change would mean no male rejection. I thought that was the scientific correlation between snip and tuck I now got the luck! Although I had walked around with this genitalia, it still never stopped me from getting laid, meeting men, getting jobs, going out, partying, hanging with family, going to the beach, living my life, taking drugs, getting laid, did I say getting laid? But my alternate lifestyle, as some right wingers would identify this as, would keep me socialized only within tranny clubs or clubs that allowed trannies to occupy them. The few times I

dated men without giving them info about my appendage, there was always a problem.

One of those Scenarios:

One day I was on the train coming home from a club. I was out all night tripping on acid and popping Quaaludes. I did a lot of flirting with men on the D train to and from Manhattan. This day was no different. I got on at 34th Street, and on West 4th Street this really fine guy sat across from me. We began to talk and he invited me to his house in Prospect Park. I asked him if he knew what was happening (my way of trying to bring up that I was a trans woman, a woman of TS experience, a woman with a penis, a queen). He said yes. We got to his house. My head was full with the excitement of just meeting someone on the train and what was left over from my acid trip. We immediately began to kiss passionately and he threw me on the bed. He ripped my clothes off and I ripped at his. I kept my panties on. He went to pull my panties off and my hand flew over what was left of my micro genitalia. He went to mount me but kept pushing in between my hand and my anus. I said, "Let me throw my legs over your shoulders and this will make things easier". The sun was shining down on our bodies and I was feeling fabulous until he pushed my arm away from my crotch and jumped off me. He began to lose it. He asked what the fuck was going on in a tone that was frightening. I told him I had asked if he knew what was up and he had said yes. He said he thought that meant that I was a whore or prostitute.

> *Now, in retrospect, why didn't we discuss money if that is what he thought?*

He told me how disgusted his mother would be if she knew that someone like me was in his house. He asked me for money and he took my ring, it was a gold initial ring my brother gave me for my junior high school graduation. I still had the same initials, RMB. I asked him for one dollar back so I could get on the train and I was getting dressed as quickly as possible (talk about something blowing your high!). As I was walking out he asked me for a blowjob. I guess his momma wouldn't mind a blowjob.

Another time. I was hanging out with this girl named Darlene. Darlene was a white hippy chick who took a lot of Tuinals and was always nodding out. Darlene and I met at the Barnum Room. She dated one of the dancers on the trapeze at the Barnum Room. His name was Blonde Eddie, and he was to die for. Darlene had a son by Eddie but Eddie and Darlene didn't stay together. Eddie was a hustler who also dated trans women and just wasn't ready to settle down. Darlene was. After all, she took so many downers she couldn't settle down any more down than she was. Darlene and I stayed friends. She lived in Park Slope, Brooklyn. I was friendly with her and her family. She started to date a biker in Brooklyn and knew a lot of the bikers in the neighborhood. One day I went to Darlene's house and her boyfriend brought this guy Poppo over. Poppo was a leader in one of the biker groups in Park Slope. I also heard through the grapevine (not the club in NY) but from his friends, that Poppo had a 10-inch … Isn't that a pre-requisite for dating someone? Poppo immediately took a liking to me. This was October of 1982, just three months prior to my final surgery. Poppo asked me out and Darlene was respecting my anonymity. One night I was at Poppo's house having dinner with his mom and he got a phone call. I don't know why I knew but I knew someone was calling to tell Poppo my 'T,' my trans history. As I heard him say I'll take care of it I knew something was wrong and I jumped up and asked his mom for my coat. He hung up the phone and said, "Let's take this outside." As I looked into his eyes I saw rage but I also saw confusion. This was the first time I could really see how frustrating this was to someone else. He threatened me and said he should kill me, but in the same breath pleaded with me to just leave. I knew he was hurt and angered by what he had just heard. He started screaming, "Why didn't you tell me?" I told him there was nothing to be told. That I was finishing what I needed to finish on January 13th and that I would be whole. He couldn't grasp it and he told me to get out of there. Although he couldn't hit me because you would just look at me and see I was a girl no matter what anybody said, he couldn't accept me either.

I left him like I left Prospect Park, like I left the guy at the Crisco Disco. I left with their disgust, I left with my internalized shame, and I left with a sense that I would never be who I was already, if that makes any sense.

Back to the morning of the Crisco Disco,
That morning Lynda and I left Crisco Disco and headed to her house in the Bronx. We sat at her kitchen table next to the Peter Max Butterfly Painting that Lynda did on her wall freehand herself. We sat there and I discussed my hopelessness. I told her that I had nothing to look forward to. I said that if she was unhappy in her life (I turned it on her) and if I was unhappy now at this point in my life, what did I have to look forward to. She tried to steer me in a different direction and was trying to play optimist. I brought up all my issues about having this surgery and how I would be perceived by others. She tried to talk to me like an older sister and encouraged me to look within for the hope, not from some sleazy brainless guy on a dance floor, or a train pickup whose momma allows for head from a femme but no fornication, or a biker whose spine hangs in front as opposed to being a continuation of his back bone. I couldn't hear her and I didn't listen. That night, which was morning, after Lynda went to sleep I went into her stash and took eight pills. Now, on any given night I would take a combination of

pills. Why I thought this was going to take me out, I had no idea. I was not thinking clearly from taking around eight other pills during the course of that evening, and the liquor consumption didn't help with my clarity as well. I woke up in the intensive care unit of Jacobi Hospital. My dad was in the hospital in Brooklyn at the exact time, but not for the same reason. He was in Brooklyn Jewish Hospital dealing with I don't remember.

Lynda was furious with me. When Lynda went to sleep I wrote her a letter saying goodbye using my dramatic energy. I took her pills and left her money, for the pills that is.

Lynda later told me, when I was already in the hospital, that she got up in the late afternoon and saw that I was not moving. She began to try to wake me up and I wouldn't budge. Lynda had to call the police to come get me. But this put Lynda in a difficult position. She was a pill dealer, she had drugs all over the house, and she was totally closeted in her neighborhood. She also became a suspect of attempted murder. Before the police came into her house she had dragged me into her living room from her bedroom. She had to answer all these questions and she was interrogated for an hour. When the EMS finally got me to the hospital and took me into the room the doctor ran out and yelled at Lynda, "Why didn't you tell us she was a transexual?" Lynda played dumb. She made like she didn't understand what they were talking about.

I woke up in ICU and was being moved to the psych ward. As my gurney was moving from one section of the hospital to another and I was coming to I met a guy being wheeled into the psych ward in the other direction. It was love at first sight! It lasted a day.

I was able to get out of the hospital on a pass to go see my dad. My dad was too exhausted to act out his disappointment with me but the energy in the room said enough. That week my aunt and uncle offered me the rest of the money I needed for my surgery. That was not my marketing strategy, but it worked anyway!

This all made total sense. If I couldn't kill myself it was important to go ahead with the surgery and start a new life when I knew the world was going to react negatively towards me when I came 'Out' to them anyway. After that month Lynda never spoke to me again.

We reconnected in 1987 when I had but a few months clean.

The trip to Colorado

I got on the plane on January 11th. I was told to take a bus from Pueblo to Trinidad. When my plane landed I missed the last bus to Trinidad and had to take a $75 cab ride to Trinidad, Colorado. I had been told what hotel I was

119

supposed to stay at but when I got there the front door was locked. How the hell could I check in when the door was locked? The cab driver was very nice and he took me down the street to a nearby motel. I checked in. I got to my room and my phone rang. The person on the other line asked me if I was there to see the doctor. I couldn't believe this. First of all, nobody knew where I was. I called the front desk and told them that they shouldn't put any calls to my room because nobody knew I was there so I shouldn't be getting any calls. That was smart to tell the front desk people that it was OK to kill me because nobody knew I was there. I immediately took a Quaalude and put the dresser in front of the door. I had two money orders and a lot of cash on me. I didn't have a checking account and I had no credit cards because I had no credit.

I woke up the next day and went to the doctor's office. I had to answer a million questions as well as be evaluated by the psychologist. The doctor brought me into a well-lit room and told me to strip. I sat there in the sunlight feeling my whole body, my soul, exposed. He asked me why I got an orchiectomy and I didn't know what he was referring to. He told me. I told him I wanted to be lovely and 'real' and that was the only way. (Don't you hate when someone asks you why you did something in the past with that sense of judgment in their tone?) He told me I had very little skin tissue to work with but that he didn't think he would do any skin grafts. I let him know how important the beach was to me and that I would hope he didn't do any grafts. He then sat me down and brought up a concern out of left field. He said he had received a letter from a Lynda Roberts stating that she believed I wasn't a good candidate for this surgery. She believed me to be unstable and this would just make things worse. He asked me if I knew her. I told him this was some jealous old broad who was stuck in a place where she wanted everyone else to be. I was furious with Lynda, not realizing she was onto something and that she was just doing this because she cared. I thought it was an evil, manipulative thing to do.

> *Did I tell you that when I went back to Lynda's house after my second suicide attempt I asked her for my money back because the pills didn't do what they were supposed to do? She gave me half the money back. So who here is manipulative?*

The doctor agreed that this woman was crazy and surgery was going to happen in the morning. The night before surgery I didn't really think about anything. I wasn't scared. I just felt alone. My brother and father called, which made me realize how alone I truly was. I had taken this trip by myself. I had taken many trips by myself and my company had usually kept me entertained. But here I was in this strange town, waiting patiently. As with any surgery they roll you in and roll you out. After the surgery I was in the recovery room and being moved back to my hospital bed. One of the assistants helped the nurse in shifting me from the gurney to my bed. I was groggy, cranky and in pain. I kept moaning fuck, oh fuck, fuck, and the assistant condescendingly, to my perception, asserted, "Now, Miss Blumenstein, that is no way for a lady to talk." I immediately woke up for a second and told him to go fuck himself. I told him I wasn't no fucking lady!

My brother would assert, "You could dress her up to look like a million bucks but you can't take Brooklyn out of this girl." And how right he was (and is)!

The next two days I was in addict heaven. I had a morphine drip and the first day I had the control. The second day, every time the nurse came into my room I complained about the pain. The doctor informed me that everything went well. When the nurse took some of the packing away I asked for a mirror. I immediately was disappointed. But that had been the story of my life. Nothing is ever right, nothing is ever perfect, and nothing is ever good enough. On the sixth day they took the catheter out and I was able to go take a shower. I had to re-learn how to pee. On the seventh day we didn't rest, but they took out the packing and that was the weirdest feeling in my life. Well, this is done, and now it is time to go back to New York. I was informed I had to dilate twenty minutes a day, three times a day. The nurses were going to drive me to Pueblo to catch my plane. On the ride to the airport I had to lay on the back seat, lube myself up, and use this inflatable dildo. I couldn't find the hole. I never had to look for this hole before. It was all new to me. I was scared to touch myself. I was scared as to what I might find or feel. "Hey, one of you nurses in the front. Could you please turn around and find my hole, will ya, please?" I requested. As I laid back with this plastic blow up doll pressing into my newly formed crack, a truck passed on the left. I gave him a wave and his jaw dropped like nobody's business. This trucker got a free pornographic show. If only he knew that this pussy he was salivating over was only eight days old he would realize he should be ashamed of himself, the pedophile that he was.
I was on a plane back to New York. I let the stewardess know I would be spending sometime in the bathroom because I just came from a complicated surgery. I didn't say what kind of surgery but told them I had to fly out to Colorado specifically to this specialist. I was a shaky girl as it was. Imagine looking for a hole between your legs and being scared to death to touch anything as well as having trembling hands. There was KY jelly all over the bathroom. I had my leg up and I kept dropping this slippery inflatable toy

that was going to keep my newly formed passageway to heaven open. The stewardess kept knocking, asking if everything was all right.

> *I felt like screaming and flinging the door open: " hey, if you come in here and find my fucking hole and get this slippery slimy thing up in me for 20 minutes everything will be OK. But if you keep knocking and disturbing me and keep making me drop this $350 piece of plastic I will be in here until 2002. "*

But I just said yes, everything was OK!
There was a kind gentlemen sitting next to me on the plane who I told I had a rare vaginal problem that only this specialist could fix. I had to sit on a donut (a blow up seat with a hole in it) and I was very uncomfortable. After the long plane ride the man carried my bag for me off the plane. This man was walking with me and my dad and his new girlfriend were at the other end to pick me up. This could be only my perception, but the look on my dad's face was much more than disgust. I might have felt that way because of his input to the first procedure I had and his reaction to that. All I thought about was nothing had changed. I was Roe long before I paid some stranger with a rare technique. He did not create me, I was me already, much before I even met the man. He just enhanced something so now I would not have to lay my hand there when I was getting screwed, which was going to be soon. Now I would be able to be totally me naked, or would I?

I had more hang-ups than a coatroom disco

124

10.

86'D

THE LOSS OF STATUS
MAINSTREAM?
WILL MY MIND EVER REST?
DADDY DEAREST
MOVING ON UP

10

86'D

The loss of status

Since 1976 all I knew was the club scene. I hung out, I worked, I played, I socialized, I copped and sold my drugs, and I got laid predominantly in an environment that catered to trans-people. I had a family of origin and I participated in holiday festivities, but the club scene was my family unit. I didn't realize that my new surgical status would relinquish my ties to these surroundings. My best friend Lynda didn't want anything to do with me and my old boss Sally let me know that it was time for me to go completely stealth and back into mainstream. I was not prepared to be thrown out of this lifestyle. Hey, I've been thrown out of better places than this, ya know!

I still worked for this Madam as her receptionist once in a while but also felt a sense of isolation with this group as well. These were pre-op women and I felt like my genitalia became something everyone would be allowed to critique. Here I was, 23 years old, without a place in the world. To many within the trans club and ball communities I was a success, I was whole. So why did I feel more devoid of life than ever before? I spent a month recuperating from this surgery and feeling more alone than ever. Now it was time for me to move on, but on to what?

Mainstream?

A job was a main priority. Losing my newest virginity was another.

I began scanning the want ads. What was I going to do and how was I going to deal with these new objectives in my life? I had worked at Macy's when I was eighteen. I had sold make-up and perfume. I had also worked at Rainbow Shop, shut up. I did not have an extensive job history that could be considered mainstream work. Let's see, I delivered newspapers while my mom drove, I performed fellatio for $10. I won a Cher Contest and lip-synched to the greatest hits of the '60s and '70s. I worked in a coat-check, I was a cocktail waitress, I was a cashier at an after-hours, and I sold drugs. How do you go about marketing this?

I looked from A to Z and could not figure out what I was qualified for. When I was a kid I was smart, but I wasn't sure what I was now. I knew that I could party and hustle and take multi-various downs but never fall out. I knew I had style, I had grace and Rita Hayworth and I gave good head, I mean face. What was I going to do to support myself? I was 23 and I lived at home. My dad paid the bills and I chipped in when I worked. And when I didn't I didn't. This was too overwhelming so I decided to concentrate on my other goal, getting laid.

The doctor said I could engage in sexual activity after four weeks. I was single so this was going to be a challenge, nah! When you're a virgin you want your first time to be special. This was going to be my 30th first time losing another virginity (… *see losing many virginities*). I decided I was going to give the Crisco Disco another shot. After all, this time if I met someone I didn't even have to say anything, or if they asked I could deny.

> *What a great way to heal low self-esteem or internalized transphobia, lie about it!*

I went dancing at the Crisco and met this guy and we decided to go to a hotel by the disco. The hotel was called the Hide-Away Inn and catered to short stays. It was on 12th Street and the West Side Highway. It wasn't the Ritz but it had beds, towels, a sink and a door. We got up to the room and got undressed. Oh my god I was going to lose my cherry, the last cherry on the vine. I was so excited and nervous. I told him that I was a virgin and he had to be gentle.

> *DING DING DING. I told him I was a virgin and expected him to be gentle and loving? This guy I just met and picked up in a sleazy after-hours joint. I am stoned and dressed provocatively. And I expected him to be loving and gentle and kind and he doesn't even know me? Sometimes I could be so delusional.*

He mounted me and started hammering away. The pain was excruciating. I was begging him to slow down but to no avail. He got off me and looked down at my crotch which was now soaked with blood. "You're a sex-change," he asserted. He quickly dismantled me and said he was going to get us a soda. Forty-five minutes later I was still lying there by myself wondering what had happened. I was soaked with blood, my vagina was throbbing, and I felt emptier than ever before, except of course for my new found cavity being filled with, whatever his name was, semen. I did the only appropriate thing to do. I ran to Ginger's house on the lower east side and banged on her door. "I've been raped," I told her, "and I need help." I wasn't sure if this guy had done any damage to my new vagina and I couldn't say I had picked up a guy who had called me what I was and then dumped my ass. My medicated ego took over and led the way to this story of rape. Ginger was as kind as she always was when it came to a crisis and she took me to a doctor in Queens who was familiar with this surgery. As I waited to be seen by the doctor the police entered the picture. They needed to take down a statement. This was one of three times I was engaged by the police to discuss my victimization status. I had been raped a few times for real but never got the police involved. The police were only involved when I was left at a hotel and was robbed in my sleep by a guy who picked me up at a disco the night before, or when I prefabricated a story like this one. I told the cops I didn't want to press charges because I was scared.

> *That night left me with a ripped urethra and bladder incontinence for the next eighteen years. Hmm, do you see a correlation between men and lasting physical and emotional tribulations?*

After that night I thought it be best to focus on work again.

I interviewed for a job I saw in the paper two weeks later. It was a marketing company. Actually the company's president just came to New York from Florida. She was tall and energetic, just like me. The interview was a success and I got the job soliciting portable massage units door to door. I quickly became a manager and slept with two guys from my team, in that order. When you meet someone in a disco it was very different from meeting someone in mainstream. The guys were loving and respectful and my belief that I would never be allowed to be whole diminished. When you meet someone from mainstream within a working environment and you are not 'Out' or 'outed' it is like you are allowed to be more yourself. I was just 'Roe' at this job and I loved my anonymity.

It turned out that the president of the company was going to be the next Mrs. McMahan. Pamela was a lovely woman who had all her managers sleep over one weekend, not with each other, but to discuss new marketing strategies. She was cool, warm and inclusive. Cool being hip, warm being genuine, and inclusive meaning ... duh! I made some great friends at that job. It was a good time in my life. I worked for East Coast Enterprises until the summer of '83 and then I needed to take a break, and spend some time on the beach.

Valiums and Alcohol

Life, mainstream, and the pursuit of happiness were interconnected with a Valium and alcohol addiction. A day would not go by without me ingesting 10-30 mg of prescription Valium. And when my script ran out I would go to Union Square to cop my Valium. I was ignorant of my addiction problems. I didn't put together my impulsivity, my suicidal ideations, my mood swings with my drug use. I had no idea that I was physically addicted to benzodiazepines.

I would find out in detox in 1987 that Valium was one of the most difficult drugs from which to withdraw.

This was going to be a great summer though. It was the summer of '83 and I would never have to tape tuck again.

I love/d the beach and have the skin to prove it. Before my last surgery I would use surgical tape to keep my genitalia in place so as not to lump up the bottom of my bikini. I would sit on the beach for hours not being able to go to the bathroom. This was one of the many sufferings I would undergo just to 'be.'

This summer was going to be all about freedom and I was going to enjoy Pier 6 of Brighton Beach like I never enjoyed it before. Pier 6 was a section of the beach where all the 'popis' hung out. It was a lot closer than Union Square and I would be able to cop, get high, party, meet men, and socialize all at the same time. I had a ball in more ways than one. I made friends with all the lifeguards and purchased sand property on Pier 6 that summer.

Will my mind ever rest?
One hot summer day I got on the D train heading to Brighton Beach in Norma Kamali. I got off the train and headed to the beach. I couldn't believe my eyes when I saw Poppo right in front of me. We looked at each other for what seemed like hours, but was only a second. I looked good and I asked him if he wanted to go up my skirt to see what he could find? He was not amused and walked away. He looked beaten up. He looked a little sick.

I would find out later that my girlfriend Darlene got the shit kicked out of her by her boyfriend because she had never told Poppo that I was a ... I also found out four years later that Darlene would die from AIDS, and that is what Poppo looked like in retrospect.

He looked gaunt. I realized that junkies who were kicking would look that way as well. Part of me felt like a fool for acting like that with him and another part realized how much I liked him and wanted him to experience me, the 'me' that was now supposedly whole.
Now that I wasn't hanging out in clubs much anymore I became more and more closeted about my past. But the more stealth I was, the more frightened I was about people finding out about my history. This did not make me happy and I needed more pills to deal with the internal conflict. I began to make up so many stories about who I was, what my life was about,

129

and where I was going. Although it was a great summer, my mind was not at ease.

Daddy dearest
Moving on up
My dad put up with a lot. Although he was never there emotionally, he gave me solace in having a roof over my head. But things were getting uncomfortable at home. He was with this woman for four years. Holidays were a joy and it seemed that my dad was entertained. Dotty, my dad's girlfriend, had a younger daughter who was dating a young man with a lot of problems. Dotty's daughter Noelle was sixteen and I was 23. Noelle's boyfriend was also sixteen. He, Noelle's boyfriend, and I got along great and we fooled around one day. What was I thinking? My thought process was always a little off. My dad came home and found Noelle's boyfriend at the house. My dad hated this kid and I think he began to hate everything I had become. It was time to start seriously thinking about moving out again.

11.
FANTASY-SEX
PREREQUISITES
GEARED TOWARDS
MY PH.D AND
ADDICTION PROGRESSION

RETURN TO 42ND
UP THE DISHEARTENED HILL
DOG DAYAFTERNOON
MOP MAN
THE POWER OF SEXUALITY
THE OPPRESSION SURMOUNTS
COMPETITIVE ANONYMOUS
WHY CAN'T I BE BEAUTIFUL?
CUT HERE AND PUMP HER THERE
WHERE'S MY PILLS?
9 1/2 WEEKS
HAPPINESS IS................
FUCK YOU / FUCK ME
ANTICS, MY FRIENDS MOVE ON

GOTTA BAG?
MY SWEET HEROINE
DETOX...ING IN PUERTO
DETOX...ING IN THE BAHAMAB
MY HATE SURFACES
I WISH I HAD CLASS

11

Fantasy-Sex Prerequisites geared toward my Ph.D. and Addiction Progression

Return to 42nd

I went to work as a receptionist for an outcall service and I met a beautiful girl by the name of Leslie. She worked for the madam who I was the receptionist for, and also a friend of. Leslie was an escort. Leslie was very friendly with the madam of the escort service and was also the biggest moneymaker for that agency. When the three of us got together, the madam, Leslie and I, our varied personalities clashed.

Leslie was from out of town. She grew up in Pennsylvania and had just spent the last three years in Florida and New Orleans beginning her transition. Ginger, the madam, was from Texas, and had transitioned a few years back. Ginger had style and grace. She had an easy time blending into society. The three of us had many commonalities. They began their transition early and had an easy time being accepted in society. I had begun my transition earlier and had the same experiences (regarding blending into society that is).

Leslie was a character and her energy was refreshing. In my earlier years I had spent more time with trans women with a different attitude. Leslie was from out of state and her life experiences were very different. Leslie was always clowning around. She had the ability to make everyone around her laugh. She also got people involved in doing many mischievous things like egg and penny throwing at strangers, out of cars, and out of her apartment window. Leslie lived in Manhattan with one of Sardi's, *the famous restaurant on 44th Street,* children.

Like most of my moves, I moved in with a woman I became friendly with. I moved in with Leslie, Sardi's daughter, three Doberman pinschers, one German shepherd and four cats. Leslie and I shared a room. I was now back in Manhattan and away from my dad's lectures. I worked at Luchows Restaurant on 51st Street as a coat-check girl in addition to my receptionist work with Ginger's Out-call Service. The woman who owned the coat-check was a coke fiend and I would be able to get high, work, get high, and work. I hated cocaine and I always did it. I loved jobs that allowed for illegal drug activity.

Leslie and Ginger decided to go to Colorado for their 'surgery' and I was surprised that they chose to go to the same doctor I went to. All the grief I got about my vagina from these women and they were going to the same place. Although they were not totally excited about my surgical results, back then we didn't have many choices around surgeons performing this procedure. But I was still surprised they were off to Colorado. When I had had this procedure done all I cared about was not having what I used to have and I was happy it worked.

> *We didn't study, research or scrutinize the work the way that many tranny women do today. The Internet has afforded many transexuals an opportunity to access international information with regard to advanced surgical procedures.*

Because of my drug addiction and my wavering sense of self, people around me had the power to make me feel good or bad. If a man rejected me and/or spooked my vagina, I was crushed. If he thought I was the best thing since sliced bread, somehow I was distrusting. But if he thought I was beautiful and sex was the greatest, somehow I felt better. It depended upon my drug and alcohol consumption. If friends criticized me, I always took it personally. And since I looked up to these two women, anything they said affected how I felt about myself. I just never let on to them that they had so much power over me and my self-worth.

Ginger was a brilliant, talented woman and although I didn't care for her false southern hospitality, I looked up to her. Leslie was beautiful on the outside and I appreciated her magnificence. I felt inferior and superior to both of them. I was one thing they both would never be, and that was cool. That, and a token, would get you on the D train. They both had so much going for them and now they were headed to have this surgery and I knew I wouldn't be the special one anymore. I was excited for them but also jealous that they were doing this as a team.

When Leslie and Ginger returned from Colorado they needed to find a new way to make money. The escort service Ginger ran catered to men who wanted a woman with a little something extra. They didn't have that anymore. Leslie heard about a peep show called Les Gals. She had a friend who worked there. The girl was a beautiful African-American 'change.' Leslie went to interview and got the job. That night she came home with $125 and I came home from the coat-check with $55. The next day I went with Leslie to Les Gals, back to, you guessed it, 'the deuce'.

Up the disheartened hill

This was the first time I was ever inside of a peep show. Hey, I am not lying!

Seriously, folks, I found another virgin element to my identity. The outside of Les Gals was all lit up. There were neon lights blinking 'live naked ladies' and '25 cent movies' for all of 42nd Street to see. The entrance of Les Gals was a storefront of an office building. On the right of Les Gals there was an international newspaper stand where one could read about any current events from all over the world. When one walked into Les Gals one could look at international genitalia spread open from all over the world as well. There were sex toys and videos proudly displayed all over the first floor. In the back of the store there was a grey-looking black man selling tokens for the booths on the second and third floor.

Leslie and I walked in and passed the men salivating over the XXX magazines. I felt like I was invading their privacy and I felt their heat and uneasiness as we rushed by. On the other hand, maybe it was my heat and energy I felt and the men were paying no attention to me. Right before we left our house to come to Les Gals I popped a 10 millie (10 mg) Valium, so I had some control of my feelings.

Leslie led me up the stairs past the booths with pictures of the porno movie that was showing in that booth. We walked to the back through the smoke and strange scent that I would later find out was a combination of sperm and disinfectant. The different smells were like oil and water, they didn't mix. We got to the dressing room and I was trembling. There were three rowdy women sitting in front of a wall-to-wall lit mirror. They were sitting on bar stools, bare-ass naked, applying paint, not on the walls but on their faces. Leslie smiled at everybody as if she was hoping to be crowned Miss Congeniality.

I was standing there not sure what to do so I put my hand in my bag and pulled out another Valium. I coughed up some spit and swallowed, a talent I learned early on in my pill-taking career. The manager walked in to see how many stank hoes, I mean booth babies she had available to work that day. Leslie introduced me to her. Tina was a short, middle-aged woman with raven red curls. She was polite, dainty, but a little rough around the edges. Leslie and I walked up to her and we towered over this woman. This immediately kicked up my internalized transphobia and it made me self-conscious. Tina asked me what I had to wear and had I ever worked in a booth before. I showed her my black teddy, black heels, black whip, and I said I had never even seen one before, a booth that was. We walked up to the third floor where there were six booths in the front, ten in the back, a cashier station, a manager station, and a big stage. There were also three pails with mops in them. Tina told Leslie to show me to a booth. I realized that the girls were territorial about booth assignments and certain booths were placed where more people could see you. Specific booths were reserved for the moneymakers. Tina told Leslie and me to take booths up front, *the visible section,* because we were tall and white.

> *The peep show business ignored all discriminatory clauses that are set in place today. The industry was racist, sexist, homo and transphobic, in addition to many other politically incorrect challenges it included.*

I put my clothes and bag in a booth but was told to stand by Leslie's booth. We opened at 11 a.m. and up came the men, in more ways than one. The men had to buy one-dollar tokens to see you in a booth. You were on one side and the man was on the other. There was glass between you. Actually, there were two floor-to-ceiling glass windows with a vinyl curtain in between that was electrically controlled by the drop of a one-dollar coin. (Picture an early Madonna video and you'll understand.) You'd stand outside your booth and entice men in. They'd go in on their side, drop a coin, curtain went up, and you would pick up the phone to talk, but not about the weather.

A man walked up to Leslie immediately and asked if he could enter, the booth that was. She smiled, as usual, and asked if I could come in with her. She explained that I was new. He excitedly said yes. I got the hang of it right away and wanted to go to my booth since Leslie had already made a few dollars and I wanted to as well. I was told we would make 30 per cent of the tokens that were dropped in our booth. I got into the music and the action immediately. I was so competitive I wanted to make sure I would make my share.

The year was 1984. I was now a booth baby. I was hanging out and living with Leslie in a zoo and working in this peep show. I was having a great time, but physically I began to feel more incomplete than ever before. My perception of self was immediately changed by this industry. I had small boobs (36A) and I had never had my thyroid shaved. I didn't buy into any of that because I had transitioned at sixteen and always blended in. There was no desire to either look like a Frederick's of Hollywood model or the need to get rid of what some would consider old masculine character traits. But working in this industry made me more self-conscious than ever before. I was competing in a world that I was not familiar with. I always wanted to be pretty. But now I felt I had to be more seductive, more voluptuous, more ...

Many of the women in the Peeps were schooled on the street. This was 42nd Street and this was a 42nd Street cultural milieu. Leslie and I were new. We also had a different energy about us. The men wanted what we had. The power and head trip I went through as I opened my curtain (the booth had a curtain behind a glass on my door in addition to the electric curtain in-between the client and myself) and saw a line of men waiting to come in my booth was invigorating. I would always sneak a look over to Leslie to see if she was busy. It became a competition for me and I would secretly compete with all fifteen women working on the floor. Leslie and I were always neck and neck as far as our sales were concerned, but I always left with more tips. I knew that other girls used toys and did all kinds of things in the privacy of the show with the client but I wasn't going to stoop to that level. I didn't have to. *Or so I thought.* Never say never!

Dog day afternoon
One day, I was sitting in front of my booth and in stepped this loudmouth woman. I knew she was a 'change' from far away. She was larger than life. She was overdramatic and boisterous. She looked at Leslie and I and I knew there was going to be trouble. There was a rumor around that Leslie and I were TS but Tina didn't question anything. We were making the company a ton of money.

> *I loved working in an environment that exposed all your sexuality while I was closeted. It reinforced my identity and made a powerful statement concerning my worth as a female. Just having a line of men waiting for me challenged all notions concerning gender constrictions*

Being confronted with another tranny, other than the closeted African-American woman, threatened my newfound power. This woman looked like a tranny, and back then that was disconcerting. As I looked closer at this woman heading to a booth I realized that it was Liz Eden. The movie Dog Day Afternoon was about a 'TS' who wanted a sex-change operation so badly her boyfriend robbed a bank to get the money. Al Pacino played the starring role and this movie was about Liz before she transitioned. Liz Eden sued the film company for not paying her for the story. And that is how she got her surgery. Her boyfriend was in jail and Liz now worked in Les Gals with her movie-making pussy.
May she rest in peace.
In the Peeps, anything went as long as there was money to be made on it. 'Changes' were allowed to work with the other women but I still didn't want to be identified as a 'Change.' There was also a peep show specifically for

women with penises. They were marketed as 'she-males.' The adult industry used that term even though many of the women didn't identify with that negative idiom.

Although 'changes' were allowed to work there, most of the 'changes' were of no threat to the other non-trans women. Leslie and I were making a lot of the money so we were a big threat to everybody. I knew Liz Eden was not going to be a threat to anyone because of the way she looked. But she truly acted like a prima donna. We eventually became friendly and Leslie and I terrorized her in a fun, juvenescent sort of way. She was no star, and I needed her to know that. Also, Leslie was a big kid and needed to act out her internal aggressions, and Liz was a good target.

Working at the Peeps drove Leslie and me crazy. The whole scenario was difficult for any ego to deal with.

> *Incorporate the stress of this intense sales position selling dreams of sex and sexuality. Then add a TS history intertwined with the goals and objectives of this position and you will comprehend.*

As a woman in a booth you had to allow every man to see you naked for a dollar token. In addition, your marketing objective was to keep them in there as long as possible. You wanted them to spend a lot of money in the booth and put cash in your hand. To achieve this goal one must use the body as the enticement. You would sit on the stool and spread your legs wide. Men would view the genital area and some would masturbate. Some came in with flashlights. Exposing my vagina to these strangers kept me in a state of 'fight or flight,' a state that all of us experience when in an extremely stressful position. I didn't know if they were going to run out of the booth when I spread my legs or if they were going to get more excited. I was not in control of their reaction and I always felt vulnerable when I was asked to spread my legs for their eyes only, remember Tula and James Bond?

> *The whole vocational experience was about power and control. My addiction issues were about power and control. And when I was vulnerable, like sitting on a chair being ordered to spread my legs, I was not in control of their reaction and I was in a vulnerable position, literally!*

Leslie and I wanted to laugh and have fun, so we became quite rambunctious. Men would mill around looking at all the girls. They would stare at us up and down until they chose their attack. This would make us nuts. How dare they be so choosy and how difficult it was to stand there barely dressed and be judged by these men. I would stand, pose, and fascinate the crowd, and if they didn't choose me I felt like I just lost and I would go into my booth to look at myself to see what was wrong with what I looked like. I can't say that others went through and dealt with this insecurity, but in retrospect, I know this work damaged the esteem of many young women. This was especially disconcerting to those of us who identified as hetero and wanted the attention of the good-looking men who would come to the Peeps.

Mop man

In the booth, a man, and/or couple, would go into one side of the booth and drop a token. When the curtain came up you were on, just like in the theatre. When I met people outside of this work and they asked what I did for a living, I said I was a performer off Broadway, and I wasn't lying. After all, there was a curtain. I would go on stage at least five times a day, and 6th Avenue was off Broadway.

I would pick up my phone and sometimes the guy on the other side didn't even want to talk. He just wanted to look at me and masturbate. Being the healthy individual I was I would be infuriated if they didn't do what I wanted. On the side of the booth there was a slit where I would push a paper asking for a tip. That was my priority, a tip. "Hey, you got a tip for me babe. I'll give you a great show!"

It was mandatory for me to be naked. The place advertised 'Live Naked Ladies,' so that is what I had to be for a dollar. The rest was up to me. The guy would either dig in his pocket before he dug into his zipper and would put a tip in my sheet of paper. And thus the show began. I had a bar stool with a towel on it and I would sit and spread, sit and play, sit and fondle until he would spew his future children all over the glass. We would say our goodbyes or get dressed in silence and then I would proudly assert over the pounding of 'Girls just want to have fun,' "Hey, mop please, Mop Man," and some non green card holding, illegally hired, sweet or nasty man would roll the mop on wheels over and mop up the floor and window. NEXT!

The power of sexuality

Each day I would learn more about the business and would become more disgusted with the fluidity of these men's fantasies. I had businessmen in suits and ties come into my booth and, as they opened themselves up and bared their inner selves, they exposed their true wears. Under their suits they wore panties, silky panties, the tackiest nighties, bras, or corsets. They would ask me to tell them how pretty they were. The better they tipped, the prettier they became. I was disgusted and/or appalled by these men.

How interesting it was that a cross dresser disgusted me back then. Did it kick up stuff for me or was it that these men got to celebrate their male privilege and, behind closed doors, they showed their true colors. Was I jealous that they had 'respectable' jobs and a secret? Or was I humiliated that they had power over my money situation and I wanted to be in control? I compare this to black on black oppression, e.g. lighter versus darker skin and the hierarchy of worth within a system that places value on shape and color of skin.

We were both on the trans continuum but they seemed to live and succeed in the world while I hid in different sub-cultures.

One might think that working in this environment would make you open up with your own sexuality and free yourself from some major hang-ups. And to a certain extent it did. I became more comfortable with my nakedness, although sitting on the chair spread-eagled for man after man always made me uncomfortable. Their reaction to me made my self-worth rise and fall constantly. I did not have inner labia, which made my vagina look different. There were times when a man would enter and I would spread and he would walk out. I was left sitting on the chair with anger, embarrassment and shame rising. All of this challenged my sexuality and my sexual practices.

On the other hand, my sexuality and sense of self deepened. I began to use my anger, jealousy and embarrassment in a way that would strengthen my sexuality and I would be even more marketable. And this was the head trip folks. There were four sex-changes working at Les Gals, and two of us were the top moneymakers, Leslie and me. There was a daily chart that stated how much each booth made displayed every day, the following day. I was always one of the top three and I loved it. Leslie and I had these pasts that might take away from our ability to make money, but we were what the men were looking for and that fed my ego. We were also closeted. We were not marketed as women with a TS history. The sex industry and the money and power was my newfound addiction and I would stay addicted, on and off, throughout the next decade.

The oppression surmounts
One might think that a woman working in this kind of environment would be a strong, determined and callous individual. And I was all of these, as well as delicate, confused and more fragile than ever. I was clearing over $750 a week and thought I had the world by the balls. I was 24 years old, a high school dropout, I had a transexual history, and I was experiencing a newfound financial security. I was also experiencing a deeper sense of shame and a neo-addiction.

One day, my dad asked what I was involved in and I told him I was a dancer. I am not sure how that made him feel but I am sure he didn't run off to his friends to let them know how proud he was of his daughter who was birth identified as male but now identified as female and was stripping for a living. I am sure he didn't rave about how I followed in my mother's footsteps and attempted suicide twice. I am sure he didn't write to others saying he loved that I did not graduate high school or that I had tremendous mood swings due to my eight-year estrogen intake, or my drug and alcohol addictions. I am sure he wasn't happy that one evening while I was living with him, at 2 a.m. my beeper went off and I got dressed and left the house to go to a call at a hotel, or that he would come home to find me with strange men in his shower at any given day. I am sure this didn't feed his appreciation for me. The shame of what I put my dad through was always with me no matter how many Valiums I took. And I was high all the time.

And this peep show work, although it was an honest living, just added to some deeper sense of shame. On some level, being a stripper with a TS history was the ultimate. But to society, and my dad, this was degradation at its worst.

I could break into a deeper discussion here, focusing my thoughts on the socio-political discourse; the socio-political aspects of sex, sexuality, women and the sex industry, transphobia, the hierarchy of oppression and stigma, and personal and societal hang-ups around deviant sexualities, using the word deviant as a nonjudgmental descriptor indicating 'out of the norm.'

What internal oppression was mine and what was me buying into a society, as well as my father's ideation, that judges the celebration of deviance and deviant behaviors? And why does deviance have such a negative connotation? Why isn't there a fluidity surrounding variant sexual practices, expression, and using one's physique as a moneymaking entity? Who was I hurting? And why was it hurting me? Why wasn't I proud that I was able to market myself? After all, I spent quite a bit of money for my vagina. It was not a total gift from god. I worked hard for it. I was just making my investment back.

Years later, in recovery, I would attend women's retreats and, at one particular retreat, I sat down with the priest running the retreat. I told him I felt dirty and un-genuine and I felt like I was not supposed to be at the retreat. I came 'Out' to him and told him I thought god hated me. He told me my ego was gorged. "How could I possibly think I got through everything that I went through without the help of God?" he said. He told me that "it was god who carried me and helped me become the woman I was today." Although I have a Judaic background, it was a priest that first got me to honor and acknowledge god within my gender journey.

The reality was I dealt with multiple oppressions. I worked in an environment where I was not 'Out,' although some of the other women knew I was a woman who had a transexual history. They were jealous of my marketing strategies, it was a cutthroat profession, and they would tell customers that I was transexual, a [sic] man, or a freak.

I grew up in a society that taught me that my profession was degrading and unacceptable. I was a drug addict and could not deal with life on life's terms. I also worked surrounded by others who had their own demons. The energy was negative a lot of the time. Management loved the fact that I made so much money for them, but did not know how to engage me. They had a stereotype of my people and this dehumanized my identity, and that pissed me off. The other women were jealous, envious, battling with their own issues, and that energy was not conducive to a loving environment. The men were simply there to objectify and fulfill whatever fantasy they couldn't fulfill elsewhere. Their energy also de,-humanized me. Here I was, using drugs to dehumanize myself. I had a TS history, which dehumanized my identity, and I was a stripper/booth baby, which dehumanized my sense of self, a societal construct that was not by my own volition.

Watch any talk show on any of these issues and see how these identities are objectified, dehumanized, looked at as tragic, or simply sensationalized.

Competitive Anonymous

When you watch the Miss America Pageant there seems to be a sense that all are in it together no matter who wins. As one can remember from the 'club scene continues,' (p.111) I competed to win. And if I didn't, I was a sore loser.

What that stems from I still don't know. I know that within the development process a child needs a certain amount of support, guidance, nurturing and discipline to be able to contain criticism, to be able to handle healthy competition, and to be able to hold on to sense of self no matter what happens. In my work with addiction issues I've observed folks struggle with sense of self and how their surroundings can have a negative effect on them instantaneously. I have also studied our larger society and observed how external things falsely fill low esteem. Is this strictly an addiction issue, societal issue, spiritual issue, or all three?

Why can't I be beautiful?

Since I was sixteen years old, propped on a bar stool in the Gilded Grape, many would say to me that I had the most exquisite eyes, I was so beautiful, my legs were amazing, I had great bone structure, perfect cheek bones, I should be a hand model, great smile, wonderful dimples, the best body they had ever seen on a woman, so attractive, stunning, exquisite, perfect breasts, striking … Yet I never considered myself a great beauty. Working in the Peeps reinforced all of my insecurities. I hated to smile because my teeth were yellow and crooked. I had little boobs, my ass was flat, and I didn't have inner labia,

Hey, where did I leave my inner labia?

My voice cracked, I had big feet, my arms were too long, my face was too long, my chin was too pointy, 'yada yada yada.' I loved to paint, and I don't mean houses. I loved colors on my eyes and it would help to camouflage my pain and my imperfections. I bought into 'blonde and blue eyes' were beautiful and the rest of us sucked. I didn't think that being the biggest moneymaker at the Peeps verified my beauty. I knew I was a sales person, just like my dad. I was a good hustler. But that didn't feed my sense of vanity and that component of my identity still hungered for internal acknowledgement. After all, if you were a woman of TS experience you had to work harder, you had to be more, and you had to be larger than life. Your womanhood was not something you took for granted.

This was the belief system when I came 'Out' as TS in the '70s. The goal was that you 'blended in,' hid your TS history, and moved on. The professionals treating the TS communities believed that to be a 'true transexual' you needed to cross over and hide that part of who you were to be successful. Doesn't this sound a tad like the movie 'Imitation of Life?'

Much of my work in the '90s with the TG/TS communities focused on healing this hierarchy of realness and beauty, although personally, it still plagues me.

I didn't realize it back then but my mind was not only clouded by drugs, alcohol, nicotine and sex addiction, it was clouded by my perception of beauty. I didn't realize all the chaos from within was clouding my perception of my shell. I couldn't see past the shell. There were things about me that made me ugly and it just added to my outside imperfections. The whole scenario of this work, my history, my addictions, and a fucked up society kept me from pursuing self-actualization, or did it? My reality was I was not hiding under the covers or waiting until I was 50 to live my life. I was involved in my journey no matter how decadent or beautiful that journey was. I was there taking all the risks. I was a booth baby. This was basically a hetero porno industry and I was right in the mix. I was a top booth baby. I defied the odds. I did what I wanted to do without any guidance, much support, and within a hostile environment. And people saw that beauty in me even if I didn't see it myself.

Cut here and pump her there

When I began High School of the Performing Arts I had my braces pulled off first by me, and then the orthodontist. I didn't want to go to school with braces and nobody stopped me from doing this. The doctor told me I would be sorry, but I didn't care.

Another component of the disease of addiction is to want what you want, when you want it, and not to worry about the ramifications of that want.

I smoked around three packs of cigarettes a day and I took a lot of drugs. Working in the Peeps made me so self-conscious. Although I was the top moneymaker, I never got enough attention. Nothing was ever enough, (*another symptom of the disease*). My breasts were too small, the lump in my neck stood out, and my nose was crooked. I think being around Leslie made me more self-conscious. Besides the fact that she was gorgeous, she hated being spooked. And the two of us together caused such chaos. She was the blonde, natural beauty and I was the hard, tough looking, striking goddess, you like that self-description?

When we were around 42nd Street or by our house we would hear all kinds of comments. Cars would stop and people were always yelling at us, "...hey, mommy, hey bonita, dame toto, que rica, hey flaca, hey estos hombres ... what?"

The flirtations and the attention on the street were always disconcerting. You never knew when you were going to hear an ignorant comment in addition to all the objectification. When I was alone I would get attention, but the two of us together was ridiculous. This was NYC and people were hip to transexuals. It made Leslie nuts, more so because she wasn't raised with the people of color communities so she wasn't comfortable with 'the New York energy.' Although they pissed me off as well, I was always attracted to African-American and Latino men, so when they gave a compliment I was right there for them. Leslie was white bread and that was all she liked.

It was the early '80s and we wore cut-up sweat shirts and skintight jeans. Remember 'Flashdance?' We were flasher dancer look-alikes.

I was making money and I needed to boost my image and self-esteem. So on I went to get what every stripper needed to earn more money, bigger boobs. As time went on I would get my nose re-one, my throat cut, a little sil in my butt and face, but never worked on my teeth.

Where's my pills?

Life without drugs was a foreign concept. I never went a day without a pill, a joint, a drink, a snort ... drugs were my vitamins. Without my vitamins I would get flu-like symptoms. I was ignorant to issues pertaining to dependence, abuse, tolerance, withdrawal, intoxication, and psychotic episodes. I just knew that if I didn't take a pill, I didn't feel right. So the appropriate thing to do was get something to take, every day.

9 1/2 weeks

There were many men from the entertainment industry who frequented the Peeps and frequented my booth. Out of respect to their anonymity I will not share their name,s but I will say that these men made some of our days more exciting and to get one of them in your booth inflated the 'ego.' I had many exciting adventures working at the Peeps, and it got more exciting as I moved from Les Gals to 7/11 to Show World, the Porno Capital of the World, well, at least 42nd Street.

Leslie and I were extras for the movie 9 ½ Weeks with Kim Basinger and Mickey Rourke. All the girls were dressed provocatively in tacky lingerie and Leslie and I wore our wraparound string bikini bathing suits. I was in white and she was in baby blue. It was the bathing suit where the string from the top went around the bottom and pulled the sides up to a high V. We did not blend. We looked like California babes and this was an erotic peep show. We did not blend because we were tall as well. We did not blend because we were 'Outed' by some of the girls and that caused a stir with the film crew. I was always so uncomfortable and did not know how to deal with folks when I was 'Outed' because I was not sure how they were going to react. It was an exciting time, even though I was so uncomfortable. I couldn't appreciate being on the set with Kim and Mickey because I was engulfed in self-consciousness.

The year was 1984 and I got paid $125 for two hours work on the set of 9½ Weeks. When I came to California and signed up with Central Casting to make some extra money I would receive a $54 *paycheck for a nine-hour day. You do the math. Something is wrong with the compensation extras are receiving in California.*

Fuck you/fuck me

When I began to work at Show World I found a new happiness and unleashed some inherent pain. Working at Show World made me a false booth baby starlet. I worked at the entrance on the second floor of Show World. I worked right by the front stairwell next to a large glass door for all of 8th Avenue to see. I learned how to pose and incorporate all of my talents to lure men up the stairs and into my booth. I was now a star. I was wanted by many. I was always a sexual being, but now I became a sexual professional. My sexuality and my competitive ways were the foundation for this success. I needed to prove something to myself, to management, and to the other girls. I was on a mission. The double messages made me crazy. There was always a line of men waiting to talk to me yet there were all these women who tried to make me feel inferior because of my transexual history. There were also men who knew I had that history and loved it. And there were men who found out, or figured it out, and their negative energy ate away at my self-worth and esteem.

This is not uncommon for all women in this industry so it is not just about the TS issues. Also, this is not the way in which it affects all women in this industry, so do not label women in the sex industry 'neurotic, insecure, trauma survivors ... I am speaking from my experience and from that of some other women whom I have since counseled, not ALL.

Show World, the institution, was a circus. The area was called the red-light district, which did not equate to a broken traffic light. The surrounding neighborhood was filled with sex, sleaze, runaways, throwaways, and tourists. Show World was filled with circus decorations, books, magazines, sex toys, booths, booth babies, and an assortment of men from all walks of life. Mops and sperm were everywhere. Money was changing hands constantly. Hands were on crotches, pussies were being spread, and sex was being discussed like it was acceptable dinner table discussion. Dreams were being fulfilled, deals were being made, drugs were being sold, disbursed, used, and the energy ... When the place was busy, the energy was full of lust and excitement and power and sex and sex and more sex. Men were scattering in and out of dance booths and private booths. When the peeps were busy it reminded me of the beginning scene in the movie Guys and Dolls where everyone was energetic and scattering about.

147

When the Peeps were slow and there were stragglers standing around staring and gawking and not spending any money, it would drive me crazy. The energy I would use to break luck was emotionally excruciating. It took all of my energy and would affect my self-esteem for better or worse. If I tried to lure a client into my booth and he refused, the anger and rage from within would explode. I would become hateful. I did not like to lose. I needed something to deal with this new energy at Show World and I was about to find just the right thing.

Show World was hard core and I would need new energy to deal with this newfound position. Show World was not only hard core, it was treacherous and hard core. I needed new medicine and in the near future I would find the doctor and the prescription I was looking for all my life.

Antics

Many things transpired during my tenure at the peep shows, from the most disgusting, revolting, and odd, to the most comical. Here are just a few.

Antic

Because of my strong Brooklyn upbringing, my appearance, my vibrant personality, and my theatrical edge I was able to market myself as a dominatrix. My character was named 'Mistress Brook.' One client's fantasy surrounded being abused by me. His 'scene' was he wanted me to make him eat my shit. Every time he came into my booth he would discuss the 'shit' with me. I couldn't believe this fantasy but hey, whatever floats your boat and pays my bills. One day, he told me that he would give me $50 for my excretions. I told him to come back tomorrow. That night, Leslie and I went home after work, did our usual hair treatments, watched a movie, talked about our dreams, men and our future, and went to sleep. The next day we were on our way to work and I remembered my customer's request. Oh shit, I forgot. We ran back upstairs and, luckily, Leslie had to go, *to the bathroom that is*. She got tinfoil and a brown paper bag, wrapped up the lunch bag and we hauled our butts down to work. Thank god I didn't bring lunch with me that day. I might have gotten the bags mixed up. My client showed up in the afternoon and I handed him the bag as he handed me a $50 bill. He went into his side of the booth. And as the curtain went up he immediately cried "Mistress Brook, please don't make me eat it, please don't make me eat it." I hit the window with my whip and demanded that he eat it. The curtain went down and I peaked out my other curtain to see who my next prospect might be. I thought about make-up, I looked in my mirror and checked my face and I waited patiently for the curtain to go back up again. I got ready for my cue, and when I heard the noise of the coin drop and the curtain rose,

I got ready for my close-up. I put my mouth to the phone and immediately got out my aggression and demanded that he eat it. The client was leaning against the glass eating away and, as I choked and gagged at the sight of him, I told him to "eat my shit." As I gagged and choked again I said, "Eat my shit." I turned my back and whipped the window facing the other way.

Nothing like a day's work and a spoiled appetite! It took around seven minutes and the client came out of his booth. He said, "Bet you never been asked to do that before?" Hey, somebody better tell this guy about bad breath and hepatitis A and B. No, his name wasn't Divine!

Antic

Leslie and I would dance together on the big stage. On the stage there were around fifteen windows where a person's head would be peeking in at you, just like another of Madonna's older videos.

The stage was a half circle with two poles. The wall was mirrored. The clients would drop a 25-cent piece and the light went out over their heads and they would get to see a dancing girl, a live sex show before 1986, or a wrestling match.

Leslie and I would act out our frustrations at being stared at all day by wrestling on stage. If you did a lesbian sex show you got ten dollars added to your weekly check. That was $10 extra you would make in twenty minutes. It added up in the long run.

Remember the show/movie 'Pajama Game' and the song 7 1/2 Cents?

This was another way to market your talents. Many women would come up on stage and truly get into it. Many women were lesbians and were looking for a partner to letsbefriends! Leslie and I did it to break up the day. We would start off serious and then she would whisper in my ear, "Hey, throw me into that window, he looks like he is having too much fun." And I would. Smash, bang and then you would see his door fly open as he ran out annoyed. Some days we would get away with it and some days the manager would run up to the stage, enter the side door, and scold us like we were children, which we were!

Other times, we would chase each other around the stage, bumping into things swinging from the pole and running up to a window and sticking our butts out at folks. We were just having a ball. Oh, the innocence of a peep show babe!

Some guys would laugh but the hard-core guys, the ones that wanted to be serious and get their money's worth, they were not happy campers.

Antic

Working in the sex industry kicked up a lot of sexual energy. As one stood in front of one's booth looking at the passersby, when you ran into 'a cutie' it would make the day more electrifying.

Imagine a construction site but the tables were turned around. We would objectify the men as much as they tried to objectify us. But we were out of control. Some of the men would be offended by the catcalls and some men appreciated the attention. After all, if it wasn't for Show World they would never be harassed by a 'New York City Slicker Diva.' Besides, weren't they asking for it? How familiar does that sound?

On the whole, I considered myself shy and not a risk taker. But in this realm, as these characters I portrayed, I could be bold. A cute guy would walk by and I would do what Diana Ross told us to do, 'reach out and touch.' It was like being a kid in a colorful store, or a fabric shopper, you liked something, you grabbed at it.

Antic

Some days the sexual energy would be so powerful you just wanted to ... There were actually some really fine-looking men milling around, and when they were willing to spend some money on you, it was great. There were a few times that I actually snuck around to their side of the booth and got more than a feel. Shhhhhhhhhhhhhhhhh!

Antic

The first few months of working in the Peeps Leslie and I experienced a culture shock, but it slowly became a cultural norm for me. I was lucky. I had my trusted pills and pot to keep me in check. But I needed more. Leslie and I usually worked straight across from each other. Leslie, the instigator ,would be eating a piece of candy and decide to throw a piece at me as I was posing for the voyeurs. We quickly involved ourselves with throwing things at each other across the traffic of men. We threw candy, pennies, paper and spit balls. *Was this third grade?* It felt like it. We would amuse ourselves. Sometimes we would laugh so hard we would pee. Imagine standing in a sex booth with a g-string and pee dripping down your leg? Where's the mop man?

Antic

When I became a heroin addict I needed someone to cop for me and bring me my drugs.

Remember the doctor and his cure? Heroin was my new prescription.

The booths that we worked in did not have a slot for tips but did have spaces and cracks. I would fold a piece of paper and push it to the client's side and ask him to put a tip in the slot, slit, slot. Some of the booths had a crack at the bottom. But that was usually where their headaches, their business pressure was released. Get the picture? Sometimes I would pass my tip paper through the bottom slit and I would retrieve more than a tip or a bag of heroin from my delivery boy.

Antic

Leslie and I would do almost anything for a laugh. If I was performing in my booth and the client refused to tip me I would still have to be naked, secretly thinking about my revenge on this tightwad. Sometimes a guy would come into my booth and not want to talk on the phone. He would stand there and direct me to undress and spread my legs so he could masturbate. Now this really made me feel objectified and inhuman and I had my boundaries. But I had to undress. Between his control issues and my control issues I sometimes lost, which infuriated me. I didn't like that feeling. I would sit on my chair with my legs up against the window and all of a sudden conk out. I would close my eyes and drop my hands to my side and my head would tilt like I couldn't hold it up any longer. Roe, play dead, good girl!

Sometimes the client would stay there until he was finished doing what he came to do and some clients would storm out of his side of the booth. One time a client even ran up to the manager to tell him that there was something wrong with me. He was worried, how sweet!

Antic

Imagine standing around for nine hours being sexy and provocative. And imagine having to go up on a stage where all you saw through little glass windows were beady eyes looking back at you? Dancing on the stage was a punishment some days. But you had to fulfill all the requirements of the job description. So, on to the stage I would go. But there were days when you felt completely sexless and men would pick up on that. In addition, you would have a man walk in a booth, drop a coin, look up, and then walk out. I always took that personally. To alleviate some of the pressure on my ego, instead of dancing sexy I would begin to lose it on stage by doing a Jerry Lewis dance. I would kick up my legs and act ridiculous. It helped release the tension, it really did.

Antic

Leslie and I needed to entertain each other to get through the day. If it wasn't for her being there I would never have been able to deal with the day, no matter how many pills I popped. Hey, if it wasn't for her, I would have never been there in the first place!

On the door of the booths there was a curtain that was set up like a shower curtain. When I was bored with a client I would begin to swing from the curtain back and fourth opening and closing and knocking myself into one wall and then the next. I would make like I was falling off my bar stool and swing the curtain back and fourth. This would cause a ruckus and men would look at my booth. This would also make Leslie *make*.

These were just a few antics of my tenure within the Peeps.

Working in a booth in a peep show let me know exactly what animals feel like at the zoo. I was in my cage and folks walked by, stared, fed me, ignored me, made faces at me, and reacted to me like I was an animal alive for their entertainment. This was not an unproblematic career!

My friends move on

Leslie and Ginger decided to move to Texas. This meant a few things. I would be left alone, I had to move out of Sardi's house, and I had to find an apartment. I moved back in with my dad for a month and then found a place in Brooklyn. In looking for an apartment I was told by the real estate agents that even though I was working nobody would want to rent to a stripper. So I was supposed to take whatever apartment I could get. They put fear and anxiety in my heart. This was discrimination, but I didn't know any better. This was my second solo apartment and I was 25 years old. Lucky for me I had my newfound partner, heroin.

Gotta bag?
My Sweet heroine

When I was working for the marketing company in '83 I had met a guy who worked at a pharmacy. He became my sidekick, and when I was looking for drugs or needed someone to bring me something to my Show World office, he was always available. *Every day I say a prayer and ask god to take care of people. I say a prayer for Adrian.*

I began my relationship with heroin in late 1984 and Adrian was my initial delivery boy. Using heroin finally made me realize I might have a slight problem with drugs. Until my heroin use I truly thought I was in control. Heroin taught me otherwise. Heroin was the boss and I became subservient to its every whim. I ate when it told me to. I slept when it told me to. I jumped as high as it wanted. I was controlled by its every desire. I loved heroin so much and I believed it loved me. When I even thought about getting it in my hands I would begin to gag from just the thought of its warm relief in the deepest part of my soul. It didn't take long for heroin to tell me that I had to wait for it to enter my system in order for me to make money. I began to work at night instead of the day. I would be in my booth at 5:30 p.m. and, if heroin wasn't in my arm, I would be a zombie until it showed up. As soon as it came I began to live again. Heroin held the light in my eyes and heroin shut that light out.

Toni and me
I became friends with another woman at work. It seems throughout my life I always had the ability to make friends with other women, and Toni was a woman I quickly became fond of.
Toni loved to drink and I loved heroin. We would clash a lot concerning our relationships and our belief system but we would also help each other stay sane in an insane environment.

Detox ... ing in Puerto Rico
Tracey and AIDS
Back to life; getting off in the Airport
It was February of 1985 when I began to realize that my new lover, heroin, was abusive. I needed to get away from him and I decided to go to Puerto Rico to detox. I didn't even know what detox meant. I did not understand withdrawal or that my body had become physically dependent. I had no understanding of neurotransmitters, dopamine, serotonin, endorphins or whatever chemical heroin reproduced in my brain. All I knew was that I was going to drink a bottle of this orange stuff called methadone, take two bags of 'D' with me on the plane, and I would be fine, somehow. This was my first trip alone. I knew of a girl in San Juan and we were going to get together when I got there. She said that she was not feeling very well but if she was up to it, we would see each other.
I got on the train in my orange danskin and white skirt and met my friend Adrian in the city. He would give me the methadone and two bags to take with me on my trip and this was my detox plan. I packed a bunch of summer clothes and made sure I had a pair of scissors in my purse just in case someone tried to mess with me.

> *I had never been a violent person. I had never harmed anyone physically and I had no idea what I thought I would do with these scissors. But I knew I was going to a foreign place and I was told I would need protection, and they didn't say bring condoms.*

As in every airport one must go through a detector. The clerk saw a scissor in my bag and told me to come with him. I told him I didn't want to miss my plane and asked how long was this going to take. He reinforced that I needed to go with him and two other police officers into a private room. I was not thinking clearly. I had to show them ID. I was asked all kind of questions. I told them I did not want to waste any more time with this and that I was a woman going to a foreign place and I needed some protection. They confiscated my mace and the scissors and told me that I could be put in prison. I swore they were kidding. And I didn't even think about the heroin I had in my wallet as they searched my wallet and went through my bag once more. They let me go and told me I would have to appear in court when I got back to New York. I got on the plane without scissors and mace but with my heroin. Good search, fellas!

My idea of detox was drinking excessively, taking Valium, acid, and sleeping with as many Puerto Rican men as possible. I slept with the security guard at the hotel where I was staying, I slept with the cop down the road, I slept with the DJ of the club next to my hotel and I slept with a man I knew from New York. *At least I slept! Most junkies kicking a habit have problems sleeping!*

When I arrived at Isla Verde I got in touch with my girlfriend Tracey and she told me how to get to her house in Condado Beach. She lived in a mansion. I didn't know Tracey was so wealthy. She had a maid and a butler and a large locked gate protecting her and her family's wealth from the evils of the poverty-stricken area right outside her doorstep. Tracey did not look like herself. Something was wrong. When I first met Tracey she had the most beautiful long brow mane, and now it was cut short. She looked gaunt. We went to the beach one day and her body seemed like it was deteriorating. Tracey confided in me that she had AIDS. She was the first woman I knew who had this disease. This disease was so new to so many of us and here she was with all this wealth surrounding her and no possible cure. Part of me wanted to be her. It seemed like a chance to get away from this world, but it is always easier to say you want something when you don't know the consequences of that want. One day Tracey and I went to the beach and we were going to pick up a man for both of us. You see, Tracey had had her surgery but never had the opportunity to be with a man. Tracey had had a blood transfusion and contracted HIV from that transfusion. Our plan was that I would fuck him, whoever he was, and then she would. When we found our boy-toy I decided to let Tracey go first. She used a condom. When they finished, she walked with this condom to the bathroom. The condom was full of blood and I decided not to fulfill my plan. Back then I was ignorant of the virus and its transmission. My internal plan was that I would contract the virus from her passing it to him and me getting it. My mind was not thinking about this man or Tracey.

> *I was caught up in my self-centered web that most addicts seem to describe when they are using, and/or attempting detox.*

I did not plan on Tracey using a condom. It was through god's grace that Tracey used a condom.

I was supposed to stay in PR for two weeks. I stayed for a month. After one year with this monkey on my back, PR had helped me get though the pain of opiate withdrawal. But as soon as I got packing and was headed for New York, I called Adrian to meet me at the airport, with heroin. I was dope sick as soon as I got off the plane in Nueve York. And I was cured as soon as I saw Adrian and my lover 'heron.'

Tracey, may you rest in peace.

Detox … ing in the Bahamas
… My hate surfaces
… I Wish I had class

In September of '85 Toni and I decided to go to the Bahamas. My relationship with Toni was competitive and confrontational. My relationship with every other female was like that. I didn't know anything about the Bahamas. I didn't even know where it was geographically. I just knew that there would be sun and heat and an opportunity to get away from heroin again. It was so hard to be in love with something so much and know how bad it was for you. It was exhausting loving something so abusive with such a positive and negative impact on your life. I needed to get away and I needed to get away now.

We landed in the Bahamas and I couldn't believe that everyone was Black. Toni loved black men and, although I dated men of all colors, I was not fond of them at that point in my life. Remember, I was working on 42nd Street and the black men around the deuce were violent and hateful. My ignorance in connection with my stereotyping in connection with my jealousy of Toni's sexual promiscuity in connection with my withdrawal process interfered with my delightful personality.

As soon as we got to the Hotel Toni and I went by the pool to wait for our room.

Here's the picture:

Toni and I were strippers. I thought I had more class than she did. She wore tacky 'Rainbow Shop' clothes and I wore more tasteful attire, so I thought. Toni had on a lime green lace tank top, matching headband, and had a white bra under it, the blouse that is. I wore a hot pink, low back danskin. I was much more classy, no headband.

We sat by the pool and tied one on, the initial procedure for detoxing of heroin. I fell asleep and woke up to a man staring at Toni's ass. I was furious and started to yell at him. I asked him who he thought he was. He was as polite as could be and Toni began to flirt with him. I was really mad that he wasn't staring at my ass and he was looking at Toni's. Pina coladas, rum, weed, and a group of Italians from New Jersey carried me through the ten days we spent in the Bahamas.

One day I was asked to be in a fashion show around the pool. I thought this was my big chance. As I paraded in the locals' fashion around the pool I saw that Toni was fast asleep. We had a big fight and I almost threw her stuff off our terrace. I told her I knew she was jealous of me and that was why she didn't stay up to take pictures of my fashion show participation. Toni explained she was just tired. I knew better.

Hey, I have a week's vacation coming up. Anybody want to travel with me?

As soon as we got off the plane I headed, bags and all, to the lower east side. So much for staying away from my lover!

Bottoms
UP

12.
ANOHER BOTTOM

Sony Dies, Hello Frank
Suicide III
the Blue Book {N.A. Text}
My Brother's Stint with Death...
...Brain Surgery
HELPPPPPPPPPPPP
My DETOX 4 REAL
On Finding Home

12

Another Bottom

Sony Dies

There are many agencies all over the world that try to support young people with mentors and role models. There were no organizations that I knew of supporting young trannies or gender questioning youth. The role models were the girls in the clubs who were living and celebrating their identity. The role models were in the ball culture where houses were exemplified and older, more experienced trans-people would play the role of father and mother. It didn't matter how they were living. The fact was they were 'living' and competing in contests and that was the success. It also proved that it was possible 'to be' and not have to hide one's strong desire to just ' be '.

I wanted to be a role model for Sony. Sony was a young mulatto girl who was birth identified as male. She lived (*existed*) in the Times Square Motel on 43rd Street between 7th and 8th Avenue. Sony shared a hotel room, one double bed, with her mom. Her mom was the woman who bore her but had a difficult time mentoring her or accepting her. Sony's mom was an active alcoholic and a welfare recipient. Sony had addiction issues as well. But she was also full of life and excitement and her lifestyle with her mom did not taint her personality. Her mom must've been doing something right.

Sony's face was the perfect mix of her black father and white mom. She was petite in her 5'11" frame. To support herself Sony became an avid booster. She would go to any major department store and walk out with numerous expensive things. I supported her boosting profession by purchasing clothes, and I also supported Sony emotionally when she would turn to me for guidance.

Sony got very involved with heroin. She was an IVDU. She went to prison and got out and went to prison and got out. Sometimes she would spend days with me after she was released. I trusted her and loved her like a daughter. I wanted more for her than she wanted for herself. I wanted her mom to straighten up and accept her daughter.

How interesting that I focused on her and her mom's addiction issues and did not look in my own backyard to see all the destruction drugs were causing me and those around me.

One time Sony came out of prison and stayed with me in Brooklyn. Her boyfriend was coming out as well and he stayed at my house too. Some money was missing and I was furious with Sony. We didn't speak until she landed in the hospital with endocarditis almost a year later. I went to see her not knowing I was there to say goodbye.

How do you say goodbye to someone you've spent too long being mad at? How do you reconcile anger and pain, especially within a community in which most of what is felt in correlation with self-celebration is anger and pain?

A week after I saw Sony she died and I took up a collection at Show World. I met with Sony's mom at a local bar where she was medicating her loss with Mr. Jack Daniels. I gave the money to her mom and wished her well.

Another vibrant human being, another young aspiring wannabe, another angel of god, another trans-woman of color, gone!

Hello Frank

I cannot tell you how many different sized, shaped, sculptured penises I have seen. That would be a book unto itself. However, there are a few that stick out, in my mind that is.

There was one Asian fellow who when he came into my booth and dropped his pants. I had to call in my friends just so they could see what I saw. This man had 'basketballs' for balls. He had this little shtick *(a.k.a. penis)*, and these humongous balls. I couldn't get over it. It was so entertaining.

I was not, in any way, politically correct, or aspire to have, any social conscience. I did not realize this was considered a deformity or a disease. And I was not thinking about this man's feelings. I just thought it was entertaining that this man had NBA gear holding up his little weewee.

Even though I have seen more weenies than I should ever tell new boyfriends, there were certain ones that kicked up the heat within my own groin and there were ones that no matter how far they spat or what tricks they were taught by their owner, I was not impressed.

One night I was standing leaning to the right side of my booth with one boot slightly crossing another and sucking hard on a cigarette while moving my white g-string with my right hand up on the right hip so that my frame would look just right. All of a sudden this man from heaven stood in front of me and asked, "Hey, you beautiful creature, is it alright if I get tokens and come to talk to you?" What he didn't know was that I would have given him the money to come into my booth.

I flung my cigarette cause I truly believed maintenance was there to clean up after me and I said in my surly, sexy, shaky, raspy, high-pitched voice, "Hurry up and get in here." It turned out his name was Frank and he worked at the post office just around the corner. We immediately began to date. Frank had the cock of life (a penis that was very attractive to a lady of my standing and desires). Frank was also a loving, caring soul and I believed he always wanted the best for me.

Frank moved in with me a month after we began to date. Frank was an ex-addict. He was an IVDU but stopped using three weeks before we met. He had just been released from Conifer Park, a drug rehabilitation center in upstate New York. Frank found out I was addicted to heroin and every time I wanted to kick he was there to help. He didn't ram 'getting off junk' down my throat. He rammed other things down my throat though!

He told me that he went to a rehabilitation program and then went to a program called Narcotics Anonymous for a week and stayed clean a day at a time.

Frank had a sad, mysterious side to him. I was never sure what it was and I was not emotionally available to get too deep with him.

> *Later in my recovery I would realize that getting clean without a program, or something to assist you with the pain of addiction, was like leaving an open wound uncared for.*

I never told Frank about my trans-history so neither one of us allowed our relationship any true depth. Frank would bring me around his family and friends and I feared that somebody might have seen me in the Peeps or that someone would figure out that I was a woman with a transexual history.

> *I didn't realize that we all have fears of rejection for various reasons and I would find out more about Frank from his wife when I was two years clean (and sober).*

There were many times I would be dope sick, dealing with withdrawal symptoms, and Frank would take me to the lower east side, downtown Brooklyn, or the methadone clinic, to cop. Frank went out of his way for me and I loved the man for that. He came to me with little judgment.

In fact, on some deeper perceptive level, I believed I could tell Frank what I had been through as far as my identity was concerned and he would've been able to still see 'me,' the 'me' that I was, and not the stereotype that so many place upon me or people like me. After six months of our living together Frank had had enough. Between my using, my antics, and his own closet filled with deep, dark secrets, Frank packed up and moved out.

When I was two years clean, Frank's wife called to tell me that Frank had died from complications due to the AIDS virus. She said that she had been told to call me after he died. She also told me that she had spent her time with Frank jealous of a stripper girl she never knew because Frank would constantly discuss this amazing woman with her, referring to me.

I assured her that I had been tested numerous times and had turned out to be HIV-negative. I also tried to support her in her grieving process and I asked how she was holding up. This was a sign for me that my road was to work with people around their own healing process. Frank's secret was that he never told me his HIV status and we never practiced safe sex. We both had secrets. Hearing about Frank reinforced my hypothesis surrounding HIV concerns. I always wondered why so many of us who had been in high-risk categories would turn out HIV-negative. I wanted to know if there were studies being done as to why so many of us kept turning out HIV-negative and others contracted the virus. I had a hypothesis that is not based in any particular science. I did, and do not, turn to science for all of my answers anyway. It is an elitist, exclusive system that has been granted too much control and has not earned all the false legitimacy that it possesses. Back to the story, shall we?

My heart was crushed that Frank was now dead but I felt like I made his widow's life easier by not losing it.

Frank, may you rest in peace!

Suicide III

The day Frank left me I was beside myself. Of course I was! I think since I was born I have always been there, beside myself! I was upset and couldn't think straight, is that better? I had a bag of phenobarbitals that Adrian gave me, the little Latino man from the pharmacy. I just kept popping them thinking I didn't want to live alone. Then, in a split second, my mood changed and I decided this was a bunch of bullshit and I am not taking myself out over a man. So I did the next two smartest things to do. I stuck my finger down my throat, believing this would bring the pills back up and into the toilet where they belonged, and I decided if I wasn't going to die I would need to get my hair colored. It was late August and a few highlights would do the trick. So I walked out of my house from Kings Highway and East 24th Street to East 19th Street and Kings Highway to a salon I was familiar with. As I walked, the streets seemed to get more curvy than usual. I was used to walking these streets in a blackout, stoned on D, or coked up. I always got myself home and I always got myself where I needed to be. After all, I was in charge of my feelings and affectations. I was in charge of how these chemicals would react in my body. I was in charge, or so I thought!

I entered the salon and sat down in the chair and the next thing I knew I woke up in ICU in Coney Island Hospital. I woke up with one long white-blonde streak intertwined with the charcoal they used to pump my stomach. My old friends Carrie and Ellen came to see me. I told them I didn't want to kill myself. I mean I had, but I came to my senses and that is why I had only one blonde streak. It all made perfect sense to me. And as soon as these girls left I knew what I had to do. Across the street from the hospital there was this great apartment building. I would go see what their prices were for apartments. After all, isn't that what I needed? I needed new scenery and a new place to live.

I called my father to come get me and he said he was already at the hospital. He had picked up my clothes and was not coming back. I left the hospital in hospital attire. As soon as I left the hospital I went home, changed and I went right to the hairdresser. Besides not finishing my hair, I wanted to know if they knew where my money and jewelry went. My hairdresser told me what had happened. She said I sat down and conked out and fell right out of the chair. They took off my jewelry and money before the ambulance came. They didn't trust the ambulance folks because there would be no witnesses on the way to the hospital to say if there were any belongings to be handed over if I made it out of there. I thanked them and explained that someone had given me some medication that I couldn't believe was that potent. They believed me! I got my hair done and gave them a huge tip. As I walked out of the salon with a slight sense of shame, embarrassment, and brassy Brooklyn blonde streaks, I went home. Every time I walked by that salon I was reminded how unmanageable my life had become and how tacky they did my highlights.

The Blue Book {NA Text}
I was told by the social worker in the hospital that I had a drug problem and I should call Narcotics Anonymous (NA) for help. When I got home I realized that Frank had given me a book from NA. I picked it up and looked it over. I even made a call to the NA Help Line but I was not ready to face

my addiction issues. I did the next best thing. I called up Adrian to cop some D and some coke and told him to come on over.

Life went on and I kept using. I was offered a modeling photo shoot for Pineapple Sportswear in Soho, New York. When I arrived I was dope sick. The photographer knew how I looked when I got myself all together. The owner of the store didn't and he was disgusted when I first entered the store. "Look at her," he said to the photographer, "she's a mess." The photographer asked him to give me a chance and they directed me to the bathroom. I pulled out my little beauty bag and snorted it all up. I brushed out my hair and added a fall. I put on the leopard leotard and I put on a little make-up. The heroin lit me up from within. And when I stepped out of the bathroom the owner was all apologetic. He couldn't believe the goddess in front of him, me! Heroin became my life and I did not live without my life in hand. I would go to any lengths, any extreme just to get that life in me. Without it I was doomed. With it, there was no stopping me. Which would you choose? Did I say something about NA and its text, oh forget about it!

My Brother's stint with death … brain surgery
It was March of '87 when I received a call from my father who told me that something was desperately wrong with my brother. I agreed to meet my father at the airport the next morning. I got to the airport just in time. One of my drug-dealing boyfriends took me there. He also gave me enough cocaine to keep me awake for the next 24 hours. I had partied all night, not really taking whatever was going on too seriously. When my dad and I boarded the plane I felt like this was a rare opportunity for us. We would sit together for an hour and possibly discuss our lives. My dad was distraught and the last thing he needed was to sit next to his coked-up daughter. I would not shut up and I kept going back and forth to the bathroom to inhale more cocaine. I hadn't thought that I could've been searched at the airport or that I was carrying illegal substances on the plane or that carrying cocaine and heroin onto an airplane would somehow interfere with our travel arrangements. I gave this no consideration. I was caught up in my drug addiction, the rarity of traveling alone with my dad, and my brother's newest struggle for his life.

I was rambling on when my dad turned to me and told me to shut the fuck up. He was tired of me and all my bullshit. He told me I disgusted him. As high as I was that was how low I went. His words cut me like a knife and I spent most of the time in the bathroom, sniff sniffing, in more ways than one. We arrived in D.C. and went right to the hospital. What I saw would change the rest of my life.

> *I didn't know back then but this was a whole new beginning for both my brother and my self.*

My brother Marc lay in that bed with half of his head totally shaved. I looked at my big brother and all I could do was fall apart.

When reality hits a junkie it is not a pretty sight. After all this time controlling my emotions I was not able to control the despair I felt and the belief that my brother could die. The doctors and my brother's friends spoke with my father. My brother had an aneurism. It turned out that he had a heart murmur. When a person has this condition the person is supposed to receive antibiotics before having a dental cleaning or any other dental work. He did not receive antibiotics and began having headaches, then severe ones, and then was rushed to the hospital. They got to the aneurism in time. But they felt that my brother was not going to be able to walk or talk the same as before. He was lying there fighting for his life and I was standing in front of him trying to slowly kill myself. I wanted so much to change places with him at that moment. But then I realized that half my head would be shaven and how long it had taken me to grow my hair. I quickly changed my mind and told god to ignore my last statement.

At that instant I was of no help to anyone. In fact, I was a burden. Marc's friends were trying to console me and I wasn't even the patient. Talk about being self-centered!

> *It turns out that my brother survived this catastrophe. He has had some medical issues since then and has undergone heart surgery and back surgery but he is doing great. He can walk and talk (in fact he very seldom shuts up) and he is a productive member in his society, with his child, with his temple, and within his occupation. He is an amazing man who has achieved and conquered many obstacles in his life. He was the catalyst, without even knowing it, for me getting clean (and sober).*

HELPPPPPPPPPPP

When I arrived back in New York City I quickly called my connection and went on another crack run. I went to work at the Peeps all the while yearning to get this monkey off my back. I met a man at work who told me he would gladly pay for a detoxification program if I agreed to have a relationship with him. I was in the business of selling dreams and this was just one more. I had never experienced a detox and I knew I could not get clean on my own. I could not stop using drugs no matter what happened around me. And now I was having a difficult time showing up for work. In the past, no matter what, I had been able to stay responsible to me, my bills, and my addiction. I was having a hard time getting out of bed and putting myself together for work. Everything was painful. Looking in the mirror hurt my spirit. Water in the shower made me cringe. And I didn't have the energy to do my hair or anything.

This client got me a bed in Danbury Connecticut Detoxification Unit. When I checked in they asked me if I had any medications with me and I lied. I had two bags of dope and some pills. I was told to take a bath. My body was so weak I couldn't move. The feel of water was like ripping at my skin with a razor. The pills they gave me in combination with my self-meds were making me weaker and weaker. I couldn't take this detox and I didn't want to have a relationship with this man, so I did the next best thing. I left the hospital AMA after three days. I hitched a ride from Connecticut and somehow wound up at a bus depot in Newburgh, NY, where my father lived. The truck driver wanted something from me while he was driving and I found some energy within me to tell him to fuck off. And that is when I was dropped off at the bus depot in Newburgh.

I arrived at my dad's house and his girlfriend, not he, was home. I flew into their house literally throwing up all this poison. I told her I wanted to die. I told her that there was no hope for me. And she told me that I should leave and not share this with my father. She was not my mom and she didn't care about me. However, her main concern was her boyfriend, my father, and she wanted to protect him. I called up another client, a sugar daddy by the name of Mark. He came and got me and took me back to NYC. I was a whirlwind and I was poisoning everything around me.

We made it to New York and I quickly copped some dope. To have my savior back in my arms once again was all that was important. The blissfulness of re-connecting to my true lover gave me back my hope and desire for life. I enjoyed throwing up and I enjoyed the peace, but only for a moment.

For the next month I had taken off on another run. This was the run to end all runs. I would cop and get high. I would be on the lower east side copping and needing to get high as fast as I could. My impulse control was at an all time low. I would snort a bag walking, throw up, swallow it, defecate on myself, keep walking, throw up and repeat as necessary. I was not a pretty sight. My friend Mark took me to the Pines in Pennsylvania to a wonderful resort where I could kick and he would try to get in his romantic weekend. It was a disaster. The relationship with him was one of the most difficult relationships to bear. He was a great guy and a big financial help. In turn he wanted my love. I was never attracted to him, I just needed his financial support, and our interactions with each other both came from unrealistic places.

I will always be grateful to this man for seeing me through some hard times though.

My Detox 4REAL

Mark drove me to a detox called Central General in Long Island and paid cash for me to stay there for seven days. When we checked in I had all these secrets. I checked in with three suitcases and a portfolio. I told the staff that Mark was my uncle. I had so much shame, I was sick, and I didn't want to answer another personal question. I was quickly given methadone and I began to feel amazingly calm. For the next day the methadone truly enhanced the withdrawal process. I was wondering why I never felt this way when I used to drink 90 and 100 mg of meth that I bought from a friend. I realized later that what I was buying was diluted meth and that this meth was not diluted. I met a guy in detox and we became quite fond of each other right away. He had a wife who was eight months pregnant and I had an uncle who thought he was my boyfriend. As we sat in NA/AA meetings we started our own intimate relationship. Our rooms were across the way and we began to flash each other at night. All the patients were told that there would be no tolerating any sexual activity. If you engaged in sex you would be thrown out. This was my first challenge surrounding my impulsive behaviors.

> *My new boyfriend was a man with a wife who was about to have a baby and my sugar daddy was my fake uncle who wanted to have sex with me. So you can see I was stuck in fantasy and self-centered behavior. I had a long road ahead of me in order to become the person I am today.*

When I first entered the hospital I told the psychiatrist that I had a transexual history. But I assured him that my history had nothing to do with my addiction or my problems in life. I did not tell him about my mother's suicide or my own suicidal ideations. I wasn't in the mood for another psych ward.

After the week was up I decided to go to a rehabilitation center. I was told to lie and say I just had an alcohol problem. That was the only way I was going to get into this inexpensive treatment facility. My new boyfriend also went into this facility. I was never so scared in my life. It was the first time that I was clean and I didn't know how to deal with any of my feelings. I was told we had to make our bed up with hospital corners and, because I didn't know how, I slept on top of the covers. I was told when to shower and, because I was scared, I would not sleep so I didn't miss my shower time. I was so deathly afraid of folks finding out about my trans history, my working in the sex industry, that I had a sugar daddy, yada yada yada. In the treatment center there were meetings. We would sit in a circle and pass a book around. I was deathly afraid to read in public. My whole body shook. Everything was terrifying and all I wanted to do was have a sexual relationship with this guy. We were told that on no uncertain terms were we allowed to fraternize. After six days, two days after my 27th birthday, I called up Mark and asked him to pick me up and take me home. When Mark arrived this guy was leaving with me. I told Mark that his wife was coming to get him from my house. Mark dropped us off and left.

I had never had sex with a man without the use of drugs. How do you do it without drugs? I went into a cabinet in my kitchen and took three pills. I didn't even know what they were. The sex was uncomfortable and so were we. The rehab was right. The next day he went back out on a run and so did I. A week later I showed up at an AA meeting in Brooklyn and signed up for aftercare in Long Island.

On finding home

A lot of people experience finding home when they enter a 12-step program. I felt like I had so many secrets and I needed to keep closeted or else. Although I didn't feel at home I quickly made friends and began the process of what is now known to me as 'recovery.'

It was almost fourteen years since my mom's death and fourteen years of not having a home. It was now time to stop running. It was time to look down at my feet and figure out what life was all about. It was now time to take risks. It was now time to find a home from within.

(1)   Working at the 220 Club

(2)   Loving at the 220 Club

(3)   Auditioning for 'Vera,' a woman of the '80s with Danny Bonaduce of the Partridge Family

(4)   My 21st birthday - stoned

(5)   Hanging out at the Casa Dario

(6)   Performing at the Grapevine

(7)   Sony, Me, Mara and Tracey. Sony was dead by her 22nd birthday. Mara and Tracey died before their 27th birthdays. Something is very wrong with this picture! May they rest in peace.

(8)   Sony at 16, already in the scene

(9)   Performing theme from the Valley of the Dolls

(10) 23 years old with family at my cousin's bat mitzvah, from L to R my brother, my father, me and Dotty

(11) Pineapple Sportswear shoot/Soho, NY

(12) Working the door of the 220 Club

(13) Working the Kamali on Brighton Beach con uno de mucho popis

(14) The Lovely Sony and I

(15) Me and Blonde Eddie, Darlene's EX

(16) The sweet Miss Sally and I, may he rest in peace

(17) Sal and the Infamous Taxi

(18) Blondie goes Brunette at the door of the 220 Club. It's me, silly

(19) Mark Reboy Shoot; makeup by Danny Wintrobe

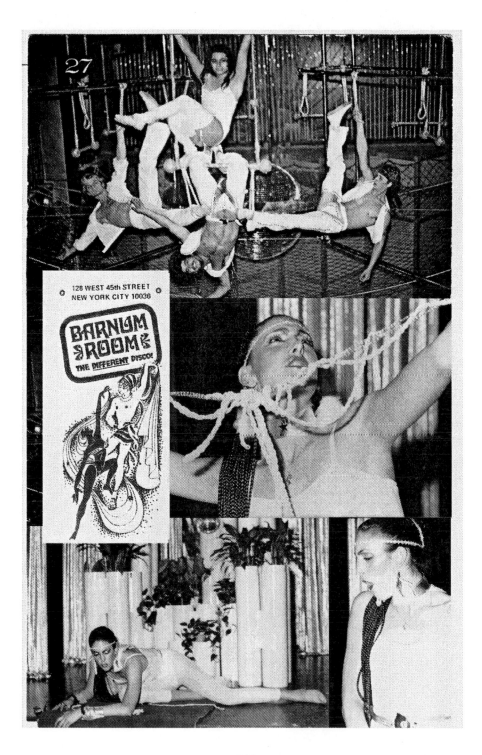

(20) Me, my monkey and Robert, who broke my heart, Robert that is

(21) Working the door and Lynda's Left Foot, not my left foot

(22) Dondie and me, he broke my heart as well, those damn Latinos☺

(23) Ginger, my Bro and me 'Discoing' it up

(24) Hanging out in Norma Kamali, yes, Precious, very '80s

(25) Hanging with the bouncers

(26) Downing it up with Darlene, may she rest in peace

(27) The Barnum Room Dancers. I auditioned once and fell flat on my face. April, the girl on the trapeze, was amazing. I know for a fact at least two are deceased. Blonde Jimmy, far left, and Blonde Eddie, far right. I forgot the man's name on the bottom, not under me, although I have forgotten most of their names.
Lower/Bottom, me performing for Missed Gay New York

(28) Show World Center on the north side of 42nd Street and Eighth Avenue. Miss T and me posing and hungry for fame and fortune

(29) Right before I went to detox. I made that hand/finger in camp and I bought that skull head when I was twelve. That's a whole other story. Call me some time and I'll tell ya all about it

(30) My first month clean, me and whitey

(31) L to R my pals, Barbara Perina, Executive Director of the Queens LGBT Center with her amazing life partner Debbie Perina

(32) One Police Plaza Event NYC

(33) The day the New York Center officially changed its name to the LGBT Center

(34) Receiving my MSW Degree with supportive colleagues, from l to r, Alan Rooney, ACSW; David Schwing, CSW; Michelle Billies, CSW; and Thom Hill, MSW

(35) Speaking at One Police Plaza to the NYPD

(36) Filming with German documentary filmmaker Rosa Von Praunheim

(37) 2002 Halloween Party at the Harry Benjamin International Gender Dysphoria Association Conference in San Antonio Texas, l to r Jude Patton's partner, my friend Leslie Townsend, author of 'Hidden IN Plain Sight,' and the amazing therapist Jude Patton.

(38) On the cover of the San Francisco Frontier Magazine, photo by Loren Cameron

(39) Still performing in recovery. I co-produced and directed 'They Lived it 'OUT,' a night to remember

(40) Beware the Reaper ... Off Broadway Pantomime Theatre. Even the Reaper's gotta go

(41) Grand Marshall Brooklyn Pride. Lynda made that outfit out of kitchen curtains

(42) My Heart, My Lynda, Rest in Peace

(43) Grandmother and me at my other cousin's bar mitzvah in '93

THE JOURNEY OF RECOVRY

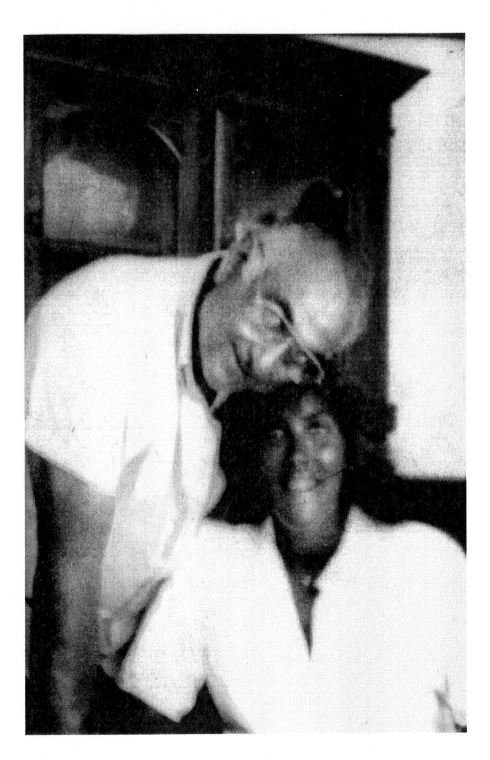

13.
RECOVERY

Hello 12 Steps

the Long Wounderful Summer

In the Closet

My First World Convention

Friends

Sharing the Darkness

13

Recovery

Hello 12 Steps

12-step programs are supposed to be anonymous. The traditions are set in place to protect the program and its individuals for a variety of reasons. However, I will get into how these programs have changed my life.

The first meetings I attended religiously happened in Sheepshead Bay, and Midwood, in Brooklyn. It turned out that my neighbors across the street were also attending these 12-step groups and they were also new. They had participated in programs and drug treatment in the past but were now revisiting their addiction issues. They were a husband and wife team and at that time they had two children. I had met them at a meeting when Vicky, the wife, came up to me to ask if I lived on Quentin Road. At the time I did not have a car, I did not know how to drive, and I didn't even dream of that being a reality in my life. They had a car and they offered to drive me to meetings. There is a saying in 12-step programs that asserts 'there are no coincidences.'

I would see minor and major miracles happen in 12-step programs. There is no way to explain it nor do I want to try to make you understand. I just want to share with you the miracles I have experienced since I've been clean and the miracles that have taken place since I have participated in this healing process.

I was scared to death going to these meetings and meeting this couple assisted me in my initiation into working through, not running away from, all my fears.

To take one step backward I want to share some information. Preceding my arrival to 12 steps in May of '87, I went to this after-hours joint in the West 30s in NYC. I picked up and took home this handsome white man who unlocked my gated window in my bedroom before we left my house, which I didn't know until later on. I went to stay at my girlfriend's in Bensonhurst to baby-sit while she went boosting and copped heroin for us. You understand, your average normal day!

When I came home I found my house burglarized. I called the police and filed a report. Unfortunately for me, and to my embarrassment, although I knew who had done this, I didn't remember his name, exactly what he looked like, or where he was from. This has happened to me many times while under the influence of drugs and alcohol, but not a house burglary.

I couldn't believe this man had robbed me when I had gone out of my way to show him a good time. On one level I was streetwise, hip, cool, and on a whole other level I was so naïve, trusting and vulnerable. What do you mean, bullshit? You don't know me! Don't pass judgment unless you've walked a mile in my size 10 - I should really be wearing an 11 - shoes.

It turned out that when I got clean my insurance company decided to pay me for the robbery and I now had money to live on. This meant that I didn't have to work in the peep show and I didn't have to sleep with my sugar daddy. I was free to focus and apply my energy to these new things called recovery and fellowship and what I later identified as a 'new life. Again, there are no coincidences!

The long, wonderful summer
It also turned out that there was a beach in Coney Island that people from AA/NA inhabited during the day. This was an opportunity for "fellowshipping" during the day as well as cruising, getting a tan, and learning how to socialize without the use of drugs. In retrospect, I believe I had few skills in engaging regular people as Roz.

> *Some more detail. My name on my social security is Roe. My name on my birth certificate is Rosalyne. When I entered treatment and was told that 'being clean was about change' I decided to call myself Roz. I did that because saying Roz controlled my essential tremor somewhat. I now had to speak in public, if you can call sitting around a table in the main area of a detoxification unit or a church basement public. The 'z' in Roz helped control the tremor somewhat and they said it was about change, so I called myself Roz. Although, to my dismay, when I said, "Hi, I am Roz and I am an addict," they would say, "Hey, Roxy," since my tremor took the 'z' to another level. Call me on the phone sometime and you'll understand the phonetics.*

I was scared to death to read in public. I was scared to death to raise my hand and share my feelings in an NA meeting. I was frightened of talking to people one-on-one. I didn't know how to socialize with others without using some kind of mind or mood altering medication. And I was not familiar with hanging around folks from Brooklyn, although I grew up there. I was going to meetings in Sheepshead Bay, Bensonhurst, downtown Brooklyn, Park Slope, Red-hook, Coney Island, and Midwood, and I was meeting all different types of people from all walks of life. Being part of a 12-step program and having a desire to stay clean a day at a time was all that mattered to people. On the whole, people didn't care where you came from, who you were, what you looked like, how much or how little you had, but just what you were willing to do about staying clean or the desire to stay clean a day at a time. What a fucking concept! And what a gift to a person like me who carried around six garbage bags filled with issues relating to shame, remorse, embarrassment and the inability to be a productive member of society. The fellowship literature even spoke about 'social acceptability did not equal recovery.' And on some subconscious level, even though I didn't believe it, this meant I was just as welcome as the women who weren't prostitutes, or the girl who had a prestigious profession and was not green around her social etiquette like I was. This was another valuable gift that offered me an opportunity to hold onto one of those folding chairs in each and every church basement that I sat on during that summer of 1987.

One of the suggestions in the program was to get a sponsor. A sponsor is an individual who had preferably a year or more clean. S/he needed to be involved with the 12 steps and 12 traditions on some level. I met this wonderful nurse who was loving and supportive. Her energy made me feel accepted. It seemed that the summer of '87, its energy, was helping me heal from many years of self-destruction. This statement is not to say I hadn't experienced great rewards and fun adventures from life. It is to say that this was a new experience. The summer of '87 I was not in a smoke-filled peep show, or a disco with strangers who at any moment might harm me emotionally or spiritually. The summer of '87 was about meeting new people from all walks of life and learning how to negotiate life clean. In my first week of recovery I met this amazing woman, a Nancy Spungen wannabe. We took a liking to each other, although we were so completely different. Puma and I began to travel to meetings, much as I did with Vicky and Peter. Puma had two children and so did Vicky. Puma came from a place of despair, much like I came from, although our history was completely different from one another. We bonded and we walked through those very first days of recovery side by side.

> *Although I made friends with everyone there, people would break into cliques. Mine was a motley crew. There was a beatnik, Rick, a Jewish nurse, Annette, a welfare heiress Puma, and a stripper who happened to have a TS history, but this was not discussed, yet. To*

this day, Puma and I have stayed friends through a lot of changes. Puma is an amazing woman who brought up two wonderful, progressive children. Puma has graduated from many years of living on welfare to be an extremely important social worker who truly helps the disenfranchised as well as educating and supporting an important CBO in NYC. Rick and Annette, I have little contact with, but are people I always wish the best for.

Unless you've been down a road that has been destructive to your life, your self-esteem and your spirit, you might not understand the healing that needs to take place in order for you to move forward, to change, to progress. I needed time to heal. I needed time to just breathe and learn how to become a human being again. After all, between working in the club scene, being thrown out of my house and high school, living on the streets, doing drugs daily, being an escort, a stripper, a performer, I had no idea what it was like to be Roe, Roz, Rosalyne. In 12 steps they say your maturing process becomes stagnant when you first started drugs. In addition, I transitioned, challenging the constructs of gender. So where could I possibly be at 27 years old after fourteen years of drug use and eleven years into my life as Roe, Roz, Rosalyne? Hey, anybody got a Pamper and a rattle?

The summer of '87 was the foundation for this new life called recovery. Who would've believed that my life would begin once again on a new and more loving journey within church basements, Coney Island beaches, and with down-home regular Brooklyn people with children and families, and would provide more love than I ever could've deserved.

In the closet
This part is not about instructions focusing on making the most out of the space you have. It's about hiding for all the right reasons!
In 12-step programs people talk. We talked and talked and talked and talked. Some who have participated in these programs feel that it's a place where people sit and bitch, sit and complain. Well, there was more to it. Back then we smoked and drank coffee in addition to bitching and complaining. However, through the smoke, the fog was lifted. Through the caffeine people became energized. And through the bitching and complaining people identified, felt less unique, connected, and healed. Whatever was going on people were showing up day after day, night after night, and many were staying clean, changing, exposing themselves, sharing their lives, and building stronger, more genuine relationships.

When I first got clean I was 25 years old (that's what I said), I had a daughter who lived with her dad (that's what I said), I was a model (that's what I said), and I was closeted (that's what I didn't say). I listened and watched and followed direction from others. I began to talk about myself at meetings, on the beach, and on the phone. But I also lied about many things. I invented a child. I talked more about modeling and less about performing. I truly believed that I couldn't be myself. In fact, I truly did not know who 'myself' was. But I did see Jerry Springer and Phil Donahue shows and I was not that, although that 'that' is not a bad thing to be. But that is who I thought people would see and that was not what I wanted to deal with in the heart of Brooklyn. I wanted relationships, sexual relationships with men in the program. I wanted to bond with other women. I wanted to be normal. I spent most of my life trying to be 'more than human,' 'bigger than life,' 'extravagant,' 'powerful' and 'fabulous'! And now all I wanted to be was 'to be.'

In early recovery you always gain weight. You find a new addiction, which to some of us, many of us, became this obsession with food. You would hang out at diners and talk and eat. I wanted to be and look normal. So I dyed my hair real blonde and started to buy a lot of collegiate sweatshirts, and I got myself some blue contacts. Now I was not a ravishing seductive dominatrix peep show hostess anymore. I became a lovely, chubby, college girl. I looked more normal, more down to earth, and less like a wannabe superstar. Recovery was about reinventing yourself and starting new. But it was NOT supposed to be about making believe or hiding parts of who you were. I couldn't get to that place of disclosure. My spirit would've been shot if I came 'Out' and folks turned their backs on me. I didn't want to face rejection surrounding a part of my life that I had always internally rejected myself. I couldn't and wouldn't take that risk.

The program involves a process of becoming honest, open-minded, and willing. I was honest about not being totally honest. And why was I not honest? Because I was honestly being, and if I came 'Out' folks would have engaged me as who they thought I was, not who I was. Or was that my perception?

At the time I didn't know many things, but what I did get from my history was that I was intuitive enough to know how to engage others on some level. I stayed in the closet. This doesn't mean that rumors might not have been going around. After all, drug addicts did not live sheltered lives and people were hip to certain things. I simply tried to cover my tracks and keep my little secret. In 12-step programs they say "you are as sick as your secrets," and that was as sick as I wanted to be.

My first world convention

I was about to have 90 days clean and I was off to a world convention in New Orleans. One might say 90 days is absolutely nothing. What is 90 days clean? It was, and is, a major achievement in 12-step programs. You count your days and you announce them with pride. For me, it was a miracle that I wasn't taking anything to show up for life a day at a time. Some might say how easy it is to stay clean when you are not working and you don't have any responsibilities. When I got clean I didn't even have a checking account. I didn't know how to balance a checking account. I didn't have any credit or credit cards. I didn't know how to drive. I didn't really know how to cook anything. I didn't really make plans or pay taxes, or show up for anything except drugs and parties and trying to look pretty and my efforts were aimed at getting dressed up. Staying clean 'a day at a time' I began to learn a little more each day. And going to a world convention and getting a 90-day key chain in front of thousands of people was a major achievement. I hated getting up and walking across a room without drugs. I was so self-conscious. And I would rarely blend. I was 5'10", bleached blonde, and busty. So people took notice when I walked across a room. My head would shake when folks looked at me. I was a wreck but I was excited about life and my newfound recovery.

The conference was in a hotel right in the heart of New Orleans. Rick and I were getting close and I was staying with two women I didn't really know well. One woman was a schoolteacher and I had a hard time with her. She was smart and sassy and had manners and self-esteem. Being around her made me look at my actions, things I would say or how I would act. I felt inferior. But I didn't run away from those feelings. I stayed and I placed those feelings somewhere for future reference. On the other side of this adventure things started to become a little too real. New Orleans had a whole red-light district that brought things too close to home for me. Being clean was my new fantasy life and being with friends and seeing female mud wrestlers, working girls, drag performers, and other transexuals frightened me and my closeted place in recovery. To most in the rooms of NA, Roz was this beautiful, shaky, nervous, ex-stripper, not a woman who was transexual. I was adored by many and treated like every other woman in recovery. That's not really a compliment but it was what I wanted to own at that point in my life.

Walking around the streets of New Orleans with my new friends and coming across things that reminded me of what was in my closet shook my foundation. Although New Orleans was a great experience I always felt like it could all be taken away from me if I was exposed! After all, to my knowledge, there was absolutely no one else like me in the rooms of NA in

Brooklyn, New York. And here I was in New Orleans and I still didn't see, meet, hear or feel like there were others like me who were clean and sober. Nor did I want to meet anyone like me for that matter.

Friends
-A person attached to another by feelings of affection or personal regard-

Within five and a half months of staying clean I built a foundation of friendships that would give me the strength to begin to build a new world for myself, one block at a time.

It was October of '87 and my insurance money was running out. I needed to figure out what I was going to be when I grew up. I signed up with a temp agency and they sent me on a receptionist job in midtown. I brought a pair of white shoes to go with the perfect receptionist attire. After all, I knew one thing and that was how to dress. I went all over looking for white shoes but couldn't find any. I finally found a pair but they were a little too tight. I bought them anyway. This was going to be my first real job since Luchows Restaurant in 1984 when I was coked up in the coatroom closet. I walked from the train stop of Grand Central to this building on Park Avenue. My feet were killing me. And when I looked down there was blood all over my new white shoes. There was a saying in NA, 'Look down at your feet. You are right where you are supposed to be.' I was a bloody mess. Was this what they meant?

I got to the office and was put in a cubicle. The phone rang and I was supposed to announce over the loudspeaker who the phone was for and what extension it was on. This could be a simple task for anybody but me. I was self-centered, shaky, nervous, bloody, and as soon as the phone rang, I answered it. I quickly turned on my loudspeaker and announced who the call was for. All you could hear was a screaming crackly chipmunk. I had no control of my vocal chords and as soon as I turned on that loudspeaker I saw every head in the agency peak around the cubicle to see what the fuck was happening. I was asked to leave with my bloody shoes and all. I immediately called a friend. I was uncontrollable for about three minutes. I was hysterical. I was incomprehensible. And after three minutes that friend had me laughing and joking and looking at all that went right in addition to all that went wrong. We realized that a receptionist position was probably not the best place to use my talents. We also talked about finding out what my true shoe size should be. The gift of friendship is unlimited.

The summer of '87 had passed and the winter was slowly exposing its ugly face. Seasonal Affective Disorder (S.A.D.) was beginning to set in and I was spending a little more time isolated. Everyone needs some structure in their lives, especially recovering addicts. I didn't have a job and the pink cloud of being clean was becoming grey. My history was right in my face but I didn't know what to do with my future. I became more and more negative and hopeless. I became angry and argumentative. But I had these friends around who knew me and wanted to see me through whatever I was going through. There was too much reality setting in. I needed to make money but didn't know how to do that besides working in a peep show. I needed to talk about my TS history but didn't trust the process of exposure. I needed to grow up but didn't know how. It was right before Thanksgiving when I decided at the inception of our first winter snow that it was time to go back to my love, heroin.

If it wasn't for my friends, if it wasn't for the man I was dating, if it wasn't for the fellowship of NA, I would not be in Hollywood right now, alive, writing this book. Did someone say shoot the drama queen?

Sharing the darkness

The saying goes 'it is always darkest before the storm.' What does that mean and why did I just share that with you? How the fuck should I know? You think I know everything?

I immediately called up my friend Adrian, my connection to heroin and crack. All the while I was getting high with him and his partner I talked about the rooms of NA and the life beyond drug addiction. I talked about how great it was to stay clean and how loving the people were. As usual, I could not be in the moment and I needed to either be in the past or the future. I went back to the peep show more beaten, self-involved, negative, hostile, and shamed. But I showed up. My boyfriend from NA would call and try to talk me into coming back to meetings. Puma and Rick and Annette were upset. I had not only made a decision about me and my life. My actions had a negative effect on their newfound recovery as well. This would be the first time I would actually understand that concept that what I did in my life directly affected those around me who loved me and needed me.

It was Thanksgiving and I took a train up to be with my dad and his family in Newburgh. I did not get high that day but I was still feeling it from the night before. I slept all day at my dad's house and used the excuse that I was working hard. Working hard on what, somebody should've asked me!

But as usual nobody challenged me around my lies and my deceit.

The darkness was too much for me. I couldn't see. I couldn't breathe. I needed my fix and it wasn't Adrian, Adrian's new running partner, a hot man, heroin, or crack. I needed NA. I needed my boyfriend Joey to know about my history. I needed to talk to Puma and Rick and Annette and just take the risk, and be me. I needed light. I needed to be back on track.

I really needed a lot of other things, but let's not go to the Christmas list just yet.

194

14.
FANTASY-SEX
.....PREREQUISITES GEARED TOWARDS MY Ph.D
REVISITED

REALITY "CHECK"
BACK TO 42ND STREET
BACK WITH A VENGEANCE

STOP: THEORY
THE A....OLE END
OF SHOW BUSINESS

14

Fantasy-Sex Prerequisites Geared Toward my Ph.D. And Addiction Progression Revisited

Reality 'check'

Reality was not always colorful and exciting for me. My insurance money ran out and I had to make a living. Since I was not going to make it as a receptionist, coat-check, retail makeup sales person, or market portable massage units, I knew I could go back to the Peeps, which I did. Something had changed for me. I was not sure what was in store for me but I knew that things were definitely different. I wanted to be clean. I wanted to make money, I wanted to talk about my history in a way I never did before, and I wanted more options as far as work was concerned. But I didn't know how to get from point A to point B.

Just put one foot in front of the other and it will happen.

Back to 42nd, back with a vengeance

Going back to 42nd Street made me think a lot about the past decade.

> *We were now more than half way through the '80s and there was a health crisis. Our society had just begun to really talk about HIV/AIDS not only as the gay disease but a disease that affected IVDUs and the heterosexual communities.*

I decided to look at my work as a peep show booth girl differently. I was going to be an HIV/AIDS Prevention Strategist. I felt like my work at Show World would help me to assist others in safe sex practices. As long as I was around, men would use me as a venue to not act out physically with another human being. If there were no body fluids being exchanged then we were all better off. A glass window was more protection than a condom.

STOP:

My Theory On

The a...ole end of show business

There is a direct correlation between the sex industry and the fashion industry. In the sex industry it is important that one be juvenescent, have a certain body structure, and be able to move, glide, portray, and hustle others.

In the fashion industry the 'man' is still in control over the 'woman,' even though it's the woman who is doing most of the selling and putting herself on display. In the sex industry one begins to lose faith in one's worth as those around turn away. In the fashion industry many are forgotten before their prime. In both the sex and fashion industry people utilize substances to deal, to compete, to show up. Many can argue that these stereotypes are untrue and that the fashion industry carries a sense of respect, which answers to a higher moral authority. I say bullshit! Fashion has ruled my world and so has sex. I've been a slave to fashion and I'll always be a slave to sex. Fashion makes me look good and sex makes me feel good. Fashion makes me feel good and good sex makes me look good.

Our last mayor in New York City, Mayor Rudolph Giuliani (a mayor who ended his tenure on a positive note in many an eye because of the 9/11 disaster), closed down many of the sex shops, the peep shows, the XXX bookstores. I worked at Show World Center on 42nd and Eighth Avenue, Les Gals on 42nd and Sixth, and 7/11 on 48th and Broadway, for over eleven years. We call these places peep shows, where there are live, naked ladies dancing and charming customers. When the mayor closed these establishments down or made them utilize 65 per cent of their space for non-pornographic material, I was already out of the business and into another level of social work. However, what happened was that many women, women with children, women addicted, women beaten up by life, women of trans experience whowere non-operative or postoperative, disenfranchised women, young runaway women, women seeking academic coaching, were out of a job and forced into other venues without support or guidance. Peep shows were a safe place to work

When the sex industry in Manhattan began to close its doors on X-rated pornographic paraphernalia and on the women who used this industry to support themselves and others, like their children, all of a sudden there was more sex on Broadway, more sex in the theatre, shows about sex, movies about sex. Victoria's Secret (a

197

feminine lingerie company) exposed even more of the model and her fashion, and the movie industry took off utilizing sex as a marketing strategy even more. Out of the hands of women supporting themselves utilizing a skill that they had honed, the money now fell into many a white man's pocket.

I spent eleven years in these peep shows believing that there was no way out. I spent eleven years in these peep shows being a star, a porno manic icon. I spent four years strung out on heroin, faux self-esteem, angry and hateful. However, the opportunities I had were that I traveled from Puerto Rico, to the Bahamas, to Florida, to Texas, whenever I felt like it. I spent eleven years as an independent contractor answering to no one but Tony the skeeve (management within this industry). I paid a heavy price for being in this industry and it wore me down. This is not a judgment. This is just my story.

I believe in karma and I learned a valuable lesson. I entered a peep show when I was 24 years old and did not clean out my locker until January 8, 1996. That day was a day I will never forget. I was released. I paid my dues. I was free. But I will not hide that I participated in that life or make up stories of those years.

I was and felt 'hot.' There was excitement. There was power. There were men. There was sex. There were opportunities I, as a high school dropout, would never have experienced if it wasn't for this occupation and its monetary rewards. There was violence. There was remorse. There was sadness. There was hate. There was competition. There was money. There were drugs.

And there was fashion, less of it, but still fashion.

Look at our women's magazines. Why are these scantly dressed models considered respectable but not if it is on a stage where men are ejaculating in front of you? What is the difference if they are fucking you with their eyes or their hand on their crotch?

The mayor robbed these women of the opportunity to feed their children. Disney took over, and these women went out on the streets and into an arena that is more isolated and dangerous, i.e. sex ads and one-on-one sex in an individual's home. More violence, more isolation, less camaraderie, more opportunistic infections STDs and HIV, more shared bodily fluids, and no protection was what became the norm for women in this industry.

If the city wanted to change its image, how come there is more porn than ever in the legitimate theatre? How come Daryl

Hannah, Sharon Stone, and Demi Moore can strip for a film clip but it is not acceptable or moral if someone strips in a booth or a stage? How come we accept 'Sex in the City' but not sex in the city?

Bottom line, I went back to work at the Peeps with a vengeance. I would've never learned as much about myself, society, the system, sexuality, jealousy, competitiveness, love, honor, self- respect, salesmanship, men, and life, if I hadn't gone back to Show World clean and sober. I went back to work, but not as lost or as hateful. I went back to make a living and be a role model for all the other women struggling with addiction. I went back and nurtured the young. I went back and was nicer to the clients. I went back and made more money, more money, and more money. I went back and stayed, on and off, for the next seven years that I was clean.

15.

OUT

OUT/ON Coming Home
Pushing Past Humiliation
Everyone Knows
The Foundation is Positioned

FREAK

What Shall I Be

When I Grow Up
Beauty School Drop In/Out
Welfare Recipient
The Queer Rooms
I'm Not Like You/I'm Like You

15

OUT

OUT/on coming home

I called Puma, Rick and Annette and I told them that I had a transexual history. There was a rumor about me but since I had never brought it up no one ever asked or believed it. It was so difficult to sit down with these new friends and tell them about something that carried so much shame. Each of them acted in the most respectful and loving manner. Rick, the most important because he was a man, told me he loved me. He reinforced how beautiful I was and how much courage I had and fuck anybody who couldn't deal with it. His words made me feel secure. It was the second time that I experienced telling a man and he was OK with the information. The first was Joey. I told Joey, my boyfriend, and he just hugged me and loved me and told me everything was OK. I was now going to meetings and I was going to start talking about this once and for all. I had my shield of friends to protect me and I was going to expose my deepest, darkest secrets in rooms filled with recovering, or in the process of recovering, addicts in Brooklyn. I had spent the last eleven years of my life trying to hide my TS history and I was now about to face it. It was either come 'OUT' or use, and I didn't want to use drugs any more as a way to deal with life. I didn't want to run. I wanted to stop running and start recovering.

Pushing past humiliation

In 1987 there were a lot of meetings going on each night in Brooklyn. I went to one meeting and raised my hand to discuss my relapse. And, as my voice shook and my hands were sweating, I spit out the humiliating word, transexual. And before I got home phones were ringing all over Brooklyn and people were discussing my past. I had gone to a meeting in downtown Brooklyn and when I got home in Midwood people were calling me to find out if it was really true. On one hand the humiliation of having this anonymous program become a free-for-all when it came to such a personal thing devastated me. On the other hand, all the energy took me away from thinking about using again. I was newly clean. I was counting days, I was working, and I was taking a new risk in life without knowing the outcome.

Everyone knows

Because of the phone calls I was getting I started to think everyone knew. Now I wasn't sure how folks were going to react. I had been clean for five

202

and a half months before my relapse and had some intimate relationships with some of the men in the rooms of Narcotics Anonymous. I wasn't sure how they were going to respond to me. I wasn't sure how I was going to respond to them. I mean, I knew how to act and be flirtatious as myself, but now my 'self' was different, or was it? And yes, men started reacting differently towards me. And some of the other women did as well. When I first got clean I was a definite threat to the narenonians (Narenon, Alanon) folks. These were the wives and girlfriends of the addicts. Since I was an addict, I was with their boyfriends and husbands were sitting in rooms talking and building relationships with. These women were sitting in their own rooms talking about their own issues living with addicts. And here was this hot woman, an addict herself, in a secretive space with their husband or boyfriend. From what I heard later on, they didn't trust me. They were right. After all, I talked about being a stripper so people discussed those issues outside the boundaries of the anonymous program. And I didn't respect the boundaries of a relationship at that time, so they were accurate in their inability to trust me. When it came out that I had a TS history the energy around me immediately changed and people changed their attitude towards me instantaneously. It was as if I became a completely different person.

The foundation is positioned

Out of all the things I did so far in recovery, this seemed to be the most difficult. I felt like as long as I didn't talk about my TS history I was allowed to be who I was for the past eleven years. I mean, I truly believed that I should die with this secret under my pillow. I felt like this was an identity that I was always going to hide from others no matter what they thought they knew. And here I was just sitting in a meeting and talking about it. The hardest was looking around after I would say something about it. I would look to see if anyone was laughing or if anyone's energy changed towards me. And now I felt like I couldn't be myself around the men, especially the ones I was attracted to. I had no idea what life was going to be like now but I knew that this was the beginning of a foundation for a new life. Even though I was uncomfortable with these issues, and I was unique, people started to talk about their deep, dark secrets and the meetings slowly changed and became more intimate. People began to speak a little more freely about their HIV status, their gay or lesbian identity, their attraction to drag queens, incest, bisexuality, and more. The meetings began to take on a deeper level of truth.

One day this tall Jewish guy - there were a lot of Jewish addicts in recovery in Brooklyn - came up to me at a Saturday morning church basement meeting and said, "The truth will set you free." It didn't feel like it at the time but there was some truth in that statement.

FREAK
n. a person or animal on exhibition as an example of some strange deviation from nature; monster

It was imperative that I looked a certain way so that when I was on display, at least there was something they couldn't take away from me. Although I felt like I hated being this freak, I began to not give it so much power. In fact, in some instances, 'freak" began to have a positive connotation.

> *Throughout the next months, years, and decades, this 'freak energy' would go back and forth depending on the level of my self-acceptance, how much I felt loved and supported, and all the other things around me that made me feel whole.*

There was nobody else like me in the rooms of NA in Brooklyn, but for some reason I became more a part of and less apart from, now that I was putting all my dirty little secrets out into the open. And I was staying clean.

What shall I be when I grow up
Beauty school drop in/out
Welfare recipient
There were many realities I had to face a day at a time now that I was clean and work was a major one.
I started Beauty School after spending some time in a training program called EPRA (Employment Program for Recovering Alcoholics). Although this was a great segue into the healing process of work I felt like I was sicker than most and did not belong. I was not interested in the AA fellowship back then simply because it was a different cultural experience. When I first got clean I went to an AA meeting and talked about being a stripper. This old Irish guy came up to me and told me that this wasn't the appropriate place to discuss those issues. I was so green surrounding social etiquette, as well as vulnerable, rough around the edges and defensive, that his words chased me right out of that fellowship for fourteen years. I felt if I couldn't talk about that then I certainly couldn't talk about all the other things that made me feel the way I felt, so why go there?

> *I returned to AA when I moved to California for a variety of reasons. I wanted to be around a more professionally oriented crowd and I didn't want to run into NA folks from the east coast. I*

just wanted to start with a clean, I mean sober, slate. However, although I have made some wonderful friends in AA out here in California, NA is my home, my heart, my central space for growing and identifying with people. You live a different cultural experience when you are involved with illegal activities and I need to be around people that went down that road.

EPRA guided me to VESID (Vocational Employment Services for Individuals with Disabilities). Addiction was considered a disease and there was financial support for individuals living with this disease. I decided that working as a cosmetologist I could make tips in addition to a small salary and that was not far from what I was doing in the Peeps. I wanted to go to school and not mix working in the peep show. I got on welfare and stayed on welfare for one year. The financial support helped me get grounded, but as soon as I got off welfare, I went back to the Peeps. Going to hair cutting school in Bensonhurst, Brooklyn gave me an opportunity to experience me just as a regular person again, not as this porno stripper, make-believe, model actress. Although my essential tremor (Parkinson's Disease) made me realize unless everyone wanted the same exact haircut, hair cutting school was not for me. But I finished it anyway.

I was a brazen, loudmouthed, foulmouthed broad, but I was calming down a little at a time. I loved the girls in school and even some of the guys were fun. I had a ball with the teachers, and traveling to Bensonhurst gave me a new respect for the Asian/Russian/Italian/Indian culture and traditions. Every day I walked under the L Train I could swear I saw Mr. Kotter and Vinny. In reality I did see Vinny. Around 5,000 of them!

The queer rooms/I'm not like you/I'm like you

I went to the lesbian and gay NA meetings once or twice right before I relapsed. I met this famous queen named 'The International Crisis' there who had a hard time allowing me to have issues surrounding my transexuality. And I had issues with her as well.

It is typical for the oppressed to oppress each other

She told me that I should just get over it and to stop using my TS stuff as an excuse. On some level she was certainly right. But on another she lived a completely different life from the one I lived. I was straight and attempting to acculturate myself into a system that was not open to people with a history that I had. She was a famous drag queen who lived in the context of the queer world. So, although she had valid points, she did not walk in my shoes. I didn't go back until I had a year clean.

When I went back, Crisis was dead from using too many hormones. Her liver gave out. So, luckily I didn't have to deal with her anymore.

205

I'm kidding! May she rest in peace.

But what I did find this time in the lesbian and gay meetings were loving individuals who allowed me to be on my own path and walk next to them on theirs. I met a group of folks who were loving and supportive and non judgmental. I met this really cute guy who bonded with me immediately. He and his roommate lived on the block with the Hell's Angels and I began to spend some time sleeping with him, not the Hell's Angels, in Manhattan. Hey, all we did was sleep, eat ice cream, smoke cigarettes, and talk about our dreams.

Vincent and Cindy and George did not judge me for working in the Peeps or for having a TS history. They just loved me, my energy, and my ability to make them laugh. The queer rooms began to really teach me how to love myself. I also met the first other woman like me in the fellowship, and Bianca and I became friends.

The straight rooms taught me about friendship, family and relationships, my vocational voyage, and the queer rooms were showing me the road to truly owning and loving my identity, my sexual identity, my queerness. The queer rooms planted the seeds for my future; all the work that I didn't know I was going to be a servant to.

**LOVE HONOR OBEY
NEED WANT SHARE**

**COMMITMENT DEFY
RESPECT CONNECT**

**LIVE FEEL THRIVE
EXPERIENCE LEARN**

**GROW
REGAIN**

**DO NOT TAKE FROM
ANOTHER GIVE**

Mr. R has requested that his identity be obscured to protect the anonymity of his children. It saddens me that we still live in a society that would condemn a man for being in a relationship with a woman like me, especially if he has children.

16.
LOVE WILL FIND IT'S WAY

MEETING MR. R
the BAHAMAS
BUILDING A RELATIONSHIP
the PRICE OF NO
BOUNDERIES

16

Love Will Find Its Way

Meeting Mr R

I was four years into recovery and this was an amazing journey. So much was changing and so much wasn't. I was still dancing on and off, but I was talking about my desires not to be in that life anymore. I truly believed there was no light at the end of the tunnel but I just kept putting one foot in front of the other and showing up. I was now 31 years old and I had participated in this vocation since I was 24. I was really tired of it. I was also dealing with a whole new era in my life. I was not connecting with any man on an intimate level. I mean, I had flings here and there but nothing substantial. I began to believe that being 'Out' was great but it had transformed the way I connected with men. In the past, if I wanted to get laid it would be so easy. If I was in need of a boyfriend that always transpired. But it was almost a year and I hadn't even slept with a guy. That was not my MO. Things were changing alright, and I was not sure if this was a higher power's will for me or if I was just getting older and losing my touch.

Many things transpired in the first four years of recovery. And one important change was that I was making genuine male friendships and not just sleeping with them. Having a guy as a friend was ever so complicated for me. First there was my trans history that I didn't want to discuss. Then there was the sex industry that I didn't want to discuss. Then there was my fear of male friendship that I didn't want to discuss. And then there was my inability NOT to objectify men as a whole. There was always something, is what I am trying to say. And now that I had been clean for four years some of these issues were being worked on a day at a time.

You ever go to a place in your head that tells you something will never happen? I started to believe I would never meet another man and fall in love. I came upon this belief for a lot of reasons. I now had male friends, most of whom were married with children. I had begun to make real friendships with guys in the program. But the energy that used to happen with men when I was closeted about my TS status had changed. Were they engaging me differently because I had a TS history? Or was I connecting with men on a new level that was unfamiliar to me? After all, my interactions and my relationships with men happened on the train, in a club, at the Peeps, and the central focus of the relationship was sexual. This was different. Men were engaging me in a different way and the power dynamics had totally changed. But I thought it was all about me being TS and others being uncomfortable with that. I was also still working in the Peeps so my ability to not be 'on' with men was a whole other challenge. And I wasn't. I wasn't working the rooms of NA. NA was a space where I was trying to just be me. It was most uncomfortable, but most freeing, to just try to be a human being and not all the other things your mind tells you you are supposed to be. I was in the process of learning how to be myself but I was also still a dancer, which affected me when I wasn't working. I mean, sometimes I would be at work and a guy from the rooms of NA would come in. Some of the guys would ignore me, which pissed me off. And some of the guys would come over to me and have the nerve to ask me what I was doing in a place like that since I had four years in recovery. I told them that I was there working, trying to make a living, and I asked them why they were there. After they would leave I would experience such shame as well as self-righteous anger. Who the hell did they think they were looking down on me and why was I now looking down on myself? But there were also those guys who were just so comfortable with themselves that they would just walk up to me, give me a hug, ask me if I was OK, and go on about their business. That was the type of person that I wanted to become. That was the type of man that I wanted to be with.

In 1991, Puma and I would attend this NA meeting in downtown Brooklyn on a Sunday night. Puma was dating this guy who was childhood friends with this group of men that were all clean. These were neighborhood, regular, irregular guys who had known each other since they were kids. They grew up together and now they were all struggling with staying clean a day at a time. These were big guys, tattooed guys, intimidating, rough around the edges characters. And the reality was, they were all real genuine and loving and on their own paths to healing their life's issues. It was great for me to get to know these guys. They treated me with respect and dignity. They were funny and I learned how to be myself, being 'out' with them, and I was totally accepted by this crowd. What is funny is when I first got clean I wanted nothing to do with them. I was scared of them, which made me act tougher. I was judgmental of the Bensonhurst 86th Street crowd because I felt like they would have issues with me. And this was the group that was the most engaging to me. I got clean on the other side of Brooklyn but these folks in Bensonhurst did not judge me for dancing, did not judge me when I came 'out' and did not judge me surrounding my lack of social etiquette. In fact the families, those that were married with children, opened up their houses to me and I became a part of their family. This was a new experience and because of it I was slowly healing.

I would go to the Sunday night meeting for many reasons but for one in particular. The guys there would tell me that there was a man that had seen me on the beach and he was really attracted to me. I liked hearing about any man being attracted to me but this was a special case. I wasn't sure who they were referring to but I liked the crowd and its energy. These guys were big, rough looking men and I liked the idea of one of them having the balls to let others know he really liked me. One day at the meeting, Puma and I were sitting around and in walked Mr R. This man was an Adonis. His body was tremendous. We began to talk. Our conversations were a little unsettling. I mean, I was nervous and uncomfortable around him and his energy was sometimes overpowering. But I liked the attention and I played with it. It was so difficult for me to be a real person with a man but here was my chance at practicing how to do that. I would see him every Sunday as well as at the beach. When I would bump into him I would become a kid, I would be unsure of myself and I would not know what to say. But he had this way about him that calmed me down and I liked that he didn't react to my shaky voice or my history in a way that made me more uncomfortable.

The Bahamas

Every year since 1989 a lot of people from Brooklyn in NA would go to the Bahamas convention. It became a ritual. The airfare and hotel was cheap and it gave people an opportunity to get together for a vacation. Many within the fellowship were dealing with a lot of loss. People were not only dying from drug addiction. Many folks who got clean and were IVDU were dying from HIV/AIDS related illnesses. We were going to too many funerals and going to the Bahamas broke up all the sadness we were facing on a daily basis. It was 1991 and I wasn't planning on attending this year's conference in the Bahamas. Although I was still dancing, I tried to work as little as possible. I just worked to pay my bills and stay 'clean' a day at a time. I didn't have a lot of direction although I was in a process of wanting to change. Mostly all the people from the meeting on Sunday were going to the Bahamas. It turned out that Mr R was going and that made me think about going as well. There were these two other guys who I was friends with who told me I could stay in their room. I took the offer and bought a plane ticket. I was so excited about this decision I wanted to call Mr R to let him know I was going too. I am not sure if I was trying to tell on myself, if I was completely ignorant to the boundaries that were in front of me, or if I was just a total self-centered idiot. But I called Mr R to tell him the good news and his wife answered. Oh, did I forget to mention that Mr R was already married and had two little boys?

Going to the Bahamas was always fun in recovery. Imagine taking a plane with 50 people that you knew. Although I always felt comfortably/uncomfortable around this crew of people I loved being with them. One of my best girlfriends, Donna, was going and she always made the party. Donna was a wacky, outrageous, wonderful woman who had style, was funky, and was a real party girl. Donna never judged my history or my inability to find another profession. There were also some women who were judgmental of me and they were on the plane as well. This was a mixed crowd and we all had a lot of issues. Many of the guys had been in and out of jail, many of our friends were living with HIV, some of these guys still dealt drugs in recovery, and some dealt with sexual issues. We were all working on heavy issues and we were all trying a day at a time 'to be.' So my shit was just my shit and I fit right in. The gift of recovery was unbelievable and, although there were some deep issues on that plane, we were all together.

When we got to the Bahamas Mr R and I really began to play around with each other. I was turning on my sexual charm and he was turning on his. I loved the attention but I also loved the way he was just being so up front about his attraction to me. Being in the Bahamas I didn't have to think about the fact that he was married. I was in a fantasy and on some level I didn't care about that boundary. I was love starved and here was a man willing to give me attention in front of all these people, so I took it. One day he and his friend rented scooters and took me and another girlfriend, Sandy, may she rest in peace, to town. The whole ride into town Mr R was telling me about how he loved his wife and would never leave her. All I could think about was who cared, just drive. That night he tried to maul me on the pool table in the hotel. We had still not slept with each other and this was the last night of the trip. Although I was ignoring that he was married and flirting with him, I still wouldn't sleep with him and he wasn't trying to get me to sleep with him either. This had never happened to me before. I mean, you meet a guy that you like and you fuck, right? This was not the case. And it had nothing to do with the fact that he was married. I wasn't in that place just yet. And when I say wasn't in that place, I mean I didn't truly understand that you don't mess around with a married man. After all, I was a stripper by trade and most of the men who entered the club had a wedding band on. So my cultural understanding was that men objectified me and I objectified them and no one was going to marry me so I had to be with a man when the chance came up. In addition, I had this TS history so I had fewer choices and needed to take it from where it came.

The last night of the Bahamas trip I slept with Mr R but we didn't have sex. We just cuddled. Oh my god, it had been like an eternity being in a man's arms. But being in this particular man's arms was going to be trouble. I felt protected all of a sudden. And having that protection, sleeping in his arms, knocked away one of my walls, the walls I wore to protect me from being hurt by the world. The next day reality set in as we were getting on the plane and going back to New York. I sat in the back of the plane with my girlfriend realizing this man was married and I had no right. I knew his wife. I had participated in women's retreats with her. He had children. And it all sank in that because I was who I was, this is what I would get.

> *Don't you love how my mind made me out to be a victim of the whole scenario and not take responsibility for my actions? The mind is a terrible thing to waste!*

The plane landed and there, at the airport, were his wife and children. I knew what I needed to do to stay out of this drama. But this was only the beginning and I couldn't.

Building a relationship
The Bahamas convention was in November and in January of 1992 Mr R showed up at my doorstep with his bags. Although I was totally in love with this man I was not ready for a live-in relationship. And I didn't want to start off this relationship like this, but this is how it happened. I could go on and on discussing the many gifts of the relationship because there were so many. But one of the major gifts with Mr R was learning how to be a partner, learning how to be in a committed relationship, learning how to love, learning how to accept love, learning to be a friend, knowing that there was someone with you, connected to you, in you, and deeply entrenched in your life. There were many struggles but the benefits outweighed the costs all the time. This man had my back 125 percent of the time. I could count on him always, which taught me how to be counted on as well. I watched this man own all his responsibilities to other people, his ex-wife and his children. He was the kind of man whom I had never experienced before in my life and I was grateful that we were on this journey of life together. This relationship changed my whole entire life. It changed my recovery, it changed the group I was socializing with. It changed everything. Not only did I now have a partner in life, I had two children to learn how to deal with. And not only did I get this man, I received a new family, his family. And most of them welcomed me with open arms. This relationship brought a new light to my recovery process and the light would only get brighter and brighter.

The price of no boundaries
In recovery you become aware of yourself and your actions. And hopefully, a day at a time, you work on being a better person to the world around you. I believe in karma. I believe in the law of karma. And, no matter how long Mr R and I were together, I always felt like the other woman. You see, I didn't respect a boundary. Although Mr R and his ex-wife were not meant to stay

together (he was just counting days when he got married), I had no right allowing him into my life, my bed, while he was still at home with his wife. And no matter how much time passed, I couldn't make it right in my head.

ACADEMIC RESCUE

17.
RECOVERY:
FORMAL AND PROFESSIONAL
ACADEMIA

THE HORROR OF THE MIRROR
THE DR'S PROGRAM
MEETING THE "POWERFUL" ONES
MY FIRST DAY OF SCHOOL
WEEKEND STRIPPING
WORKING MY WAY IN

17

Recovery: Formal and Professional Academia

The horror of the mirror

The journey of recovery took me many places. One of those places was to a meeting where there were others similar to me. These were people who lived with a transexual history, folks on a gender journey, and men and woman who wanted desperately to look at these issues. When I was single I was able to ignore certain things in my life. But now, in a relationship, my past was always in my face. It didn't only affect me, it affected my partner. And I needed to figure out why I had so many issues around being a woman with a transexual history.

I had heard about a meeting at this place called the Lesbian and Gay Community Services Center. Instantly, I didn't want to have anything to do with a center that was for lesbians and gays. It kicked up old stuff. In addition, there was so much anger towards these populations who told me to move on after my surgery. In the club scene these people exiled me, and it was always a challenge to own my core identity around them anyway. I didn't want to have to go through that again. I felt like I didn't belong at a center for lesbians and gays but I also felt that way about my social experiences with all my straight friends. There was no specific place where I felt totally comfortable. And there was no specific place where I felt totally uncomfortable either. So I went.

There are many suggestions in 12-step meetings focusing on new ways in which you live your life. One of the suggestions for meeting 'goers' is you come early and stay late. This gives you an opportunity to be of service by setting up chairs or making coffee. It also gives you a chance to get to know others after the meeting is finished.

I walked into the STA (Survivors of Transexuality Anonymous) meeting late and left before I had to talk to anyone. Although the meeting made me think a lot, I basically went there to tell people I hated my transexual history and it denied me the opportunity to just 'be.' And then I would leave. I was not the most optimistic in the group. I remember one woman being really supportive to me in my process of participation and that was Riki Wilchins, current Executive Director of GenderPac and co-founder of the Gender Identity Project at the center.

In that meeting I found Riki to be genuine, loving and supportive. Although I could never stay and socialize, Riki's 'keep coming back' response gave me the incentive to 'keep coming back.' I needed that meeting desperately, although I felt most of the participants were not like myself. This was a group of people in the process of looking at their TS issues, not living them. And the transexuals who had transitioned looked transexual. I experienced a false privilege by 'passing' as non-transexual, which caused me to have more shame around being transexual to begin with. I didn't understand at the time all the variables that added to my self-hatred surrounding my transexual history. And going to these meetings became the foundation to which I had a chance to do some work on these deep issues of self-loathing. Thank god for the center and STA.

The Dr.'s program
A couple of my boyfriend's buddies participated in a retreat that was held upstate at Veritas Villa, a substance abuse treatment facility. They told me about this woman, a psychologist who worked with transexuals. I decided to go meet with her even though I had never met with a psychologist around these issues before. Recovery taught me to reach out and get help as well as to take risks and do things differently. I hated how I felt as I walked into the lesbian and gay center. I was hoping the front desk staff would think I was a lesbian rather than a person with a transexual history.

Dr Warren kept me waiting, as she did throughout our relationship. She finally came to greet me. She was a beautiful, but plain-looking woman in her late thirties. Her eyes and smile were piercing and her aura was a little overbearing. Her energy and her aura, a cross between Woodstock and, intellectual Eastern European beauty, with an Ivy League education, and it was a tad overwhelming. I was not comfortable at all with her, but for some reason I knew this was a woman from whom I would learn a lot. I tried to ignore my intimidation and figure out how I might be of service to the work that she was doing. Dr Barbara Warren was doing something I had never ever heard about. She was spearheading a program dedicated to the health and well-being of transexual people. And she was bringing on people of TS experience to do the work with her. On one level she was actually taking on the whole profession that treated these communities. She was looking to the TS communities to work within their communities, and most of the profession worked with TS people focusing on the psycho-pathology of the identity. Barbara was putting her professional reputation on the line. I did not know then, nor did she, that this shaky stripper in recovery was going to be a solid component to this pioneering effort to heal these sexual minorities.

> *My relationship with Barbara, Dr. Warren, was a challenge for both of us from the very beginning. Although we argued a lot, and our communication skills were not very good when it came to dealing with one another, I will always love her in a profound way. She took a chance with me and I became a success as well as a major pain in the ass. Give a streetwise egomaniac some formal knowledge and you've created a monster. I think what pissed Barbara off the most was so many times I was right but she couldn't do anything about it. Her hands were tied and she had to try to tie mine.*

Meeting the 'powerful' ones

I began to work with Barbara as a volunteer for the Gender Identity Project within Mental Health and Social Services at the Lesbian and Gay Community Services Center.

All I wanted to do was be in the background. I didn't want to have to talk to anybody and I didn't want to socialize. Barbara would coordinate an event and I wanted to set up chairs and/or clean up, nothing else. But as I hung around Barbara and the center I was meeting professional transexual people and I began to form an opinion surrounding their discussions. I don't mean that they were professionals at being transexuals, they were nurses and scientists and teachers and computer geeks, etc. I was really impressed with their ability to be professionals. I was also very intimidated. A few were genuinely sweet and engaging and some of the folks were very weird and made me more uncomfortable. I think I was more intimidated because of my profession. I was still stripping and I was an addict in recovery. That didn't seem to me to be a prestigious professional position. But I was in recovery and I didn't want to make believe I was anything but who I was. What I did have was that no matter what I did for a living or how many drugs I took to survive life, I was a success. I lived my dream at an early age and I was a lot more comfortable in my skin than I gave myself credit for. And some of the men and women I was meeting acknowledged that, which made me feel like I had something to offer this project.

My first day of school

Many things were beginning to transpire as I worked as a volunteer at the center. One prominent thing was I knew I needed to go back to school. If I wanted to do other things to make money other than stripping I had to get a formal education. Hanging around the center and listening to the way people talked about politics and social justice and books I had never heard of made me realize how out of touch I was without a formal education.

I would later realize how out of touch they were without an informal education.

I knew I had to do something. This was the scariest thing in the world for me. In fact, everything frightened me. Everything challenged my homeostasis, and made me feel inferior. But it had to be done and I was going to do it. Barbara believed that John Jay College of Criminal Justice had an excellent CAC (*Certification of Alcoholism Counseling*) program and I trusted her academic judgment. I applied and got in, which wasn't that difficult.

In my first semester I took two classes. My first day, I went to the cafeteria to get a cup of coffee. I remember this like it was yesterday.

I walked into the cafeteria and felt like I was 80 feet tall. My hands were shaking and I could barely say anything without the quiver being totally prominent in my voice. I dropped my books. I was totally self-conscious. But I showed up and continually showed up on a daily basis. My schedule became school twice a week and papers on the weekend. I volunteered with the Gender Identity Project (GIP) twice a week and continued my NA meetings. I went to one queer identified meeting and three regular ones.

Queer = irregular

I spent the weekend evenings with my boyfriend after working all day as a stripper/booth baby. I was on this new road, not sure where I was going, but in a process. I was struggling with trying to use a computer. I was struggling with learning how to read and pay attention. I struggled with writing a paper and using the library. I struggled with identifying my TS history and figuring out how I could be a help to others. I struggled with my stripping and couldn't figure out why there was so much shame surrounding me in that profession. And I was also struggling with how to be a good partner to this man who wanted more attention than I had to offer.

I was in school and had all these new responsibilities. Although he was totally supportive, my new life began to change our relationship. After that first semester I realized something about myself. I was smart. I could have a temper tantrum, lose it, feel overwhelmed and still see a semester through to the end. I stuck with it and got two A's. I couldn't believe it. I was energized to take on another semester.

Working my way in

As I started to learn in a formal academic setting, I began to participate within Mental Health and Social Service team meetings and started to have opinions that were developed through the application of my readings, my colleagues' outlook, and my informal education. I began to realize that my street life, in conjunction with my academic knowledge and my recovery process, could be of some value to the transexual communities. But I knew

I, and the GIP, had to be even more culturally diverse. After all, this was the center and all kinds of gender non-conforming people would walk through the doors of the center seeking some support around many different issues. The center and school made me realize I had opinions that were worthy of sharing. I began to think and think and think, as I realized I didn't know anything the more I had the opportunity to think. Throughout all these new experiences, every day I had to make a conscious decision not to run away from it all. I began to slowly work my way into my skin and not away from it. I learned to sit with anger and not totally act out on it. I learned how to feel inadequate, tell myself I was nothing but a freak stripper, quietly thank myself for sharing, and put one foot in front of the other and show up for this new life. I learned how to be accommodating and go out of my way for a man who was showing up for me on a daily basis. I learned!

CERT/IFICATE

The Trustees of The Belle Zeller Scholarship Trust Fund

Are Pleased to Present the

Belle Zeller Scholarship Award

For Academic Excellence, Meritorious Achievement

And Community Service While Attending the

City University of New York

To

Rosalyne Blumenstein

John Jay College of Criminal Justice

College

Trustees

Who's Who
AMONG STUDENTS IN
American Universities
& Colleges

This is to certify that

ROSALYNE BLUMENSTEIN

has been elected to
Who's Who Among Students in
American Universities & Colleges
in recognition of outstanding merit and
accomplishment as a student at

**JOHN JAY COLLEGE
OF CRIMINAL JUSTICE
1996-97**

The National Honor Society in Psychology

Psi Chi

This certificate attests that

Rosalyne Blumenstein

is a lifetime member of Psi Chi, the National Honor Society in Psychology,
and was regularly inducted into the Psi Chi Chapter at

John Jay College of Criminal Justice, CUNY

May 30, 1996

The City University of New York
Baccalaureate Program

Thomas W. Smith Academic Fellowship

awarded January 1996 to

Rosalyne Blumenstein

Pamela V. Reid
Associate Provost and
Dean for Academic Affairs

Michael C.T. Brooker
Academic Director

Courtesy, Professionalism & Respect

Certificate of Appreciation

In Appreciation for your participation, this certificate is awarded to:

Rosalyne Blumenstein

For the success of the New York City Police Foundation's
Commanding Officer for the Day, held on September 22, 1999

226

18.

ADDICTION AND RECOVERY

SEX ADDICTIONS AND INTIMACY
MONEY MAKES THE
WORLD GO ROUND RE-VISITED
LOVE HEALS
HIDING BEHIND MY PHYSIQUE
NO SMOKING PLEASE

BINGO
SHOW WORLD/SHOW NO MORE
SCHOLARSHIP/SCHOLARSHIP/SCHOLARSHIP

18

Addiction and Recovery

Sex addictions and intimacy

Going to school opened up a new world for me, as did participating in 12-step groups. I was learning so much from books, from other students, from friends in 12-steps, and from the tools given to me in all these arenas. One of the things I began to take a look at was how my sex addiction kept me from truly being intimate. You learn how to get down to business working in a peep show. And you focus on just a few important factors like money, the ability to be a sexual being, and how big the guy's ... was. It was simple. If there was not a lot of money involved but the man was sexually appealing, it was almost acceptable for him to take up your time. If there was money, it didn't matter how the person looked, I learned how to turn it on.

But this was supposed to be theatre, and this theatre was affecting my real-life sexual experiences. When I worked it didn't matter if I came home with almost a grand, I was irritable. And so many days I would be so irritable at work I had to do something in order to release the excess anxiety. Masturbation at work did not occur in every institution. Working in the Peeps, masturbation became a component of my daily necessities, like computer programs and office supplies are to a corporate setting.

In fact, I think some sexual energy might be helpful in certain situations in all workplace domains.

> *I know I'll probably get some flak from those who have been harassed due to sexual harassment in the working environment and I understand the trauma of that experience. Nor do I want to ignore the dynamics of a power system interjecting sex and sexual energy in the work place. I have just seen and experienced first hand 'sexual release' used as a positive affirmation and as a tool, and I did not want to discount this tool that I used for a break from the stresses of the workday at the peep show. Now, does anyone have a tool they want to share with me?*

Money makes the world go round revisited

Working in the peep show I became more competitive than ever before. There was a new generation of women in the Peeps and I tried desperately to hold onto my status.

When I began my work in the red-light district in 1984, most of the women were strung out on something or beaten up by life's ugly side.

There were now all these white college women working in a booth or in the back, lap dancing. When I first came to Show World I was the minority. I was white, a person of no color. And now there were more women like me but younger, those bitches!

And now I wasn't so special. I was in my early thirties and I wasn't getting any younger. So I had to figure out ways to hold onto my celebrity status, and that meant doing things in the booth to perform for the customer that I had never thought I would do before. In recovery one learns that you can do or be anything you want. You can live your dreams. All you have to do is show up, participate, listen, learn, and work at it. I became a really good hustler and was making a ton of money, although I only worked one or two days a week. I was sharpening my skills at Show World. My dad was a salesman and I guess I had the gene. I don't think he intended for that gene to be in a booth. Well, actually, they were in my locker, the jeans, that is. And I was in the booth.

Love heals

Working at Show World did not make me a happy camper but it freed me up to study more efficiently. It was so hard for me to concentrate, so being able to have a little more time to do that was extremely helpful. And I felt something in my life I had never actually felt before, at least not since my mom. And that was love. Mr R loved me to death and I loved him. When life got scary for me he reassured me, and when life was too much for him I learned to reciprocate. And I actually liked doing it. Slowly but surely love taught me how to be me. Love taught me that it was OK to be me. Mr R's love was healing all those years I lived with guys and made up stories about me and my life just to cover my tracks. I would lie about my period, I would lie and say I had an abortion or that my kid was with his father but I wouldn't say why. I would lie and say I was modeling when I was dancing. I would lie and talk about my childhood like I was not who I was. Here I was with a man, and I was exactly who I was, and now I was on a road to becoming a whole new person. I was not making believe I wasn't, I was just growing and changing and adding to 'me' because I finally had the opportunity to be 'me' with someone else. What a gift!

Hiding behind my physique

One of my issues was my physique. My ability to turn heads had always been a priority. And now that I was working at the center I prided myself on being attractive because I felt like I couldn't compete with all those intellectuals. I guess we all use whatever we have to make ourselves feel good and my looks were something I spent a lot of time on. Mr R always told me I was beautiful. He made me feel secure about my physical appearance and I wasn't always available to do the same. It seemed like the more someone loved me the more I would be ignorant in how I dealt with that love. In the past I would use my physicality to get attention. I would dress myself up so elaborately and cause such a ruckus but I wasn't comfortable with the attention. I was now dressing a little more conservatively. I was able to wear sneakers or go out without my hair done or without makeup. Although I always used my looks to hide I was now coming out a little and not hiding behind my ability to do drag well.

> *From this short synopsis you can see the confusion. It's called growing pains. It is called peeling the onion but not sure what is under each layer. It is called recovery and discovery.*

No smoking please

I was trying to work less and less at the Peeps, something I was always struggling with. I got a job as a receptionist with a person who was in recovery. There were two other women working there as well so I felt comfortable. I decided to stop smoking after my boyfriend asked me how much money I spent on perfume. He said that my hair smelt like cigarettes and not the expensive perfume I was buying. It made so much sense that the next day I stopped smoking. I had smoked three packs a day for almost twenty years.

> *I began smoking Pall Malls and Lucky Strikes at the age of eleven and I'd smoked ever since.*

I had wanted to stop for the past year and being with a nonsmoker helped me achieve this new goal of mine.

> *They say you should attempt things in life when life gets a little simpler. My life suddenly became chaotic but I stayed on this road anyway.*

I was now in my second semester of school. I was now 32. I got a call from upstate New York. My dad had collapsed in Atlantic City and was hospitalized. At the time I didn't know how to drive and I was in the middle of my second semester in school, I had just started this new job, and I had just stopped smoking. My brother and I were not talking. I called my dad's wife and she was no help as to what I should do. Mr R drove me upstate.

My dad was always the backbone of my life. No matter what was going on I knew on some level he would be there for me. Even if he had nothing to offer me emotionally, which was most of the time, he would send me a check. I always had him to turn to and I was grateful he didn't take off like my mom did. Even when I was sixteen and I was on the streets he would get my social security check to me and, at least for one week, I had money in my pocket. My dad didn't show his emotions unless it was to yell. He never fell apart like my mom so he seemed to be the rock. I walked into the hospital and there he was in this bed, paralyzed from the waist down, and he saw me and we both started to sob. I couldn't deal with it. I didn't know what to do or say.

My life had just begun with work, the center, school, a relationship, and now, here, my dad's life was ending. My father's wife, girlfriend at the time, got annoyed that he was crying and I couldn't control myself. This was my daddy, the man that I had to turn to no matter what. He didn't offer me much but he was always there. My dad never walked again.

It might sound superficial but I didn't pick up cigarettes in order to deal with my dad's tragedy. It also might sound self-centered but I stayed in school and focused on my studies. I called my dad every week but didn't go to visit as much as I knew I should have done. I couldn't. I didn't have access to a car. Mr R had his kids on the weekends and I had to study or work. Since I had been clean my dad had been sending me money once a month to help me out a little. One day I was on the phone with him and he told me he couldn't send me any more money. My heart broke. Not because he couldn't send me any more money, because I knew that was his way to be supportive and he couldn't do it anymore.

Did he think that that was all he was good for with me, the money? I didn't know how to verbalize what I was feeling and I couldn't share my new joy with him. It was killing me. And this was about him, not me. We never had the chance to really get to know each other and here he was in a crisis and I couldn't be there more. I had to be in my life and get through school and make a living and take care of my boyfriend and try to be a friend to my boyfriend's kids, which was most difficult for me.

Slowly things were not looking good with my father and I couldn't deal with all the emotions I was trying to repress. I was in therapy but it wasn't helping. Something seemed very wrong with this therapist but I couldn't put my finger on it. I was going to Post Graduate Center for Mental Health on the east side in Manhattan. There were also things wrong in my relationship and I didn't have the energy to work on them. School was a priority as well as trying to move my way into the center.

Mr R and I decided to break up in May of '93. It was around my birthday and I just didn't want this relationship anymore and neither did he. He moved into an apartment for about a week and then went back to his wife. I felt relieved and sorry. Although I loved him I hated being with a man that had been married when we met. We were together for almost five months. It was so hard to go to work at the Peeps and then be sexual at home. It was so hard to be 'loving' to this man when my dad was not the man he used to be and I wasn't able to connect with him the way I wanted to. I spoke to my dad every week, but it wasn't my dad anymore.

Mr R took me up to see my father in May even though we were breaking up. That was the kind of guy Mr R was. My dad was drugged. He was in a lot of pain and they were giving him morphine. As soon as I got there he started yelling at me. His bed was in the middle of the living room in his house in Newburgh. And his family was taking care of him. This was a family that had been a part of his life for the past thirteen years. This was a family that was never my family, but I was grateful to them for being in his life.

> *Although his wife Dotty was an ignorant unattractive ...tch, she did give my father something he had not had in a long time, and that was a family. NA and Mr R gave me that. But I always wanted my dad to be a part of that as well. It was a shame that this group, my brother, my father and me, could never repair our family.*

It seemed like my life was really turning itself around for the better but now the men in my life were both leaving.

On June 3rd I got a call telling me my father had died. I went upstate to the funeral with a friend. I went to the funeral home before anyone else was there. I was able to hug and kiss my dad like I never did before. In front of my eyes there was my dad, a man I had put through hell. Lying there was this man who I never got to know. There was this man for whom I had done nothing to make him proud. Lying there was this broken man who had had too hard a life. I loved this man with all my heart no matter what. And I was determined to make him proud. But he was gone.

My dad was 59 years old and only one of his kids showed up to his funeral. He was not a good father but I felt obligated to him. My brother didn't. My brother had enough of the diseased relationship and had decided to let it go a while ago. Even though my dad 'sucked' as a father he put up with a child who was transexual, and that made me grateful. How sad is that?

> *We live in a world where people turn their backs on their children because they are transexual. But I was one of the lucky ones. My dad didn't turn his back on me, although now he was lying on his back, forever!*
> *I was so mad at my brother for making me do this funeral thing alone. After the cemetery I didn't go back to my father's house with his family because I felt as if I didn't belong. I was alone in the world at 33 years old. I was an orphan. And I felt empty.*
> *It turned out that my brother was in a car accident on his way to the funeral and had not been able to get there. My brother and I started to work on our relationship again shortly after my dad's death. Two men were gone and now one man was coming back in, my brother.*

It turned out that my father's wife had changed his will a week before he had died. There was no way I was going to fight this in court. And this was a turning point for me. I believed that his wife had been good to him. She was an old Italian woman who hadn't talked to her own sister in years over money. This was a greedy family and I didn't want to have anything to do with the negative energy. I couldn't believe she would rob me in the way she was and I believed in the karma so I just let go. After all, she was in her late fifties and I was in my thirties. I thought, "I'll make my own." Let her have it. And that was not me. This was a newfound freedom. Money had always meant so much to me. After all, look at the lengths I would go to make it. I needed to stay focused, and fighting this old broad for $50,000 was not worth it.

Bingo

Shortly after my father's death I went for a session with my therapist. This was at the Postgraduate Center. I immediately smelled something in the office that was unfamiliarly familiar. My therapist kept nodding off and it was hard to be self-absorbed when it looked like I was boring her to death.

> *As a therapist myself I have experienced being exhausted in sessions with clients. Sometimes it took everything I had to keep my eyes open as well. But I never fell asleep on a client, never!*

I realized what the smell was. It was alcohol. I asked her what the strange smell in the office was. And she asserted that she was sick and was on medication. The next session I could smell the same thing and I realized that this therapist was drinking. I couldn't believe I was dealing with not being sure if my therapist was sober or not. My father had just died, I had broken up with my boyfriend, I was in school, and I was trying to change my vocational life. I didn't want to deal with questioning the sobriety of my therapist in my session. The session was to focus on me, not her and her ability to stay awake. As I confronted her I realized I was not caught up in my self-righteous anger. I told her I thought her nodding off was inappropriate behavior. And whatever was going on with her she needed to do some work around it and not see clients. I did not report her. I just stopped going. This was a big deal for me. Usually when I am wronged by somebody, someone has to pay. But I was letting this one go. There was too much pain and sorrow in my life right now but I was OK. I thought about suing the institution and let that one go as well. My greed would not change the fact that this woman needed help, but she had to realize it. And what if I was wrong? I let it go. Let it go, already!

In July of 1993 I saw Mr R on the beach. He tried to talk to me and I lost it. My father had just died, my therapist was a drunk, he had moved out, and all I wanted was to hold him and feel secure. He moved back in with me the next week. On some level I felt a little better about our relationship and this triangle.

After all, he had gone back to his wife, they had tried to make it work, but he was in love with me and that relationship was over. I felt like his breakup wasn't my fault this time. I tried to use this rationale to make this relationship sit right in my heart. Mr R and I would be together for the next seven years.

So why did I call this subheading BINGO?

The year was 1995. The month was December. I had spent two and a half years in school. Things were changing ridiculously fast. I was on the dean's list every year. I was working my way in at the center and was now the coordinator of the Gender Identity Project. I was learning and growing and staying clean. But I was still stripping once a week to make ends meet. One day I was in my booth at Show World and this young man came in to see me. He looked at me and, with sincerity in his voice ,he told me "he thought I must've been gorgeous when I was young." When I was young?

I knew that day I had to get out of there. I couldn't be one of those old ladies working in a booth. That would totally crush my ego and we don't need to have my ego crushed. I just didn't know what to do. I couldn't see the forest from the trees. I couldn't see the light at the end of the tunnel. I couldn't see this guy's penis! Got ya back, boy!

For a Christmas gift Mr R and I decided to take a cruise on the Royal Caribbean. Every night on the cruise we would play bingo. And every night we would make like we won. The last night of the cruise I was sitting at a blackjack table and I made him get up and go buy us our cards for bingo. The pot was $9,600. Mr R and I were having a blast. We went to the main theatre for bingo and sat in the front row. The speaker called out the first number and Mr R jumped up and screamed 'Bingo.' Nobody laughed but us. The room was filled with a bit of upper crust, refined, boring tourists and then there was married to the mob/Mr R and his stripper broad, a.k.a. Brooklyn Barbie and Ken.

As the speaker called the letters and numbers we were filling up our two cards. When the speaker called B4, or whatever it was, we had it, BINGO. Mr R grabbed the card out of my hand and ran to the stage, without me, the bastard! We won bingo and split the jackpot with another couple. The excitement was overwhelming and we were dwelling in the attention from others. My mind started to race. I had just learned how to drive and I started to spend the money in my head. After we collected the money we went to the blackjack table. I was on fire. I could do no wrong. This doesn't happen to me often and I was enjoying the addiction, the rush, the fire. Mr R and I were sitting at the blackjack table with a guy in-between us. I started talking about how we were going to spend the money and we got into a fight. The poor guy in-between us didn't know what hit him as he saw this beautiful woman on his left all of a sudden sound like a shaking 60-year-old fisherman cussing and fighting. We got up from the table and went by the side of the ship and Mr R threatened to throw all the money overboard. If at any time I thought money bought happiness, I truly realized that at this very moment it didn't and I was confused. I wanted to get the money and have Mr R jump overboard, not the other way around. We both calmed down and went home with different ideas about the money. However, I was about to change my life one more time.

Show World/Show no more

On January 8, 1996 I walked into Show World to walk out of Show World. The day had finally arrived. I went up to my locker and began to empty eleven years worth of paraphernalia. I couldn't believe this day was here. I had waited forever to come to a place in my life where I knew I would not have to do this for a living again. It seemed like an eternity was spent in this booth, my office, this locker, this building, this internal isolated, exciting, devastating place. I looked around at the lights, the men, the workers, and the mops, and I knew I was finished. So much had transpired in this building. This is where I was financially free to do a lot of things in life, like enhance my body, cosmetic procedures, and rearrange my dreams, like lose all belief in myself.

I had spent eleven years working in an environment that on one level celebrated my power as a woman and on another level made me feel disgusting and deserving of no normalcy. I had become a porno star and a junkie. I had become a bigger liar and life swallowed up my reality and became a daily fantasy. I lived to make money and get high. I was greedy, jealous, competitive and hateful. I also surrounded myself with a lot of women with a lot of problems.

> *When I was using drugs at work I used to get so upset from being stared at, or if a client ignored my advances I might throw something at him or spit at him. One time I was working by the stairs and a man grabbed my ass as he walked by and I threw him down the stairs. I was not gentle. And neither were many of the other women.*

On the other hand I also spent seven years clean at Show World and I became a mentor to the younger women who entered into the industry. I worked on my relationships with management, with clients, and with my greed and my jealousy. I brought some love, some recovery into this work and I could leave feeling a modest sense of pride for my accomplishments.

I was leaving and I knew I was never coming back. No matter what was in store for me financially, I knew this was it.

There was one manager from Brooklyn who became a friend. Being clean in this environment, I had learned to be more myself even in the midst of 'the hustle.' He saw me and he stopped me before I left. "Roe, you have so much going for you," he said. "You are truly a class act. Don't ever come back here again."

> *His words made me feel special.*
> *My experiences in this industry did not make me feel whole but they sure filled my pockets. Within those eleven years I was always looking for a feeling that would center me. Heroin helped me achieve that. Cosmetic surgery helped me achieve that. Men and their money helped me achieve that. And now, my parting words with Show World, the simplest comment, grounded me with the exit of this journey, his words made me feel whole. I was leaving with this feeling and I was never to go back.*

It was January 8, 1996 and I walked away from 42nd Street and 8th Avenue for the last time.

Scholarship/Scholarship/Scholarship

In January of 1996 I was awarded the Belle Zeller Scholarship for academic excellence, meritorious achievement and community service. Also in January I received the Thomas W. Smith Academic Fellowship from the City of New York Baccalaureate Program. In March of 1996 I became the first ever Director of the Gender Identity Project at the Lesbian and Gay Community Services Center. It was the end of my third year in school and I was still on the dean's list. I was beginning to believe I had something to offer.

238

19.
SOCIAL/SEXUAL PROGRESSION?

A Professional Development
the Making of a Politician
Fame and It's Addiction
EGO GoGo
Working for the Good of the Communities
Graduation

19

A Social/Sexual Progression?

A professional development

My work at the center, in conjunction with my formal academic training, in conjunction with my recovery work, was invigorating. Every day was a challenge, every day was a journey into the unknown, and every day was a new experience. I loved learning and integrating my formal training with my informal education. I believed this made me more intuitive, or did it? My life took on a deeper meaning. And my work slowly became my life. I was one lucky woman. I had a loving man at my side who supported my new professional status. I was involving myself with queer social justice but not really understanding the dynamics of the politics, the players, or the long-term effect it would have on me. Initially it gave me a drive I had not experienced since I first got clean.

The making of a politician

At the center we had weekly staff meetings. We would go around the room and discuss our work. This was intimidating for me, but I had learned to speak in NA meetings and this wasn't much different. The players were different but the public speaking challenge was the same. I was going around to other agencies, first with Dr. Barbara Warren and then by myself. At first I was extremely defensive. I was also playing the role of the population that was up for discussion. Barbara was the expert and I was the 'disenfranchised population.'

I first came 'Out' in NA in 1987 and now I was coming 'Out,' or 'Outed' because of my position at the center, everywhere I went. And I was not always facing audiences that were progressive, understanding or culturally competent. I had to try to play politics with these strange bedfellows. And I had to try not to lose my temper, curse people out, give them the finger, or tell them what I really felt about their ignorance towards the trans populations. This was trial and error and there were times where I just had to tell folks exactly how I felt. I did this at the center as well as with other community based organizations I was now getting involved with. I was constantly watching how those around me would engage the public and I was slowly learning to contain while being in an uncomfortable position. However, this kind of work was unfamiliar to me. And there seemed to be something wrong with the way people were reacting to trans issues within the center as well as other agencies. I couldn't figure it out. It was also very hard to get used to keeping my clothes on at work all the time!

Fame and its addiction
Ego go go

There were few people besides Barbara and the GIP doing trans-social work using a progressive, nonpathologizing model. I was involved with cutting edge work, which had its costs and benefits. The cost was there was no template from which to start. There was no curriculum and I made it up as I went along. My heart guided me and my work. And my ego was also a central part. I began to be pulled in many different directions. I was asked to speak here and to speak there. I was asked my opinion on this and that. I was asked to be the token on this committee and that committee. And I accepted everything from everywhere. I was needed and I was going to fulfill my responsibilities by showing up and speaking out. There was so much work to be done and so little time to do it. I also had a lot of catching up to do. After all, I had just spent most of my life somewhere in a fantasy not realizing all this prejudice so many trans people were being subjected to.

> *When I went to the hospital or to detox I just went to detox. I never had a problem as to where they were going to put me or what dorm I would be in.*

I couldn't believe trans women were being denied access to treatment. I couldn't believe different programs had the balls to reject trans clients. Even before my surgery I was in psych wards and I was told not to discuss my gender challenges and everything would be fine. I didn't discuss them and everything wasn't fine. But I was never denied access!

And here I was discussing trans issues and everything wasn't fine as well. I was beginning to deal with oppression in a way I had never dealt with before. But I was also building some ego-strength and was able to face it and challenge it with a more professional demeanor.

Again, I believed that having a stable, loving, supportive relationship kept me sane. I would work in this neo-movement and battle by myself, but I was part of a team when I went home. I would go home to my very straight life with my regular, family-oriented, nonpolitical friends in Brooklyn. I was also attending John Jay College of Criminal Justice and was spending time discussing other oppressions in addition to sexual minority issues. There seemed to be a balance in my life.

241

Working for the good of the communities

Working out of the center gave me an opportunity to have a voice. It offered me access, giving me access to the world via the phone, the Internet, colleagues nationally, as well as many forums and podiums on a local level. I believed what I was doing was for the good of all the trans communities and, in addition, I was able to heal. As I established myself I began to see light in the eyes of many clients and I would bring them on as peer counselors. The trans community in New York was amazingly diverse and we needed to figure out a way to have all these voices heard. The center was a great place to do this work.

Graduation

In 1997 I graduated the CUNY BA Program and John Jay College of Criminal Justice, summa cum laude. I received the 'Who's Who among American Students' award as well as a special scholarship at John Jay commencement.

It was June 6th and there was a downpour. I walked across the stage with my brother, my nephew, my aunt, my friend Kim, Barbara, and my fiancé in the audience. And, as I shook the hand of the president, I thought about my parents. I thought about what I had put my dad through and how ashamed I was of myself always. I wished he had been there to share that day with me. And I wished my mom had been around as well. As I accepted my BA diploma I thought, 'This aint shit, it's not a master's degree' and there was a downpour from within.

I knew that I had my work cut out for me on an internal as well as scholastic level. And, although the road ahead was bright, I knew it was not going to be easy. I also knew that I had much work to do within the context of a social justice movement. The rain on graduation day reminded me of the cold rain from within. There needed to be some motherfucken healing to attend to and I knew I had a whole new 'A'Genda in store for me.

Things don't always go according to plans. After graduation I took off from school for eighteen months and then I started an MSW Program at Hunter. Mr R and I had been engaged since I was 35 years old. We were going to get married some day, but that someday turned into no day. Our lives just took on a different meaning and, after the first semester of my master's program, we split. I had spent over seven years with the same man. I had learned so much. I loved so much.

Being with Mr R protected me from a lot of my internal shame. I had a man who loved me so much, and no matter what ignorance I would encounter through my work at the center, I had the foundation of love right by my side.

Mr R and I spent seven and a half years together. In those seven and a half years so much changed in my life.
And I owe so much of my journey to him. Without him I might still have all those walls up. And those walls kept me imprisoned.
As the walls came down I changed, I took more risks, I moved forward.
Mr R and I got engaged when I was 35 but I knew in my heart we would never be married. That was the karma. In 1998 we ended that part of our relationship. But that man will always own a part of my heart. He was the first man I had ever been with who knew everything about me. And he was so proud of me. His support helped me heal and I know I will never meet another man like him again.
Today, I love him like a brother. And all I want for him is to be happy. He is now with a wonderful woman. I am overjoyed for them and wish them all the happiness in the world. He was the catalyst for many future life's lessons! He was a gift and a sacrifice! I will always be grateful for that gift.

You see, part of why I got my position in the first place was that in addition to having some knowledge I had the life experience.
I fought the title of peer counselor, even though my formal title was Director. Everywhere I went in the context of my work I became the thing the population we were discussing. And, at first, I was pretty much alone. I was the token at the center and I was OK with that. The center was a lovely place with so many interesting loving folks. I needed to change the system and the only way to do that was to be in the system. I also needed to work. I was too old to go back to dancing and that is not why I struggled with school at this point in my life. I wanted to do something different and this work landed in my lap. It was all so confusing.

My work devoured me. And I had no energy for an intimate relationship at this time. I was consumed. It seemed that something was very wrong with the climate that I was involved with but I couldn't put my finger on it. Sometimes I felt like I was crazy because they way things were done just didn't make any sense to me. My work as a health care provider gave me a whole new meaning and zest for life. But it also kicked up issues pertaining to social justice and morality. It seemed that there was little, if any, justice for the transgender communities, even, and especially, within the larger lesbian and gay movement. This was a platform from which I truly believed there would be no problem. I mean, on one level I was so loved within the center and by the people I came in contact with. And on another level there was so much ignorance and intolerance within the gay movement towards people along the transgender continuum. I mean they totally 'otherized' the trans identity and this made me crazy, crazier.

Let's take a step back;
When I first started working at the center it was easier to deal with the ignorance surrounding TG issues because I was so removed. I went to work and then went home to my life. And now I was in a master's program at Hunter for people who were already doing the work but didn't have the degree.

When we all shared what we did and what population/s we were working with, in my classmates' minds I became the population that I was working with, even though I never identified as such. Those who were working with young adults with emotional disorders did not become young and disordered to me. Those within the area of addiction and treatment did not become drug addicts in recovery to me. And those who worked with welfare reform did not become welfare recipients in the context of our discussions. But I was labeled 'Transgendered' and that threw me for a loop.

At the center, in the political arena, with other health care providers, within the profession of people working with trans clients, I was trans, I wasn't just a health care provider working within the community. And on some internal transphobic level I didn't want to be identified with the population, I just wanted to be a good health care provider. I was a provider working with and for these populations. My trans stuff was old and I did not desire for that to be the primary label of my existence, nor did I want that to be the legitimizing factor in the context of my work. After all I was working for, not simply living, the issues.

Now that I was single without a partner it was all in my face. I couldn't escape to my life. I didn't have a hetero life anymore.

So I engulfed myself into the work and that meant educating, educating, educating, especially, and primarily, lesbian and gay folks, since I believed they were the groups that would understand the most and assist with the social transformation. After all, they had experienced similar oppression. So I began to use different marketing strategies to make a point. I'd write a speech, I would send a letter, I would sit and talk, I would make a phone call, I would direct and edit a film, I would put together a lecture, I screamed, I cried, I schmoozed, I laughed, and I got angry, a lot. But I kept experiencing the same ignorance over and over and it began to get to me. I definitely needed a break. The fighting and the oppression from too many directions were getting on my last nerve.

REAL LIFE
EXPERIENCES

20.
THE
EMOTIONAL/SPIRITUAL
COLLAPSE....
IT'S ANALYSIS AND
RECOVERY Re-BAPTIZED

THE SCARIEST TIME
THE END IS NEAR
STOP
OWN IT

THE LONG ROAD TO FREEDOM
SHARING THE SPOTLIGHT
IT'S NOT YOURS TO BEGIN WITH

20

The Emotional/Spiritual Collapse ... Its Analysis and Recovery Rebaptized

The Scariest Time

It was late June, early July 2001. The warmth of the air and the sweat on my brow was bringing out what I thought was a neo-sexual freedom. I was coming into the light, I was chasing the light, I was blinded by the light, and at some point I would find out I was burnt by the light.

Here I was, a 41-year-old single woman of transexual experience working in a queer environment and living in a right wing, Republican, blue collared, family oriented neighborhood in Staten Island. "Where does a girl go to get laid?" I asked myself every night as I slipped Rocco and his hot nymphets into my VCR? For some reason the VCR never answered me. The paradox of my life! I was in the sex industry for too many years. I've had my share of life's ups and downs ... wait, that's a song. Get back to the point, Rosalyne. Oh yeah, the paracox, I mean dox.

Here I was, 41, and finally through with school. I had letters after my name! I was free and single and I defy any woman 25 and older to compete with me. Well, at least I could stand next to them and no one would push past me to get to them. I could still stop traffic. Well, anyone could if they stood in the middle of the street screaming STOP.

Here I was, 41. By the time I finish this fucking chapter I'll be 42.

OK, I was 41, remember? Why was this year so hard? Why were my clothes getting tighter and my thoughts getting more perverse and why was I feeling unnerved and a tad desperate? Whatever the reason, I was, I am, and I think I'd better get used to it. It seemed the sexier I dressed the more untouchable, the more inapproachable I became. No matter what I did, how friendly I was, very few were opting for a taste of this aging gracefully, sexual social worker with a brain, a body that won't quit, independence, an opinion, and who was also an easy lay. I mean it. You appear and I would adhere.

It was the summer of 2001. In my professional hat I was the director of a social service program within a liberation movement. We did outreach to people who were at high risk for HIV/AIDS and ATOD issues (alcohol tobacco and other drugs).

That summer we didn't hire an outreach worker, some of my staff were leaving, moving on, taking a break, and I didn't have the energy to outreach for an outreach worker. So as the director, I took on the responsibility of making sure we met our contractual requirements as well as keeping our services visible to the needy and disenfranchised.

I also had a plan, a scheme, a goal, a motive. And this one's a doozy. I put myself in a bar called Stellas. It was on 47th Street and it was a club where men hustled men. There were many rationales as to why I decided to take on this work beside the fact that I was losing it but didn't know it yet.

Hey, Stella, why don't you get over here and ... Why doesn't anyone ask me? Stella's was a club right in the middle of what once was a happening, pornographic, sleazy and exciting neighborhood, and now looks like cartoon characters and their friends from Oklahoma, the neo décor and the tourists.

I first experienced Stella's on my birthday with an old colleague and his partner. I decided I wanted to go there because I wanted to objectify the men.

> *However, when you are clean (and sober) it is so difficult to do things that you were able to do when you had mind-altering chemicals in your system. As a person in recovery you become aware of your surroundings, your affectations, your interactions with the world. It is sometimes difficult to do things without thinking about how your input into life has an effect on others.*

I wanted to get out of myself and objectify another human being. Though, as we watched the men dance and strip, all I could think about was what a difficult profession this must be for them and I began to deal with my own counter-transference around how I felt when I danced in front of men for money, power and a sense of self. I thought about how easily that could be taken away from me if I received a negative response from the audience and quickly thought that these guys might be juggling these same emotions as they swung their weenies round and round.

Watching these men I couldn't objectify them. Although I thought some were attractive, nothing sexual was occurring within my psyche, my soul, my groin. There was one Latino man who was stroking his pole, his man stick, his self-esteem, on stage, and the audience was going wild. They were throwing money at him left and right. And the more money he received the more his esteem appeared to grow, as well as his phallus, of course. All I could think about was how it felt when I had the power, when I stripped and paraded in front of men, when the audience was feeding my sense of self by reacting to me the way I wanted. I felt like I was in control, which was not reality based. I became nauseous and upset with myself that I was a component of the lion's den asking this object to be the subject of my entertainment, and it is then that I wanted to help.

Now did I want to help these guys or did I want to help me? And why is it acceptable to go objectify someone in the Broadway theatre or in a film but not on this stage?

> *Denial of your counter transference issues when one is in the helping profession occurs every so often. That is why supervision is important.*

So I decided to do outreach to Stella's because I believed that these men who had sex with men also had sex with transexual women, women of TS experience, femme-queens, drag queens, chicks with dicks, she-males ... and this was the population my program was funded to serve. Yet I believed that this MSM (men who have sex with men) group were a group who were overlooked and did not receive loving, effective HIV/AIDS prevention stratagems. I wanted to write about this experience and then allocate money through my work within the Prevention Planning Group and New York City's Department of Health. Aren't I a fucking Mother Theresa? (No disrespect intended.)

I also had other motives, as I am sure you suspected. You think you know me so well, now that you reached this chapter of my life, don't you?

One of my suppressed motivations for hanging out in a male hustle joint handing out condoms, drinking diet Pepsi and getting my labia in an uproar was my spirit was shot.

I'd secretly hit rock bottom and I didn't even know it. I had been clean for almost fourteen years so I couldn't possibly be as crazed as I was. (I didn't come to this conclusion until late July). I was in Stella's because my belief in me, my womanhood, my core identity, my hetero privilege, had been squashed and I didn't know where to turn to meet a man. My sense of self was now in question due to years of working, being around, and fighting a queer, predominantly gay movement. Oh, poor me, the victim! How nice it would be to pass all the blame onto a larger group as opposed to attempt to own some of the deficiency myself. I will, I promise, but not right now.

Since I was sixteen I have never looked back. I have never questioned whether I made the right decision. I believed I had no choice. I never questioned my inner sense of femaleness no matter how often I was spooked, or if I was rejected by a lover or if I was in a dry spell, thank god for KY. I always knew on some core, inner spiritual level that I, Rosalyne Michelle Blumenstein, a.k.a. Roe/Roz, was who I was.

I was 41 years old and I was confused by what so many queer leaders would say about the populations I was a component of. I began to question 'myself' due to all that the L and G organizations (Lesbian and Gay) stated. I began to think maybe I was a transgendered being who had no real place in a sexual society. And that my time, as a transgendered being, was not here yet. I began to think maybe "my peoples, we haven't paid our dues," and maybe I needed to go backwards instead of forward.

So I made a decision to do outreach in a male hustle bar where anything went. I made a decision to take my perfectly shaped, 41-year-old squat and dead lifted neo rear to a club where I might be *transgendered,* whatever that is, and have fun.

Yet there were more variables to this anthropological exploration of the MSM sex culture and my crack-up that challenged this undertaking.

I was now a social worker with a license and had to abide by certain ethics under this licensure agreement. And even before that licensing procedure I had never utilized my sexuality within my profession (social work, social services, drug counseling …) in an inappropriate fashion. I may always have pushed the envelope with regards to my linguistics and dress, but no one of less power has ever been given the opportunity to push anything into me for more power.

Going to Stella's gave me the opportunity to see how truly lost I was. However, I still felt as if I was attempting to give myself space where I could be a woman of TS experience, Out, popular, professional, and desirable. I wanted all these variables to fit into place.

I started my outreach strategies the end of May and stopped in August. My goals and objectives were to see it through until September, but I met a man. A man that would do me in sexually, spiritually, emotionally …

And besides, September 11 would change all of our worlds forever …

Jimmy Crack Corn, a.k.a. Pothead/borderline personality

I was walking down 14th Street in my little dungaree skirt, my belly ring exposed to anyone in eye distance, a tight leotard fitting, greenish blue hippie blouse with nipples protruding and saying 'chocolate kisses available.'

It was a 'bad hair day,' which made me and my look more approachable, meaning I was not looking perfect. As I walked past this man on the left (*which is my better side*) he looked at me and I gave him that 'I am 41and I still can't open my mouth to smile a full smile at a stranger's look so I smirk with my mouth closed and the sides of my lips go up a tad which states I am recognizing that you are looking at me but I am unsure of how I should respond' kind of look.

I kept walking.

As I passed him I saw his hands. He had thick fingers and I immediately thought about where those fingers would do me the most justice but I kept walking. As I turned the corner and proceeded east on 14th Street the same man ran in front of me and said, "Wow, you are the most beautiful girl in the world and I'd like to take you to lunch." So many things quickly went through my deteriorating mind. For one, I thought wow, this man has balls to approach me, and how curious I was to know really what kind of balls they were, I mean he had. I thought immediately about my response and attempted to control the tone and texture of the sound of my voice. I'd been trying to do this ineffectively since I was sixteen, so why I thought I would be able to conquer this feat at that moment I don't really know, but I kept trying.

I turned to him and said that I was busy with chores but if he gave me his number I would gladly call, and I meant it. He looked at me through what appeared to be a collegiate stare and stated, "You'll never call." I looked at him with my desperate, sophisticated, authoritative look …""Give me your number and I'll call you." He gave it to me and I went on about my business feeling empowered by his kind words. That night I called Jimmy.

For some reason I can't remember our conversation, but what I do remember was that it was not intimidating to me.

For the past nine years I had been around so many gay men and was out of the mating game because of my relationship with my ex-fiancé. Also, because of years in the sex industry, when I met men I utilized a different form of communication. My ability to engage men as beings, not only dollar signs or sexual entities, was the challenge. Not to mention all the other shit that flies through my head as I first would meet someone. I am talking about the old trauma that resurfaces as I meet a new man. Many times the 're' is the reinstitution of trauma because of my transexual past and the ways in which our society is taught to respond to a woman of TS experience. It would make my daily social life unnerving. I was always waiting for that negative reaction to occur within the interaction.

I don't know if I will ever have the opportunity to rid myself of that self-abomination due to too many past ignorant discriminatory responses.

That Saturday evening I had plans to perform outreach at Stella's and I had a date with Jimmy for Sunday. However, I was no longer a night owl. And when I did stay up later than midnight it transformed my internal discussions the whole next day. When I was tired from a night in a club, the whole next day I allowed myself a little more darkness within my thought process. Staying up late affects my soul and my ego, and I become physically and emotionally shakier. When I stayed out late the night before, the next day my nerves were not steady. But I become freer in the context that my reality guards are inoperative. Sunday morning I was pleased that I didn't have to wash my hair to meet this man. Less work to pull myself together was the latest phase of time management skills I was honing. As I got older my energy was utilized more for academia, social work practice, and marketing strategies around my trainings and private consulting work. It was a pleasure to wake up Sunday morning and just get dressed.

That morning was an extremely beautiful day even though it was high humidity. I was about to challenge myself and take a clothing risk I had never taken before. I don't think I had ever gone without panties in my life and I was about to lose my virginity to this experience. Ever since my genital reconstruction I had dealt with incontinence. After surgery I truly believed I would be free from the constraints of tight panties, gaffs, surgical tape or tight jeans. That was not my reality and I was a slave to maxi and mini pads as well as a need for close proximity to a bathroom at all times.

(In November of 2000 I had met with a urologist who took my insurance. He repositioned my 'urethra franklin' and, tah-dah, I was leak free. Eighteen years of June Allison commercials and now I was free at last, free at last, thank god I was free at last).

So Sunday I put on a toga-top hip-hugger skirt and a cotton beige midriff blouse and was ready to go. This beige blouse was a definite attention getter. You can clearly view my nickel-sized nipples with my bra on so I was classy, sneaky sexy. You also get a great shot of my stomach and my navel ring. If there was one thing I knew that summer, I knew I was in good shape and my stomach made sure to scream that out to passers-by. I was tired so I felt a little less inhibited even though I felt 'darker and shakier.' I also felt my first sea breeze up my skirt as I walked. That was a tantalizing experience!

It seemed that ever since my surgery, when I was supposed to experience genital freedom, a neo-imprisonment came about. And this was my get out of jail free card, which made me nervous and exhilarated. No panties, no worries, no problem!

Jim and I were supposed to meet at five. As usual I was early. I was going to walk around Manhattan to scope out a restaurant, but as I got to the corner Jimmy was there. He had some sort of sports T-shirt on that was not tucked into his trousers. He wore plain baggy, but not hip-hop baggy, jeans. He had on glasses and an extremely conservative haircut. This man looked like a typical 'upstate New Yorker,' if one can stereotype an 'upstate dude' appearance. He was not handsome, nor was he disapproving to the eye. As an outsider, one might think that this man and his look were definitely out of his league in trying to engage a woman who looked like me. After all, I looked like an exotic being from another country. I was so hot, I was sizzling. Or, to the outside world did I just look like an aging ho?

Immediately I knew I was the leader of this meeting. It put me a little at ease because I was a control 'freak.' However, I was still nervous and had a difficult time walking down the street with this man because the attention I was receiving from passers-by made me self-conscious.

It is funny how folks say, "Oh look at her all coochy. She's just loving the attention!" But when I am dressed "coochy" I am sometimes at my most vulnerable or at my least self-assured. Jim also kept staring at me, which made me think a lot. Was he trying to figure me out? Was he able to see the masculine components of my personality, of my inner core?

And did that matter? And why did it still carry so much weight within my inner sense of self? I was an 'Out' and sometimes a proud, confidant woman who has conquered obstacles and achieved many goals. I should be proud of all of me, but no matter how I bullshit myself I knew the world did not see me the way that I saw me, especially when I was 'Out.' And, on some level, I must not see myself the way I think I should always see myself.

Jim and I kept walking and attempted small talk. He kept staring at me. At one point we walked by a large mirrored building and he stopped us. He turned to the mirror and said, "I can't believe how beautiful you are. What are you doing with me?" *DING DING* DING! The man just won fifteen minutes of fellatio and he didn't even know it. I was tired, I was feeling sexy, I had wants and desires, and I was not thinking straight.

I turned to Jimmy and I said, "Hey, you wanna come back to my place in Staten Island? You can sleep over. I have an extra room. I would love the company," which I really believed. "But let me make one thing perfectly clear (*Nixon*). If you try to sleep with me that will be the last time you ever see me again." What was I thinking and where was I going with this?

Yes, I had been desperate for company ever since I moved onto the toxic Island of Staten. The island that's filled, landfilled that is, with beautiful houses and sexless, sexually looking Stepford wives and cheating husbands. This island where my clothes were stored, but my heart was not. This island where I had existed in social isolation for almost three years! I had lucked out with great neighbors, but they were not going to fulfill all of my desires and needs. So here was the deal; I ask a perfect stranger to come spend the night at my house. I am dressed very provocatively and I assert that we will not have sex, or if we do I will never see him again. Come on! Someone bring on the straitjacket! Jimmy left his car and drove with me. The warm air made me feel 'Alive' and the smell of this man next to me made me wet … Well, as wet as a woman of TS experience can be without the support of KY or any other lubricating accoutrement.

He began to fondle me in the car as I drove, and I loved it (so much for no fooling around). I was free at that moment. All of a sudden I believed I was not a part of my life and I was experiencing a sense of freedom that I had not visited in quite some time. I was high without a drug in my system, but I was high nonetheless. And because I felt high I wanted more, just like when I did drugs. As Jimmy began to lift my skirt and go down on me I drove over the Verrazano Bridge towards Stagnant (Staten) Island. And all I could think about was I wish I had a hat to throw up in the air and sing '*Who can turn the world on with her smile ...*'

We got to my house and we immediately attacked one another. I couldn't get my hands off of him and he could not ... off me. When Jimmy dropped his pants I knew I was going to be in love. It seemed like Jimmy's body, which was not toned, was not beautiful, not muscular, fit right on top and right into my perfectly shaped, extremely tight body. It seemed like his penis, his best attribute, was made for my vagina. The next morning Jimmy left for work and I could not stop thinking about the erotic sex I had had the night before. I was in heaven. I was free. I was celebrating me and my sexuality and I loved it.

> *You have no idea how hard it is to work in an environment where folks tell you you are amazing and amazing looking but no man ever wants to ... you. I mean, I don't care if they are all gay, they are still men and some of them I would've loved to ...*
> *In the very near future I would figure out that this guy was what you call a total upstate asshole, a redneck, a racist, a moron, a hateful human being. But I could overlook all that because his ding dong rang my bell louder than I have heard in a long time. Little did I know that the price of this d... would be more than I could afford. Little did I know that this short relationship would take me over the edge, the edge that I had been dangling on for too long, and the edge that I was not even aware of until I began to fall over it.*

The next evening Jimmy called me. If a man calls after he fucks you on the first date you know he is really interested. Isn't it ridiculous? If I met someone that I liked, I wanted to see if I was sexually compatible with him. And that makes me a slut? But if a guy did it, he's Romeo, gigolo, he gets high five, he's a playboy. All my girlfriends would tell me that it wasn't OK to bed someone right away. But I have always felt like I had to, or I wanted to, or I needed to. And if a woman beds a man right away they think you do that all the time, so?

This past January of 2002 I finally learned my lesson around this. At 41.5 years of age I finally realized this is not healthy for me. Not because of the judgment but because I cannot bed someone and not have feelings about it. As soon as I give my body to someone they have power over my emotions, and that does not work when you are sleeping with a stranger who might not see the you that you are and only see the (w)hole that you are.

Back to Jimmy! He called and we started this dreadful relationship. Someone should've shot me right in the head and stopped me from taking on this drug, I mean man.

I know my ex-colleague and good friend Thom Hill would say that whenever I got laid I would come to work glowing and excited about my newfound BoyToy.

But this Jimmy was different. I loved being Rosalyne 'without a past' with Jimmy. I couldn't get enough of him in me, on me, or over me. Ever since my genital enhancement surgery I would get sore after intercourse. This Jimmy could do it to me four to five times a day and I still wanted more. I guess this was all a component of my losing my sense of self, my losing control of what was really happening.

Let me explain some of the details about the Jimmy saga.

The first problem, Jimmy was racist and homophobic. The second problem, Jimmy said he had pancreatitis. The third problem, he seemed 'not available emotionally.' One day I was at his cabin in North Jersey, a cabin that didn't have a bed or much furniture and things were still packed. I should have gotten out of that relationship at that moment when I found him in his basement sucking on a pipe. He said he was going to do some wash and I went down there just to be with him. I missed him already. I missed touching him. I went around the house and there he stood by himself, in his basement, sucking. I ran upstairs and was furious. "How dare this jerk put my recovery in jeopardy," I thought. I did not think for one second that it was my choice to be there. I went crazy and started yelling at him. And as I went to leave I went right back into the house and realized I couldn't just leave like that. I needed to talk to him. His d... was too good to let go. I was hooked. And besides, my ex taught me to hang in there if something was important and Jimmy's ... was important. In addition, under all his faults I knew there was a sweet, lost, sad man who I really liked and wanted to help. Did this mean I had bad self-esteem, or my desperateness surrounding age, sex, sexuality and lack of freedom was developing rapidly?

We talked and agreed that he needed help. He came clean and told me about his problems with liquor and his stomach, how he had almost died, how he was not a good husband, and how he had no rights to his daughter. He told me he was sorry and he cried. And at that moment I knew I was in love. I wanted to help this man and I wanted to leave everything behind, queer work, queer liberation, being 'Out.' I wanted to just be Rosalyne with this hick who made me feel so physically good and I wanted to get as far away from the Lesbian and Gay Center and all its baggage.

So I began to open up a little as well. I told him that I knew what pain felt like. I told him I left home when I was sixteen. I didn't give him all the details but I told him I lived on 42nd Street. He asked me if I was a prostitute. I couldn't believe he asked me that question and I didn't appreciate the tone. I told him. Actually I phrased it in a question. "What do you think a sixteen-year-old girl does for a living when she is homeless and a runaway?" He immediately went off on me and seemed disgusted with the idea that I would do such a thing.

Imagine the balls on this man. Hmmm, those balls!

This man could not stand next to me as far as academic achievements, spirituality, as far as physicality was concerned, worth, genialness, and here he was judging me. And what's worse is the fact that I truly felt bad about myself and my past as he belittled my experience. If this shook his tree I knew that my TS history would be a total shocker and he would hate me.

Believe it or not I did not run. In fact, I took him home to my house and started making calls for 12-step groups in his area. I told him how furious I was with his judgment and I really thought I was talking to someone. I would not give up on him. Was I desperate or did I see something in this man that was worth it?

The next week I went to visit him and I met his sister down the road. His future brother-in-law was a drinker and a spitter and I couldn't believe that this social worker, this activist, this societal mover and shaker, was hanging out with this crowd. I did not blend or fit in. But we had some things in common. Jimmy and I were rebels, but I had a cause.

Jimmy had a bike (motorcycle) and I had never wanted to ride on them. But I got on the back of his bike and we drove up and down winding roads as he held me and I held him. Every so often he would rub my leg and I was falling more in love with the fantasy of not being the Rosalyne of the Gender Identity Project and just 'being' Rosalyne. I wore a workout bra and tight jeans and I looked hot behind this man with borderline personality disorder, a pot habit, a man who was chased out of Orange County, a man who had no morals, a man who couldn't eat because he tortured his body. I felt so good behind this man who had so much hate in his system. I felt so good. And I was the woman behind this man, a woman with a heavy secretive past with him, a woman who was dealing with depression and suicidal ideations, a woman who felt lost and cornered in a movement that was not healthy. I felt lost, Jimmy was lost, and together we were …

I spent the next three weekends with him. He would call every night and I dreaded going to work. I wanted to ride on his bike and be free from all the pain I was feeling in my life. This man made me feel so good and I would do anything to make him feel even better. However, this man also made me feel horrible. There was something just not right and I knew it in the back of my intellectual being.

In the third week of this psycho-drama Jimmy asked me if I would go with him to his sister's wedding. I felt like I was going to have to tell him about my TS history. I knew he would go crazy but I knew I had to do it. Also, I had spent so many years with a man who loved me just for who I was and I wasn't going to settle. I felt that after the initial shock he would get over it. After all, I was the diva. I was educated, I was gorgeous, I was fun, I was independent, and I performed lots of sexual tricks on him he had never experienced before. What more could a man ask for?

I just knew he would get over it and I was also sure he wouldn't.

All week I told him that I had to talk to him but it had to be in person. I believed that anyone could not look at me and get upset about my history when they saw me in their face, when they saw the me that I see.

He kept asking me to tell him and I refused … until Thursday. I called him from work. I had a whole plan of how this would take place. However, when we were on the phone I just got to the point.

He went crazy and called me a 'man' and asked if I had a dick before and said he couldn't deal with this at all and hung up. And at that moment, there went my other shoe! I lost my mind. I became hysterical and slammed myself out of the center and the office that I was working in and walked to the bus stop wishing for a car to run me over. I was suicidal and I hadn't felt suicidal like this since Robert Guzman left me when I was nineteen years old.

> *He left me on the A train and said he couldn't deal with me anymore. This felt just like that except I was fourteen years clean (and sober) and back then I was a Tuinal, Valium and Quaalude addict.*

I was in turmoil. I refused to accept this and allow this man to say goodbye to me. I felt like too much was at stake and I felt uncontrollably desperate. I called him twice to tell him he would be an idiot if he threw away what we had. I told him he would never find another woman like me. As if he wanted another! I told him that my transition happened 26 years ago and that I had spent my whole life like I was now. I was trying desperately to sell the legitimacy of my identity to him (*as well as to myself*). All of what was surfacing as far as the lack of my sense of self was cultivating like creeping vines and taken charge of my intellect. I was grabbing out and I told him I would show him pictures of me when I was sixteen just so he could see I was not one of those Jerry Springer folks, as if my identity was more genuine than anyone else who had trudged through this path. I was filled with internalized transphobia. I was filled with self-loathing about my TS history. I was grasping for anything to market my uniqueness.

In my professional role I was supposed 'to be.' I was understood to be the one who held it all together. After all, I was the 'transgendered' poster child on the east coast involved with the LGBT communities and the health care profession. I was the Director of a Gender Project and a spokesperson, and a pioneer, and a trailblazer for transgender rights within a lesbian and gay movement. And at that moment I loathed them (the queers) more than ever, which indicated I loathed me for being an element of them. At that moment my life and my work was meaningless.

Here I was.

Fact: I was not working in the peep shows any longer, using this as a judgment in contradiction of me as far as labeling my self-worth.

I was not a stripper. I was a respectable member of society. I was clean (and sober). I was a loving, free individual and this dirt bag was disgusted by me and my past. And I was disgusted by me and my past, and my immediate life did not help me with my intense shame.

I hadn't spoken to my ex fiancé in over a year and he was the only one who would be able to save me, so I called him.

That night my ex came over and took care of me for the weekend. If it wasn't for him I would have, well, I don't know where I would be today. However, my ex coming over was also a test. He was still angry with me because I had left and because I hadn't been very helpful to him and his esteem when we were together. And I was furious with him for not staying my friend after we split, for that was how our relationship was initially established. We had begun as friends and I missed that friendship terribly. He came over to help me but brought some uncomfortable history along with him. The whole weekend I was crying and hopeless and couldn't get this man out of my head. My ex said that he would call and I knew he wouldn't. Monday night I came home from work in a zombie-like state that had taken over the celebrated, alive, vivacious and sexual body I thought I was inhabiting. The phone rang and it was Jimmy. He said he had to see me and I came alive. I won, I won! I knew my looks, my self, would break through those stereotypical barriers because I was special.

> *In the eyes and heart of 'Lookism' I've realized how wrong this belief system is and how oppressive it is to my self, society, and the communities I work with and for. But on some level I always felt I was special and this proved it once again, or did it? I paid a substantial price by leaving home at such an early age and I deserved to reap those benefits of early transition.*

Jimmy came over the next night. He began therapy with a counselor I recommended. He began to tell me that I went against everything he stood for in his life. As if ... ! I got angry and I wanted to prove myself to this imbalanced court system, his brain. He said he wanted to know "if I had had a dick, like him, before, you know ..." I told him that if I had had a dick like him I would be Roger instead of Rosalyne and then he asked me if that was my name. I was furious. That night Jimmy couldn't get an erection and I owned it. I believed it had everything to do with me and nothing to do with his limp dick. I was beside myself. I was beside a limp dick and I was horny. This man's participation in my life was hurrying my death. I thought I had done so much work on myself spiritually and emotionally. All my hard work being clean (and sober), being a political activist, a social worker, having a degree, it was all going down the drain. And I was feeling like all of my clients who had come to me hopeless and suicidal. I couldn't be or find the tools I needed to deal with my emotions and everything seemed overwhelming, hopeless, insane, cloudy, and not recovery oriented.

> *I've utilized my formal and informal training to be a tool for the trans communities. I was a role model, I was a therapist who employed the strengths perspective. I was part of a progressive support system, I was a mentor, and I was an advocate.*
> *And here I was, lying in my self-hate surrendering my sense of self, lost in this moron's belief system, and I was nothing.*

I began to implement a short-term disability case from work. I couldn't work. I couldn't work with clients when I felt hopeless. I didn't yet have a diagnosis but what came up in session with my EAP counselor was that I was dealing with vicarious traumatization. I couldn't hold their trauma because their trauma kicked up all my old stuff before and after I entered into this position within a queer movement. In conjunction with their, mine, and Jimmy's issues, as well as every other man I've attempted to date since I went public around my trans past. I was drowning and choking in despair.

The End is Near
At least that's what it felt like. I believed I couldn't show up for one more day of work. Everyone I spoke with supported me except one colleague. That person will never know, but their ignorance at the time fueled so much hate and anger in me that it kept me alive. It kept me from being totally hopeless. I wonder if that was their clinical strategy.

My short-term disability plan took two weeks to implement. I wonder if I had got hit by a car or had a major heart attack would I have been asked to come in to straighten things out before I went out on disability? I believed I was in a crisis. It was a struggle just to get into the shower and I became enraged and saddened by this new disability. It reminded me of my past drug detoxes. I started taking antidepressants, Wellbutrin, and I threw them out.

Stop
As I began to pack up my desk and delegate responsibilities I knew my life was either ending or just beginning. I would sneak a look into my staff's eyes every chance I could, hoping to get back what I had given them. I needed support. I felt desperate and scared. I could not believe my emotions and this new medication made me feel like I was outside of my own body. Part of me wanted to run, part of me wanted to take myself out, part of me wanted to be in the arms of that sociopath. I hate labeling the man, but if the shoe fits ... And part of me wanted to just get it the fuck together and go about my business as usual. I didn't feel comfortable with this new energy of mine. I had never looked down upon anyone who took antidepressants, I just never thought that would be me. After all, I wasn't my mother anymore (*emotional, weak, shaky*), I was my dad (*strong, assertive, energetic*). My whole life I would struggle with these personality traits I received from my parents.

> *My mom was loving and friendly, nurturing, too emotional, and weak. My dad didn't feel, or show his feelings. He just showed up. I truly believe that is why he got cancer and died before his 60th birthday.*

When I couldn't cope or I was nervous I was mom, and the dad component would be inpatient with the mom component. This breakdown was mom all the way but I had one thing she didn't have, I had a 12-step fellowship, some antidepressants that weren't addictive, an understanding of mental health issues and concerns, and some truly loving and supportive queer and non-queer identified friends rooting me on. I needed life to STOP and I

261

needed it to stop right this second. I got through the two weeks before my short-term disability kicked in. I believed I would be out the rest of the summer and back some time in mid-October. At least that was my, my psychiatrist's, and the EAP counselor's plan of action.

Own It

When I was trying to set up the time off, interjections from one colleague made me feel like I was making all of it up. I felt on some deeper level I was just lying and playing a game, like I did so many other times in my life.

> *When I was a child I was always a liar and a drama queen and an instigator. And when I was using drugs I always had delightful bullshit stories to tell.*

And when I was confronted by this person, I believed on some deeper level they were right. They really knew me and saw through all my bullshit. If it weren't for a group of other clinicians, my ex fiancé, my close friends from the 12-step program, I would have never believed and/or used the tools in front of me to reconnect with my homeostasis. When I was on top of things I would still be affected by what others said about me. If there was a group of people that supported me and one who thought I was inept, I would be more affected by the one who thought I was inept.

Another character trait of the addicted personality

This emotional breakdown took me to an even deeper sense of not loving 'self.' However, on the other side something made sure I would not give up and I was in control with being out of control. I knew my road needed to be focused on 'owning me.'

Through the years at the center although I gained so much, I felt 'me' slowly disappear. I felt I was not provided with the right space and support within my work and it was all too much to contain. How strange it all was. The work I got involved with in 1993 opened doors I thought I would never walk through. The work at the Center gave me a platform from which to grow as an individual, an academic, a social worker, a leader, and a community organizer. The work offered me so many opportunities and the work terrorized my spirit, my soul, and my core identity.

As I said goodbye to my clients I was filled with sadness. But one client interaction after another held me up, kept me breathing, and gave me the mustard seed of hope I needed. One of my very special clients (*someone whom I had met when she was just sixteen*) asked me for a hug and thanked me endlessly for the support I had given her. Small things like that kept me breathing. She walked out of my office and I broke down.

I knew I could not work at this job any longer but I also knew that I had helped that young lady and so many others who had walked into my office over the past ten years.

The Long Road to Freedom
The combination of the medication, which I got back on, therapy, 12-step fellowshipping, prayers, and the love from friends assisted me. But I was not the same person who collapsed and I was damned if I was going to repeat the same mistakes and start to feel like I had felt when I left in August. By September I realized, only subconsciously, that this man was not right for me and I needed to move on. That doesn't mean I left him or took a stand, it meant that I knew, I had the awareness, that he was no good for me and I would have to let go at some point.

Sharing the Spotlight
It's not yours to Begin With
9/11 changed everything for everybody.
I knew I had to go back to work and volunteer with New York City's Emergency Medical Service and the Fire Department. Everything surrounding all of us in New York was devastating and I was trained to help people get it back together. It was time to let go of this man, this obsession, and it was time to get back to the helping profession. Besides, there was so much more genuine pain and heartache than what I, alone, was going through. 9/11 woke me up and gave me the courage to make the decisions I was about to make. I hated that it took this disaster to make me see the forest through the trees, but I should be grateful that I learned from the experience, as opposed to so many of us who never stop and think. They just got angrier and angrier, which I have done too many times.
For years my trans work was enmeshed with my internal being. It was time for me to move out of the spotlight and let others take this work to another level. Besides, I wanted a private life back. It seemed like I was in the public eye without the star status. Everywhere I went people knew all about what they thought was all of who I was, and I needed some privacy.
So what the hell did you write this book for, bitch?
As I worked with my dear friend Barbara, who was working herself ragged around critical incidence stress debriefing with the EMS workers, I knew I was going to develop a plan to leave my job and go west and have that privacy. It was time to live again. It was time to take another major risk in my life. I felt stable surrounding this decision. All my decisions had proved to be the right ones, especially when within the pit of my stomach I knew it was right. As I thought about my plan of action I thought about what I would be leaving. I thought about all the love that had surrounded me these

past fifteen years and I felt grateful like I had never felt before. People had helped me heal and I had participated in the healing process of others. And although I felt totally inept, I tried to help some of the EMS workers in their healing process, though I was afraid that this trauma was going to have a lasting negative affect on their daily lives for a long time to come.

I began to implement a move plan and set my last day of work at the center for April 26, 2002.

21.
CALIFORNIA DREAMING BACK to LIFE BACK to REALITY

21

California Dreaming/ Back to Life/ Back to Reality

On 4/25/02, the next to last day at the LGBT Center in NYC, and my final staff meeting, this is what transpired!

An in-house email sent to all the staff of the center from its Executive Director Richard Burns

"On Thursday morning I am going to Washington, D.C. for two meetings at the Capitol. A group of U.S. senators have asked sixteen queer leaders from around the country to meet with them at the Senate to discuss some of the issues facing our community. While this meeting marks significant progress for our movement, it means that I will miss the staff meeting at which we will say thank you and goodbye to Rosalyne Blumenstein. I will have the opportunity to say goodbye privately to Roz on Friday, but there are a few things I would like to acknowledge publicly. I think of Roz as a pioneer in many different ways. She and Barbara developed the GIP here at the center at a time when such a thing was unheard of at a lesbian and gay institution. Certainly, critical services were offered and a long educational process was begun, but what I think is not often acknowledged is the role of the GIP and its leadership in the creation of an organized and proud trans community here in New York. Very few people have the opportunity to play such a role in life and it is a legacy of which Roz can be extraordinarily proud. Another leadership role Roz played in the process of changing the hearts and minds of so many people in gay New York and here at the center about the place of trans people and community within this chaotic movement. With her patience, charm and sense of intelligent humor, Roz won my heart, and ultimately my mind, on an issue that now, with the benefit of hindsight, seems very obvious.

So Roz, I hope that you are very proud of your work leading the GIP, the change work you've done which helped lead to the conclusion of our branding initiative, your advocacy with government and policy makers, and the lesbian, gay, bisexual and transgender community which you leave for those that follow you.

I know Los Angeles will never know what hit them."

> *I read this email once every two months. Every time I pick it up the tears well in my eyes and I feel a sense of love and respect from a person I truly did not get to know. I know that anyone I looked up to at the center disappointed me too many times, but in my heart I*

knew Richard had to see I was right at what I was trying to accomplish at the center But most of the time the movement just didn't move!

On another level, I thought that Richard and the center's Senior Team couldn't wait for me to get out of there. I sensed they felt I was just a loudmouth, obnoxious, difficult, challenging, noncompliant employee.

Back to the staff meeting

Julia, the director of Information and Referrals (I and R) wrote and read this to the staff

"Top Ten Things I'll miss About Roz"

10. Her incredible talent for making fun of herself and others.
9. Her ability to seem charming while actually being a sarcastic bitch.
8. Her preference for tight clothing.
7. Her ability to move herself to tears while talking about her job.
6. Her general lack of shame.
5. Her unstoppable need to say the hard things that others don't have the guts to say.
4. Her glamorous aura.
3. Her bravery in the face of everything.
2. Her amazingly foul potty mouth.
1. And the number one thing I'll miss about Roz: Her spectacular, well-hidden, heart of gold.

I love you, Julia"

Julia reminded me that I was loved at the workplace. That meant so much to me, especially since I felt so bitter about all that transpired over the past few years there. I thanked her internally and externally for that acknowledgment.

As words traveled around the room the love overwhelmed me. How could there be so much emotion in the workplace? This was an exceptional working environment, this was! And it was time for me to go. At the end of the staff meeting I received a standing ovation. I had worked for the center since 1993, and that had never happened in a staff meeting before. Were they so elated that I was leaving that they all got up at the same time to show me to the door? Or did I make a mark on this group?

The next week, as I drove away from a Philadelphia HIV/AIDS-related conference that I was a plenary speaker for, I questioned. What had happened these past years? Had I accomplished anything? Had I been of help to anyone, to myself? Had I assisted in any social change? Had I even scratched the surface of oppression within the LGBT movement, within mainstream social services? And what was in store for me in California?

I knew I would desperately miss the gifts I had received working with and for queer people in New York City. However, I knew I would not miss the fight, or the struggle, or my constantly questioning what I was doing, or if I was doing it right. My inability to believe in me, my work, constantly questioning and challenging the institution around inclusion, was too much for this unstable individual to bear.

There were many really brilliant trans leaders before me, and when I began this work I looked to them for support and acknowledgment. Few of them gave me a kind word or the acknowledgement I needed as to what I was trying to achieve. One particular person who had a large voice within the trans movement would always identify me as the 'assistant to the Director of Mental Health and Social Services.' To her, I was always the silly performer, I was never her colleague. I believed in her and her work and could not get back the same kind of accolade. Elitist folks like that taught me early on how important it was to nurture my own staff, my colleagues, and my communities. That had always been my priority in addition to healing my own self-hate and internalized transphobia. I thank her for the lesson and I despise her for her inability to see me, which brings up my own ability to see myself.

As I had always fought 'to be,' **and not be branded with a 'T,'** and only as 'T,' just because that is only a part of my eclectic heritage, I had fought to be seen as a healing agent of this growing 'T' movement. I also struggled with some trans leaders to acknowledge the work that the GIP had succeeded in doing by giving a voice to all within the 'T' movement.
To those that did, have, and continue to do so, I humbly thank them, for the 'T' movement desperately needed, and needs, that diverse voice and all its support. The GIP was a service desperately needed not only for trans people along the continuum. It was needed to challenge and recreate social structure surrounding the fluidity of gender within social services, the queer movement, and society as a whole. I am sure the work will continue with its most talented and hard working social worker, Miss Carrie Davis, MSW. I was put in a position where I needed to take care of others and there were so many days I needed that for myself. Carrie helped to take care of me as I to her. She will take this work to new heights and the community/ies will only benefit from her stability, her brilliance and her dedication. I know Melissa Sklarz will do the same within the local political front.

California Dreaming

Racism, sexism, classism, and elitism are alive and well in the queer movement as within the larger society and I wanted to drive as far away as I could to get away from it all. I am dreaming 'California,' give me that chance to be, to believe, to breathe again.

California dreaming

will give me the opportunity to heal.

will give me the opportunity to write this book.

will give me the opportunity to go back to the social justice fight with a stable sense of self and a different outlook on how I might be a tool for social change.

HERE SHE IS, BOYS
HERE SHE IS, WORLD
HERE'S ... you get the picture!

LGBTLGBTLG
BTLGBTLGBT
LGBTLGBTLG
BTLGBTLGBT

The Essentials: Political and Social Reorganization

The next pages condense my personal and professional struggles within the gay and lesbian movement. I hope to give some insight focusing on how I tried to work with the defiance.

THE ESSENTIALS:
POLITICAL AND SOCIAL ReORGANIZATION

APPENDIX I

ADDICTION/RECOVERY AND A SOCIAL/SEXUAL PROGRESSION?

Appendix I

Addiction/Recovery and a Social/Sexual Progression?

Or, why am I even having this discussion?

Is the world ready to digest the LG with the BT (Lesbian and Gay) (Bisexual and Transgender)?

In her writing, Susan Stryker,[1] a trans-identified professor in California, uses the words transexual and transgendered interchangeably. In The Gay and Lesbian Journal Stryker wrote "… work in transgender studies will consist of definitional wrangling until a better consensus emerges of who deploys these terms, in which context, and with what intent." (Stryker, 1998, intro.)

Gays and lesbians are utilizing words like 'transgender,' 'transexual,' 'drag,' 'poly-sexual,' 'transvestite' et al. to describe widely varying gender experiences. Many are confused as to what means what and it depends on varying degrees as to which term fits, or might befit, which identity. And since none of this is standardized, words are used interchangeably. The discussion, the debate, of who identifies as what, is political and sometimes oppressive.

The focus of this dialogue is predominantly around the oppression of the 'transgender experience' within the LGBT movement. However, there are other oppressed groups within the acronym as well as subcultural experiences within the acronym that are oppressed and silenced individuals. But for this appendix (and my sanity), the discussion is the 'transgender experience.'

Gays - and for the politically progressive, gays and lesbians - have had the opportunity to direct what academia categorizes as 'Identity Politics' since the Stonewall revolution. The Stonewall revolution afforded Gs and Ls their own political identity, from within which they have had the opportunity to slowly and surely educate and transform the attitudes of a homophobic society at large.[2]

It is understood that Black drag queens, lesbians and bisexuals (some of whom might have identified as pre-op, non-op transexuals, butch, dykes …) were out on the street fighting the police during the evening of the Stonewall riots, but what came out of that evening was the **Gay Rights Movement, not the 'queer diversity initiative.'** Did the drag queens, transexuals, lesbians and bisexuals identify as 'gay' Did they have an opportunity to use language that was supportive of their sexual minority status? And does the continuum of so-called 'aberrant' gender identities known to us as 'transgender, or the transgender experience,' have a place within the gay movement today?

Does this movement embrace and celebrate diversity or does it practice, as Freire states within his book 'The Pedagogy of the Oppressed,' the oppressor oppressing the oppressed?[3]

I am asking these questions because so many have asked me if the T of the LGBT belong together. So here is an out-loud discussion you should have with yourself, your friends, socially conscious colleagues, and/or your church and synagogue.

The Pro: These are sexual minority categories that together will have power in numbers.

The Con: The LGBT movement has silenced many constituents under the belief that to truly celebrate the diversity of its sub-groups would create more ignorance and confusion in society at large with less progress achieved more slowly.

The Pro: In 1973 'Homosexuality' was removed from the DSMIII (Diagnostic Statistical Manual Third Edition [see chapter 1]).

The Con: But in 2000, the DSMIV still identified Gender Identity Disorder (GID) as a disorder within children, adolescents and adults when there is "a strong and persistent cross-gender identification (not merely a desire for any perceived cultural advantage of being the other sex)." (DSMIV p. 246)

The DSMIV goes on to state that among adolescents and adults with this disorder the "disturbance causes clinically significant distress" (p. 248) {302.6 in children, 302.85 in adolescents or adults, and 302.6 Not Otherwise Specified NOS}.

The Pro: Here we the have lesbians and gays able to buy, challenge relinquish, or possess enough power within the American Psychiatric Association to vote out a 'Homosexual diagnosis' (1973).[4]

The Con: However, T of the LGBT, identified now as GID (Gender Identity Disorder) is still listed in the reference guide around disorders, deviant behaviors, abnormalities. Also, a part of the population that falls under T are confronted with, and controlled by, guidelines and gatekeepers involved in stating how we work with, support, advise or manage gender 'dysphoric' identities and behaviors.

The Pro and Con: Trans-people, specifically transsexuals, are made to jump through hoops, and others identified as LGB and not T do not have to. There are no guidelines for:

Sodomizing one's intimate partner when both identify as the same sex
Appropriate ways to perform cunnilingus and fellatio.

I don't recall ever seeing international guidelines on these subjects so one can assume that people invented their own through supportive sexual interaction and not standards of care.[5]

In fact, many along the transgender continuum have figured out ways in which to deal with their transgender identity without following guidelines that are sometimes oppressive or archaic in knowledge. To have, live, and survive an identity that is not celebrated, but is a diagnosis, is emotionally challenging, to say the least.

If one read Paulo Freire's 'Pedagogy of the Oppressed,' one would understand that the oppressed become the oppressors when they still feel oppressed.

Although the L/G lobbyists are in Washington side by side with the political hetero communities, many L/G people are still isolated, shamed, silent, closeted, and in pain surrounding their sexual orientation.

As the movement struggles with self-acceptance it is difficult to want to be associated with people within the movement who seem to be less acceptable within the larger society.

Sexual Minorities is the umbrella term identifying LGBT, and those even questioning their sexual orientation or gender identity. Valentine, an anthropologist with a progressive mentality, states in his dissertation titled 'I Know What I Am ...' that there are "leaky boundaries between sex/sexuality/orientation/gender." (p. 136). The connection and/or the fluidity of LGBT identities would mean that the Oppressor would have to think twice about claiming a description or label specifically for the 'LGBT' and would have no certainty or power on how to describe these populations, and this is disempowering to the oppressors.

Because of all the stereotyping, confusion and disempowerment queer people face, many do not want to be identified with one of the other categories within the whole LGBT acronym.

Gay drag queens (e.g. many members of the Imperial Court of New York)[6] do not want, desire, or accept being identified as transgender, although there is a handful of women of transexual experience within this philanthropic organization.

Men and women of transexual experience who identify as heterosexual do not have any voice within this LGBT movement and do not want to be identified with it.[7]

In addition, the straight or bisexual cross-dresser is silenced from the whole discussion.[8]

Some within the movement use the umbrella term 'queer' (not sexual minority/ies) as an all-inclusive idiom. Older 'queers' are offended by that term, so many use 'gay' as the umbrella. But gay speaks to a male dominated system and also is focused on an identity that is deeply emotionally, physically, sexually, spiritually connected to another of the same identity/sex. Doesn't this silence the whole bi and trans experience? So why is it used so often?

> "... Gender and sexuality are so intimately connected in practices, discourses, and ideas, that it becomes difficult to disaggregate them from analytic and political purposes." (Valentine p.136) [10]
> "... The category 'transgender,' with its recent origins in U.S. identity politics, is becoming a tool for the cross-cultural description of non-normative genders as a way of avoiding recourse to the category 'gay' but without recognition of the meanings attached to it." (p.136)[11]

Is the LGBT movement moving?
I worked at the Lesbian and Gay Community Services Center in New York City for years. The center had added a tag line to its letterhead and to the sign in front of the building.[12] Then the center changed its name officially unofficially. There's progress at this institution and there's progress at others. But many are still utilizing 'gay' as the umbrella for LGBT.
For some reason, most of the political lesbian and gay leaders, executives, fund raisers, activists, academicians, sociologists, social workers, and editors have a difficult time assigning transgender, this experience, this continuum of gender identities and expressions, into their comprehension of what LGBT means. There is a constant refusal and noncompliance to celebrate the transgender experience as a legitimate expression of gender. (Transgender includes all sexual orientations.)[13]

Those in control of LGBT media, those in control of the naming of the movement, those in control of policy, those in control of representation, those in control of money, those in control of large community centers refuse (or ignore) the damage that LG is doing by not including BT within the apex of the movement. Although we've come a long way around inclusion within the 'queer' movement, there is still such a long way to go. And as the leaders of the LGbt movement stagnate, argue, or are not available to 'hear' what they need to 'hear,' the education that is taking place on a grass-roots level within public space, e.g. Mental Health Services, Department of Health, Health Commissioner's Office, the Judicial System et al., is wrong and is doing damage to a percentage of people of transexual experience who are silent, silenced, closeted, or are not involving themselves with the queer agenda/movement*. It is also doing damage to all those nelly fags, bull-daggers, femme men, butch women as well.

Again, David Valentine, Ph.D., whose dissertation "I Know what I am: 'Transgender' and the Space Between Gender and Sexuality" communicates how the category of transgender was named in order to separate sex, sexuality, gender and presentation in order to own some false privilege within the political structure.

Here are some examples of the silencing of the 'T' within the LGBT movement from 2000:

The Lesbian Gay Community Services Center (LGCSC) membership committee sent out a letter to women encouraging them to become members. The envelope had pictures of women from the center's community. I was on the envelope along with one of my counselors, Ms. Carrie Davis. Throughout the promotional material it only identified women as lesbians and only detailed programs that worked effectively with "lesbian parents," young women, lesbian movie night, and lesbians with substance abuse problems. It never mentioned women of transexual experience, phallic-women, bisexual women, or women who are questioning their fe-MALE identity.

Queens Pride, the GAY and LESBIAN Pride Committee acknowledges and integrates LGBT but never discusses specific 'T' issues. They state QLGPC is Queens' largest multi-service lesbian and gay rights organization.

A fundraiser at the center (LGCSC) marketing a transgender theatrical persona, Lypsinka (now I do not know how this person identifies, but within the definition of transgender, if one utilizes the gender role of another identified sex, one would fit within this continuum). An E*Trade Evening benefiting the center — "Please join us for an "E*Trade Evening as we celebrate our continued support of the **gay and lesbian** community."

Empire State Pride Agenda (ESPA) consulted with communities around the 11/7/00 vote. They produced a **2000 Statewide Voter Guide**. They consulted with **lesbian and gay organizations** throughout New York State.[14]

The Journal of Lesbian and Gay Studies had not yet become a Journal of **LGBT** Studies.

The Gay/Lesbian/Bisexual/Transgender Public Policy Issues, a citizen's and administrator's guide to the **New Cultural Struggle,** stated on its first page, "This book covered the range of public policy issues that face the **gay/lesbian/bisexual/transgender** community, using case studies and personal anecdotes. Its strongest chapters provided analysis and guidance for public administrators and citizens to develop programs and policies to overcome hurtful stereotypes and promote acceptance of

gay/lesbian/bisexual/transgender people in all areas of contemporary life. The author gives insights on the experiences of **NON-HETEROSEXUAL** people in our society ..."

LGNY News: Responding to protesting transexual activists (what gender identity/sex is a '**transexual**' anyway, and how are we defining **TS** here?) who entered the Michigan Womyn's Festival grounds and women who opposed them, festival organizers have reaffirmed that an annual event is for "womyn-born womyn" only (which means?).

NY Times magazine 5/28/2000 identified the war widow of Pfc. Barry Winchell who was murdered for having a **gay lover**. Gary's lover was **a woman of transexual experience** who was led by **LG leaders to speak out**. "In order to turn the murdered soldier Barry Winchell into a martyr for **gay rights**, activists first had to turn his girlfriend, Calpernia Addams, into a man." (p. 24).

In 2003 the Advocate in their May 27th magazine did the same exact thing and even put two men on the cover who were playing these characters in a Showtime Movie.

The Advocate, the national Gay and Lesbian News magazine, had two people on their 5/25/00 cover, famous swimmer Greg Louganis and actress Alexandra Billings. They identify the two. "Greg – **this man was born gay,** and Alexandra – **this woman was born a man**." My and my staff's opinion - If Greg was born gay then Alexandra was born a woman. If Alexandra was born a man, then Greg was born straight.

Heritage of Pride 1999 (HOP) Rally (a rally in which I was one of the speakers) identified themselves as **Lesbian** and **Gay** pride.

In HOP-Pride of 2000 it did not change to LGBT. In 2002 I think it did.

The Advocate ran an article titled "Cunning Linguists" written by a lesbian by the name of Nora Vincent. Within this article Nora talks about "**transexuals as being body mutilators.**" The Advocate is supposed to be a Gay and Lesbian magazine focused on queer issues. I wonder if they have ever run an article that terrorizes the **GL** communities or that negates the whole sexual orientation that is other than hetero? Nora has written many articles against the 'trans-identity.'

I began to challenge many of the *LG* Institutions around LGBT issues. This does not mean I am not grateful to them for the work that they've done and the work they will continue to do. This just means that I think, no, I know, there are massive changes that need to take place within the *LG* movement.

Notes

[1] Susan Stryker is a community-based scholar, freelance writer, and transgender activist. She is currently working on Ecstatic Passages: A Postmodern Transexual Memoir (Oxford University Press, forthcoming).

[2] Stonewall was a bar by Christopher Street in NYC that queer identified people frequented. It used to be raided all the time. People who were identified as homosexuals or who were dancing together and of the same sex, or people who didn't have at least three pieces of clothing that matched their sex (their birth identified sex), were arrested. The night of Stonewall, many queer identified people outside of the bar got tired of the police harassment and fought back. So began this 'neo' revolution.

[3] I have used Freire within my work as a social worker, activist, educator and counselor. His explanation of oppression, stigma, jealousy, and internalized shame is classic.

[4] It took a tremendous amount of effort, organizing, lobbying, money, and time to challenge the APA surrounding the removal of homosexuality as a diagnostic category. G and L leaders worked their 'butts' off. The 'T' doesn't have nearly as much power, money or people willing to do this work. It is important that the LG groups support and assist in changing the DSMIV, which at present few within the APA's GLB 44th division are willing to even look at.

[5] As a society we need to look at how we engage each other around healthy sexuality and belief systems. To date, this is not in place. Look at the language when someone says "suck my dick," or "you're a scum-bag," or "shove it up your ass." Then think about how this "common" language is used and then move it to the level where people are participating in this behavior or are attempting to negotiate condom usage. Things that make you go hmmmm, or ouch!

[6] The Imperial Court of New York has been extremely financially supportive to the Gender Identity Project (*a program I was the director of*). Their philanthropic dollars have assisted with many outreach strategies. Yet few of their members ever participate in the support groups or cultural events for and by people who outwardly identify as trans.

[7] Most straight-identified people of transexual experience **do not** participate within the LGBT movement. Is this because they are closeted about their transexuality? Or is this because the LGBT movement has never made it a priority to make room for heterosexuals and bisexual people within the movement?

[8] Within a patriarchal system femininity is identified as the lesser components of the society, e.g. the weak, the disempowered, the second

class. A cross-dresser is usually identified as a man wearing women's clothes, and not the other way around. Although there are many male-identified cross-dressers within our society, there are very few ways in which to celebrate that identity/behavior/role. Therefore, many are silent or silenced, and are isolated.

[9] Bisexual identity is not celebrated within the LG movement and this must change. There are so many issues that I can't touch upon within this book, but somebody needs to.

[10] 'Preference' utters choice, and some might feel if it is a choice why not just choose to be hetero. It places a moral value on your sexual orientation.

[11] I had the pleasure of working with Dr. Valentine for a year when he asked to work within the GIP. I was enrolled in an undergraduate program and he was doing his fieldwork for his doctorate. I was leery of him because he wasn't of trans experience and he was too smart to work for me. I am so grateful for the opportunity I had to work with him, to learn from him, and to have him learn from me. The experience taught me so much about myself, and the value system around formal and informal education. David is my most favorite anteater.

[12] The center's sign has stated Lesbian and Gay Community Services Center serving the lesbian, gay, bisexual and transgender communities since 1983. I believe that there is no discussion around changing the name at this time, which is not only problematic but also damaging to the L and G communities. However, I also understand the ramifications of being inclusive and disrupting the homeostasis (no pun intended).

This was in the year 2000. In 2001 the Center became the LGBT Center

[13] It is hard for us to comprehend something when it is not our experience. That is why it is so important for social workers to be out there in the communities experiencing what others are experiencing. Sex and gender is cemented in our heads as pink and blue from the inception of birth. It is so difficult to challenge these theories.

[14] Many of these these gay and lesbian organizations support the bi and trans identity or identities. But they will not list it as such.

Fall of 2000 and the Union of Language

Here we are at the Lesbian and Gay Community Services Center in New York City. It is the fall of 2000. It's the end of a new beginning, or is it the beginning of the end?

It's an election year and many are scurrying around attempting to win points for possible funding on a local, state and federal level. Some of the center staff, our allies, and LG political leaders are setting up those dominos, aiming them to fall in the direction of choice. There's discussion on a national level about gay rights, gay marriage, gay support. There's a major bill being worked out around hate crime legislation and it has moved up a few notches within the game of politics and civil bureaucracies. The Hate Crimes Prevention Act, S./H.R. 1082, brought together many communities that waited patiently until all had a seat at the table. However, there are components within the queer populations (specifically certain sexual minorities) that have been left out. These are people identified as people along the Transgender (TG) continuum. Some identify as gay, lesbian, bisexual, omnisexual, pansexual, and/or heterosexual, but what is left out is their right to gender identity or gender expression.

There are also those on the TG continuum who are angry, experiencing self-righteous anger, and they are being strangled by their feelings of hostility. And as Nina Kebenoff, Ed.M., C.S.W., C.G.P., [1] asserts, "they can taste the blood of the meat in their oral cavities even though they are celebrated vegans." Nina, a therapist, states that anger is power and energetic. So even though folks on the TG continuum are angry, there is a place for that energy. It's the fall of 2000, the end of a new beginning or the beginning of the end?

In the lobby of the Lesbian and Gay Community Services Center (thecenter that serves lesbians, gays, bisexuals and transgender people since 1983), within the back of the lobby by the coffee house, there's a sign for a play called 'Boys Don't Wear Lipstick,' the story of Brian Belovitch. Brian Belovitch is a man, a gay man, a gay, androgynous looking man, a gay, androgynous looking man with a gender different history. Brian lived fifteen years of his life as Tische, a voluptuous, egocentric, self-centered, West Village drag performer who at one time married a man and lived in Europe. Brian (Tische) was also a drug addict who did a stint as 'a crack addicted hooker' in midtown. The center has an advertisement for Brian's play in the coffee house. Brian is also doing a benefit for GenderPac.[2]

> GenderPac, the Gender Identity Project, and the center's Public Policy Department hosted a fundraiser with Academy Award winner *Hillary Swank and the cast of* **Boys don't Cry**[3] *and GenderPac hosted a fundraiser with Brian Belovitch as well.*

'Boys Don't Cry,' 'Boys Don't Wear Lipstick,' what else don't boys do?
One might think this is a paradox of terms when we look at these two stories. What value (*if any*) is being executed by supporting a play like *Boys Don't Wear Lipstick* at the center when the LGBT movement is at this socio/political stage of its development?
Confused … Here are more details:
Brian is not only the writer and performer. This play is about his life. Brian is also someone I have known and admired since I was sixteen years old. Brian spent most of his life addicted to something, and when Brian, then

Tische, got clean and sober and started to look at her life, Tische knew she was not going to be able to have sex/gender realignment surgery and decided to live as the gender that she was birth identified as, a man, a boy, *a boy who doesn't wear lipstick,* even though he's wearing it again to perform 'him' as 'hir.'

More confused? Good! Let's call this Identity Politics.

This play is about a person who wakes up from a fog of drugs and alcohol, wakes up in time to be true to himself, the man that he's supposed to be.

The power of language!

All of this can be factual for Brian. This is Brian's story and he is living his dream by telling it, making money from it, and allowing himself to perform within the '*Ticshe*' persona again. That is wonderful for Brian. He should be supported and nurtured around his creation, his work, and his talents. He gets to play himself as herself and gets to feed that inner component of him that will always fall somewhere on the trans-continuum.

But does this set up precedence around the gender movement within the larger queer movement? Is this a smaller representation of what the larger **LG** controlled movement is subconsciously positioned at? Is the center an acceptable place to advertise a play about a trans-person who, after they get clean and sober, cleans up their act, starts to recover, and then their trans identity is realized to be just a persona that belongs on a stage and has no relevance to 'real' life? Drugs and alcohol kept Tische alive and sobriety buried Tische then marketed Tische. Sort of like what drag does for the whole gay movement.

Is this acceptable?

The construction, deconstruction and reconstruction of gender identity mergers are just about play? It's preference not orientation? It is not a legitimate identity? It should not be taken seriously?

By celebrating this play, GenderPAC, and the center, are relaying a message. And at this point within a struggling LGBT movement, a movement that is brittle and vulnerable and still uncomfortable to the **Bs** and the **Ts**, doesn't this feed into the likes of those horrible writers (well, not bad writers, just schmucks) like Janice Raymond, '*The Transexual Empire, the making of the she-male,*' writer-archaic activist like Jim Fouratt, and Nora Vincent, writer (*Village Voice and the Advocate*)?

Advertising 'Boys Don't Wear Lipstick' in a lesbian and gay center, an amazing center that houses the only gender program that is progressive, is like adding salt to the wound, just enough so that it stings.

The **BT** communities are in the most need of unconditional positive regard and support. In 1969, right after the Stonewall riot, gay and lesbian people felt invigorated but still vulnerable, abused and confused. Many were juggling internalized societal induced self-hatred. Does one think a play focusing on a gay man or lesbian finally deciding to live the 'straight life' after coming off LSD would be politically/socially/emotionally beneficial to other gays and lesbians? Especially if the movie was housed right within the only place that felt a little safe?

Within the scheme of identity politics do we think that would happen?

Brian's story is Brian's story and it should be respected as a valid, very influential, uplifting, entertaining tale.

But the Power of Language is amongst us! Within this movement, at this time, this play should not be used or advertised as a fundraiser or something the center supports.

Cultural competency and diversity initiatives are about these issues!

In my T Town Two speech (*see Appendix II speeches*) I proposed "that some day the truth will set us all free." In the words of Martin Luther King Junior, "None of us are free until all of us are free."

Language has the power to break our spirits.

Language has the power to destroy our souls.

Many activists of trans and bi experiences, many allies, many gay and lesbians will not give up without a fight. But many of us are hurting.

I identify myself as a leader, a hetero woman, a passionate, uneducated, educated diva, and a social work practitioner. I will fight for what I believe to the very end. I will challenge those before me to do what is right as I hope those that experience the same integrity will do back to me when I am wrong.[3] I have loved this movement. I have the utmost respect for Brian, for the center, and for what the mission of GenderPac could be about. I will not sit back and be silent when I see, feel and hear what I believe to be wrong.

Notes

[1] Nina Klebanoff is a Systems Therapist who assists people in learning how to contain their feelings, experience them by staying in their appropriate role. Nina has been facilitating a group for around twelve years at the center. The group began when clinicians, social workers, therapists, counselors and substance abuse practitioners needed a place to go to learn how to truly deal with all the death and dying that was happening around them. It was in the middle of the AIDS crisis. And so this group began and is still going strong, but not at the center.

[2] GPAC is a national organization that states its mission is for racial and gender equality on a national level. Now this is only half true. The Executive Director (an amazing person who in the past has identified as someone on the transgender continuum) was one of the first truly visible people challenging our society around transgender issues within the political arena. Her name is Riki Anne Wilchins, author of 'Read My Lips, sexual subversion and the end of Gender.' GPAC brings up many racial

inequalities on a national level. GPAC utilizes these points of reference, e.g. hate crimes, discriminatory practices, murders, to secure a position within the political arena, both mainstream and within the queer, predominantly gay and lesbian, movement. They have brilliant ideas but I think they are challenged by true diversity initiatives surrounding class and race and I hope they are working on it.

{This one is not even worth a *}

Jim Fouratt and Nora Vincent are assholes who have constantly had some space to voice their opinions, usually around June, what some queer people call 'Gay Pride' month. Every June, when people are looking to experience pride around their gender identity and/or sexual orientation someone always gives Jim and Nora a plateau in which they can denigrate the trans-identity.

[3] 'Boys Don't Cry' was the story of Brandon Teena. Brandon was brutally raped and murdered in Nebraska by his friends when they found out that he was identified female at birth (this is my language, not the way it was explained in the movie or the way it was marketed).

You should know that Carrie Davis, GIP counselor (at the time), sent an email to the center's Special Events Department and also had some very constructive dialogue with them. Carrie also spoke with allies from the center's Information and Referral program and they immediately took down the 'Boys Don't Wear Lipstick' sign. Someday this will not happen in the first place because it will be on everyone's radar.

The Downside to false fame

As you could read, Life, and this work, was getting too complicated. I've been handed a plateau from which to make statements concerning the future of the transgender communities. I haven't played the game with the same rules as many others within the LGBT movement and I came from a different cultural background. I was taking a lot of things a little too personally. But I believed in my heart I was coming from a loving place. I juggled the institutional constraints, the needs of the TG communities, my job description that kept growing, lack of quality guidance through the struggle, and all of my own personal shit. Becoming a poster child took away something I had worked so hard for, a right to be 'me.' And sometimes I just lost it. A component of my being adored, the new fame, fame I had not truly earned. I just took on a job that nobody else wanted. I was there and it was offered to me. It allowed me to act out a fantasy that made me an important individual, someone to listen to, a smart woman. And on the other side, I am really no one. Just a loudmouth broad from Brooklyn who had the balls to say what she felt. Fame, how quickly it can come and without delay it can be gone.

The Professional Perspective
Social Work Practice and the Power of Language

It is important to note that culturally competent practice within the communities that identify as gender different, gender variant, gender dysphoric, gender euphoric, gender oppressed, gender challenged, gender confused, gender free, is infrequent. In my work as a director of a gender program I received too many calls from social workers around the world utilizing negative, pathologizing language and verbal bias that they didn't acknowledge. I do realize that they were the ones calling, and that is the first step. I can't imagine how many social workers are dealing with trans-clients and are doing these clients a disservice. I have many anecdotal stories but will restrain. Although there are many health care providers interested in working with clients of this experience, their care is still of grave concern to me. In all the trainings I've been involved with in the past eleven years around gender identity issues, I still have a small list of people who I would feel comfortable referring trans-clients to. There is a definite shortage of trans-culturally appropriate care.

Language is an important component of care for these communities. I observe health care practitioners, academicians, as well as the organized gay and lesbian communities, utilizing language that is wrong or offensive.

The trans-communities compile diverse people around gender as well as diversity in all other areas including, but not limited to, age, color, class, education, ethnicity, comprehension of their experiences, as well as status and growth around their trans-issues. The easiest and most effective tool that I have to offer is to utilize good social work practice by meeting the client exactly where they are without holding onto an internal, bipolarized gender/sex agenda.

When it comes to intake, psycho socials, basic demographics, or filling out forms for your contracts, ask the clients how they identify with regards to gender, with regards to sex, with regards to color, with regards to ethnicity.

If your form has few choices, add 'other' and give them the space to self-identify.

If your form is computerized, attach a cover letter with your monthly or annual report. Get involved in challenging the language as well as supporting the identity of the client. Be honest and supportive and respectful and assist that client in exploring these ideations around gender and identity.

This might be the very first time this client is offered this opportunity. You will be surprised how much help this is for them. Language is a powerful tool. Use it wisely. And know that when NASW (*National Association of Social Workers*) states '**First do no harm,**' that includes attempting not to use language that is offensive. Gender inappropriate language with a trans-client is offensive.

I have never slipped up with a Jewish client by calling them a ... I have never slipped up with an African-American or Latina/o client by calling them a ... I have never slipped up with a gay or lesbian client by calling them a ... or a ...

When a client identifies as one specific gender (and not all clients will, especially when they are in an exploration phase), but when they do, it is not acceptable to slip up around pronouns. This only means that when you do, you must realize that you are not hearing, seeing or listening to their core identity and you are working from stereotypes and biases as well as incorporating a belief system that does not legitimize their identity. **Know this, work on it, and go on.** I have made slips around clients who I am not always familiar with. But I make sure to learn from the experience so it will never happen again. With clients such as the deaf, or the physically challenged, or older clients, or youth, or clients where English is their second language, or clients who have been physically structured differently, I make sure that I am able to see them, the 'them' that they see, the 'them' that they are.

That is the 'true' them. And that is the 'them' I am supposed to be working with and for.

Within social work practice it is essential that we rethink and reevaluate our perceptions of gender, identity, sexuality and sexual orientation so that all who deviate have the opportunity to live outside of that rigid system, free from self-judgment, hate and fear.

As clinicians, we identify and we diagnose, utilizing our advanced degrees, justifying our assessments with empirical, rigid, testosterone dominated research. We compare our patients, clients, consumers, friends, family and colleagues to categories within the DSMIV. We need to rethink the process.

As a profession that works with and for the more vulnerable populations we need to be aware of these personal and societal biases that affect all of our lives. If we begin to own this knowledge we can move from a condescending approach to an approach that is grounded in respect and integrity for **all.**

Appendix II
Strategies for
Social/Sexual Justice

Appendix II

Strategies for Social/Sexual Justice

Speeches
Paper

A true thespian challenges the forces by way of stirring oration

Narrative Expression
the spirit of the journey contained by a queer hetero-woman's discourse:
1994-2000

During my tenure at the LG, now LGBT Center in New York City, I received many opportunities to express my personal and professional positions concerning the Sexual Minority/ies Social Justice Movement that I was now formally affiliated with and energized by. I, like so many others, was informally involved with this neo-revolution just by challenging gender constructs or deviating from what was considered to be the 'norm' surrounding sexual orientation and gender identity presentation.

Throughout the ten years I spent at the center I was presented with a variety of podiums from which to speak up and speak out. I tried many strategies as I learned to use my personal and professional voice. Here are some of the speeches I used to educate, advocate, challenge, embarrass or connect those with power to see, feel, experience, hear and understand the need to change and expand the exclusive gay movement into an inclusive queer movement.

Note:
I did not edit these speeches for your reading pleasure. As I grew academically, so did my use of linguistics. The essence of the speeches speak for themselves. And the significance of my grammar is secondary.

1999 Speech presented by Rosalyne Blumenstein
at New York City's Heritage of Pride Rally June, in front of 3,000 people at Bryant Park, 42nd and 6th Avenue, NYC

People of transgender experience, bisexuals, intersex people who look queer, indigenous peoples. We will not be silent any longer!
We are now 30 years succeeding Stonewall. This movement is in its adult phase of development. It is now time to own our responsibilities by taking care of all of our families, not just those which some feel are <u>satisfactory</u> members.
<u>*Our blood and our security lay within the hands of this movement*</u>. We must own that reality. It is now time to call out the *healers* and leaders of our communities. All of us, not only gay or lesbian identified people, need to heal from significant emotional, spiritual and physical injustice.
People of transgender experience have been a part of this movement since its inception, irregardless of our sexual attractions to those with different, the same, or variations of genitalia or secondary sexual *characteristics*. Bisexuals have also attempted to participate within this movement, yet the movement seems to want to silence them repeatedly.
Martin Luther King, Jr. said, unless all are free, none are actually free.

Transgender identity and bisexuality are equal issues deserving of top billing. People of transgender experience or bisexual people are not subheadings of a gay and lesbian movement. Make this movement responsible for bringing life to these voices or else this movement will die. It will amalgamate into only those of us that look like we don't belong within this movement anyway.

What is 'LGBandT' Pride and how do we all obtain it?

The movement's responsibility is to bring all to the table, drag queens, cross dressers, intersex, bisexuals, *people of transexual experience that identify as straight, bi, lesbian, gay, pan-sexual or omnisexual, black, white, yellow, red, rich, poor, young and old.* Everyone should be served, not only those that look, act or present as non-queer or those that blend acceptably.

Your responsibility is to make this voice heard. Let every f**king lesbian and gay organization in this country know that the time has come to change their name. The time has come to either make room at the table or give the table up. It is time to support those of us that are starving for access, those of us that are bleeding to death on the streets and not being acknowledged.

Brandon Teena is dead! Mathew Shepard is dead

Televised and Sensationalized

And what about all the transgender people of color and of no color that are thrown out of their houses at an early age and are tortured murderously every day? What about transexual people that are tortured by a system that pathologizes their very existence and refuses them adequate health care? What about all the bisexual peoples that are 86'D from too many of our communities because of their eclectic approach to sexual and emotional intimacies? What about the intersex person that is stigmatized at birth, and lives with that stigma until the day they die? And what about all of our people that challenge gender expression on a daily basis and are harassed on our city streets? No one makes a stink, and they are our responsibility. They should, and will, be taken care of.

Leslie Feinberg states, "when we allow ourselves to be split along lines of oppression we lose," and Riki Wilchins asserts, "will you let your pain make your heart smaller and smaller so it only holds your own troubles and you seek your own liberation? Or will you let your heart grow larger so you're open to the troubles of others?"

Our blood and our lives are in the hands of this movement!

We will not be silent any longer! Will you?

Or will you keep attempting to silence us?

I beg of you, let Empire State Pride Agenda, National Gay Lesbian Task Force, Human Rights Campaign, the NYC and L.A. Center and all the Queer Community Centers around the U.S. know about their responsibilities to these communities

ROSALYNE BLUMENSTEIN

Have a good pride and thank you. ©1999

Twenty-three years ago there was a sixteen-year-old transexual girl roaming aimlessly around our city streets. This adolescent was asked to leave her home in Long Island, and was asked to drop out of her prestigious high school in NYC. Family and school officials demanded her to exile merely because she identified herself as transexual and was willing to challenge gender constrictions, those gender constrictions that so many of us were and are brought up with. Through conniving, hustling, illicit activities she roamed the streets for money, food, housing, acceptance, and love. This child found solace in the nightlife, with the support of drug addiction and prostitution. Our society designates these as the deviant sub-cultures yet, to so many, this is where home is fabricated.

Well, a lot has happened in 23 years.

This child survived those arenas, survived drug addiction, survived the streets, and survived the physical and verbal self and societal abuse that she and so many others like her have had to confront in their lifetime. This young transexual female has survived and has experienced many opportunities to turn her life around. She is extremely fortunate to stand before you this evening and graciously accept this award. But why hers when so many of her compardres are gone, dead, defeated?

My good friend and colleague Lynn Walker states it best, "We are judged by the color and shape of our skin". Is it that my looks and my features are not so threatening or challenging to a society that values features, some of which I present? Do we think it's because society has allowed me "to be" because I blend? Why is it that this aging gracefully woman is allowed to position herself in front of you owning a false sense of privilege while so many of her brothers and sisters of transgender experience are mistreated and abused. Is it not too difficult to accept someone who looks like someone who deserves privilege?

And how many of our LGBT queer brothers and sisters and others are not able and do not blend into these categories? How many of us experience privilege to walk around free?

Courage to me is all the young adults that are roaming our streets. We've attempted to chase many of them away from 42nd Street, out of the peep shows, off the streets, out of the SROs, and into the dark ends of the suburbs so that they may be quietly murdered, taken advantage of, and thrown away. These people are out on the streets for many reasons, but one reason is because they believe within their core that their transgender experience needs to be visible and celebrated no matter what the DSMIV, the media, the church, their family, or their neighbors say. That is courage! That is chutzpah!

I want you to think. Think about what a young gender questioning, transgender, cross dresser of color has to do to survive their community from which they have been reared. If we were able to assist them with life skills, substance abuse treatment, access to health care or any direction, support and respect, where could they go from there? You try surviving the streets at night. If we could help them to place that energy somewhere else, how powerful and beneficial to our society could they be?

Many of us are challenged because we do not look like Barbie or Ken. Not me, I identify as aging Barbie, not Asian, *aging* Barbie. I spent many years being told that as long as I did not look like what I was, I would be successful. Well, my success then is only supported if it's external? Internalized transphobia took me to places which hospitalized me into Kings County, Coney Island and Jacobi. We need to change our perception of what is acceptable, what is valued and how we deal with difference. How many of us do not speak the King's English, we do not come from privilege, and we have not been educated within the best school districts? How many of us do not look or care to look like Barbie or Ken? How many of us need to be supported around our diversity? So how do we celebrate that challenge as opposed to devaluing those of us that deviate from that societal standard of practice?

My work is not just about transgender issues and concerns or the rights for sexual minorities, it's about celebrating diversity and not being fearful, hating, or being able to abuse and mistreat someone who is different, different looking, or has a distinct way of celebrating their gender.

I accept this award in honor of those that have undeniable courage and I accept this for the work that I am involved with at the Gender Identity Project of the Lesbian and Gay Community Services Center, the people, the trans-identified people, my peers. I thank those within the hierarchy of the center that have allowed me the space, this opportunity to be involved with the work that I do.

To GOAL, Dear GOAL one day BTGOAL or TBGOAL or LGBOAT or queer officers action league, I thank you so, so much.© 1999

2000 Outline for speech presented at the NY City Council Members of the Manhattan Delegation Black Latino/a Caucus.
The focus of the speech was for changing the city's Basic Human Rights ordinance to include "perceived gender and gender expression" so that people of trans-experience would be protected under the law.

I come to you today exhausted with worry yet with a mustard seed of faith
I thank you, Margarita Lopez, and the rest of the city council for putting yourself out and truly attempting to understand the importance of the situations that gender variant/gender different people face on a daily basis and the discriminations that we are subjected to within our society in 1999.

I am currently the director of the Gender Identity Project. I work three jobs and juggle seventeen credits within a master's program. I am honored to have the privilege to challenge myself intellectually, emotionally, spiritually, academically and professionally.

But I will never forget my adolescence on the streets, homeless, hated, denied access to many institutions, denied health care, denied compassion from the dominant literate and illiterate society. Every day I go to work and I see TG people on the street. I think so much has changed for me, but not changed in 23 years.

What can I do? What can we do?

To start off with, it would be nice if they knew that they had the right 'to be,' that they had the right 'to live.' It would be nice if they had that right.

Whose children are on the streets? Whose lost adults? They are our brothers, sisters, mothers, fathers, cousins. They are our children.

To quote Social Work Practice, "Our society is only as strong as our weakest link."

So what are we asking for?

We are asking you to legitimize our diverse experiences, gender variant, gender transgressors, of transexual experience, the list goes on and on and includes MANY people. It includes fem gays, butch lesbians, bisexuals, heterosexuals. It includes all of us that have challenged or challenge gender identity or gender presentation.

I've been weakened by the battle. Coming 'OUT' is not easy and so many of us do not have that choice. We are Outed daily and we face hate, discrimination, oppression, stigmatization, violence, and little access to too many things. There is so much work for us to do to change societal ignorance.

Let's start with amending the Human Rights Code

Again, Just Basic Human Rights.

Thank you for your time

2000 The Day After ...
In March 2000 the Lesbian and Gay Community Services Center
(LGCSC) hosted what was cosponsored by the Gay and Lesbian
Independent Democrats (GLID), the National Lesbian and Gay Task
Force (NGLTF) et al. The vice president came to speak at the center
and this was a first.
*This speech was made by Rosalyne Blumenstein at the center's weekly
staff meeting the day after ...*

I come to you today with a mustard seed of faith that somehow this cry, this plea to this institution, this village with its amazing tribes will somehow share, thereby lessening my anger and frustration.

For many of us, these past weeks have consisted of wonderful history in the making. For many staff here at the center it has been more stressful than one could imagine. The schmoozing, the entertaining, the setting up, the taking down, the being on, the turning off. As an institution, we've all played an integral part – for us, for an institution, for the LGBT movement.

Some of us could not participate, we had to seek out neo-social work interns for the coming year to assist in healing our communities in days that follow. I was supposed to go to the Intern Day at Columbia, but I chose to be here with you, with us, with the vice president.

Some of us swept floors and set up chairs for these events. Some ran around like chickens without a head making sure things were organized. Some of us were attached to telephone lines giving directions to our communities that wanted to see history in the making. Some of our co-workers strategically planned what they were going to say so that there might be more money allocated to the center and other queer identified institutions, more job opportunities, a stronger infrastructure, and a brighter future for us all. But was and is this for all? I ask you!

From the top down I know, and I believe, this is a difficult time. We are growing, and evolving. There is money stress, there are race tensions, there are class concerns. However, we work together for the common good – our informal mission – All queers need not die alone shamed and filled with self-hate.

We need to remember. We've faced an AIDS crisis that is still not over. We are not losing people in large quantities anymore.

Yet I am here to tell you, you are still losing people but not by literal death. We are chasing people out the door and we need to stop them before it is too late.

These weeks' history has been fabricated. It was an opportunity for all to feel like we've arrived but someone, somebody, some group made the decision that only some of us would experience that joy.

From Bradley, the Center Women's Event, the Hillary Swank appearance, Hillary Clinton's arrival, to yesterday's Al Gore speech, things became clear, this is not for all of us.

Standing on the side waiting for Bradley to arrive, sitting with my Housing Work's clients, by my side, I felt the energy of the room, I emotionally applauded the room and all its constituents. I felt proud and honored to be a valuable servant of this center. After all, it is ALL of our participation and cooperation that encourages things like this to happen. As I looked around I tried to ignore the exclusive banners, L and G, not B or T. I tried to ignore the exclusive buttons, the exclusive National Lesbian and Gay Task Force Study that was handed out as one walked into the Lesbian and Gay Community Center. I tried to ignore the exclusive faces that surrounded me. I looked in front of me, there ya go, there's the center's banner, "The Lesbian and Gay Community Services Center," and there's the tag line vaguely appearing behind and under the heads and faces of the lesbian and gay communities. The tag line appeared as if from a shadow of a dimly lit late afternoon sun. If you had some knowledge of the center you knew it was there, but it was just as easy to ignore and deny its presence.

A conundrum!

One by one speakers ignored bi and trans. Political people, the communities, our own center staff. Yes, two speakers threw "trans" into their speeches and one speaker threw "bi and trans" in. If I was Bradley, Clinton or Gore, I wouldn't have understood the importance of the diversity around what LGB and T means either.

I left these events slowly beaten, tired and frustrated. While the Empire State Pride Agenda, the Gay/Lesbian Independent Democrats, The Lesbian and Gay Community Services Center, and the Lesbian and Gay Communities experienced a newfound sense of self and freedom, my people and other insurgent groups, we went back to the fields with our spirit downcast. But we did not sing to heal, we did not come together to repair. We, in fact, left separate, isolated and some, self-hating. Some internalize the rejection while some of us challenge the audacity of those that experienced the freedom.

Each day was supposed to be filled with the hope and desire that somehow the next event, political performance, would be different. And each time it was not.

Back to the Gore day:

I'm sitting with staff celebrating a vice president coming to the center. I look up, same signs, same literature, but I hope this will be the day I experience the accomplishments of my work, experience my value here at the center. And there, oh my god, on stage, I see, a woman of transgender experience, Melissa Sklarz. A woman that I and my supervisor have had the opportunity to nurture, mentor, work with for the past seven years. I sit up and back in a proud stance, like a nurturing mother.

One by one the speakers address us. My life, my power, my soul, is shattered as bi and trans is excluded from speeches of the officials on the stage. The officials that I've attempted to educate appropriately within the constraints of the center and its unofficial communication policy. A center that I've wanted desperately to feel a sense of pride and value from because of my contributions. Somehow Melissa's face becomes distorted up on stage and looks like a piece from which another puzzle, she doesn't seem to fit and I'm not sure where I placed the other box, the other puzzle.

Yet, as the last speaker from the center, our executive director, speaks and utilizes language that is inclusive LGBT, I internally break down and sob. I thank him in my heart, knowing this brief interaction of inclusion is not enough. No one hears and no one cares.

And as for Gore, he discusses how this audience, this audience filled with lesbian and gays, it looks like every other audience he speaks to. He states we all want the same thing, we all deserve the same opportunities, we are all involved with the same kind of struggles around family, work and survival. And as he speaks I look in the back to see if there are any sixteen-year-old runaway/thrown away, coke addicted, homeless, transgender or gender questioning youth who resort to prostitution as a survival profession, I look back to see if they're around, sitting down, or trying to get in. I look back to see if Brandon Teena (Movie: Boys Don't Cry –A young trans-man who was brutally raped and murdered in Nebraska by a group of men that found out he was born identified as a woman) might somehow be in the back while Gore discusses Mathew Shepard's death. (Mathew Shepard was a gay college student who was brutally murdered by some guys he knew and left with from a bar in Wyoming. Mathew's death caused a national wake-up call to look at the way the judiciary system identifies and tries bias and hate crimes towards gay and lesbian people.)

As all this is going through my head I somehow keep thinking of the words 'fairness' and 'integrity.' They just keep flashing through my brain like a subliminal strobing advertisement.

I walk outside to taste some clear air and the New York Blade asks me to make a statement. I'm consumed in thought, reviewing my life as I discuss with the Blade's reporter, stating "how the center is a role model nationally for the national Lesbian and Gay Community Centers to show how LGBT people can come together and work effectively for the common good," and as my stomach turns I somehow am not believing a word I'm saying.

Don't get me wrong. I think we work for an amazing institution. This institution has given me great opportunities to succeed. This institution has afforded me the opportunity to take a small project and make it a world-renowned program. This institution is an institution that I want to continue to work with and for. We have to change! And I am at a loss. I am not speaking for my staff. I am speaking as a spectator. I've worked here for seven years. I have been dealing with negotiating gender and gender oppression for 35 years since I was laughed out of nursery school. I cannot fight the institution and have any leftover energy to do all the other things I must do to change the ways in which the world deals with gender, transgender, transexual issues and concerns. What is each and every one of our responsibilities around changing this conundrum?

Some of you might be saying how self-centered I am to take up this time and shove this diatribe into your hearing canals. And all I can say is that I don't even identify as bisexual or transgender, this is not a fight just for myself. I am fighting for all of us, those that assimilate as well as those that don't. I am fighting for those that participate as well as those that don't.

We, as an institution, must be collectively responsible to make sure that this never happens again. All of our hard work, our work within the diversity initiative, will mean absolutely nothing if we don't have an action plan for future inclusive events. "Bi and Trans" must be included across the board if we really want to represent these populations.

Again, I ponder the word, 'integrity.'

Bisexuals and people of transgender/transexual experience need to stay here. We have assisted in building this movement, this center. I want the larger queer movement to reap the benefits of our energy, our talents, our integrity. The people I work with and for have so much to offer. Don't cheat this movement, the center, out of this.

© 2000

2000 Brooklyn Pride Parade, June 2000.
One of four Grand Marshals for the parade
Here is the speech prior to the parade

It is such an honor to celebrate with y'all here in Brooklyn and to be on this stage with Paul, Daisy, Colin, the borough president and Sonia.

A visionary of the civil rights movement asserted many years ago
– unless all are free, none are actually free. Today, we celebrate in Brooklyn, LGBT Pride. Yet so many of us are still not a constituent of this experience! So many still hide in closets, experience too much societal and intrinsic trans, homo, and bi phobia. We still have so much work to do personally as well as politically. One of our responsibilities as a movement

is to realize: if we are exclusive, too many of us die, literally and figuratively. Yes, our diversity is sometimes overwhelming.

But if we do not allow /all to have a voice, /all to celebrate /all to be at the table, that table is devoid.

I am here today to be honored, but to also remind you about all of our responsibilities. We summon this month Pride. Pride equates some semblance of freedom. Freedom is for all, and the only way to connect to it is to love and honor our differences. Look back in history. Although enslaved, many survived the cotton fields, the concentration camps, workhouses, whorehouses, reservations, various captures. They did it through connection with others. Too many of us are still isolated, chained, separate, and silent. Please let us begin today by ending the isolation of others. Do not sell out our sundry communities for the sake of false privilege. Gay is not the umbrella term for all of us.

I am a straight woman of transexual experience. Half of the clients and communities I work with along the transgender continuum identify as bisexual or heterosexual. Do not silence their identities. Do not hate your effeminate gay male friends or tell them to act less like who they are. Do not cringe when you're with your butch lesbian sister because she outwardly celebrates her identity. Do not silence the bisexual or transgender communities. Do not judge one another by the shape and color of their skin, or their use of language, or their abilities, or their age, but by their inward search for integrity!

The only way to change this society is to be inclusive, together, not exclusive and alone.

We are all an integral part of this queer movement and if this movement is stagnant then it is not a movement any longer. Please, Love/ Honor/ Celebrate/ Unite/ Include/ Legitimate/ and Value one another! Challenge those that are ignorant, discriminatory, prejudice, and blinded, because those are truly the ones that are lost in some falsified Pride.

Within the organized exclusive Gay and Lesbian Political Arena, they think we need to be attractive and appropriately presentable to have a seat at the table, so, I ask you, how much more presentable can we be and why wouldn't anyone want all of us at the table!

Happy LGBT Pride © 2000

2000 Rosalyne Blumenstein MSW
Director Gender Identity Project, LGCSC NY, NY
Evening Clinician Housing Works Inc. NY, NY
T Town Two Speech for a Town Hall Meeting discussing Violence

At what price freedom? De que precio, la libertad? Be-eyzeh Me chir ho-fesh? Ah kel pree La Lee behr Tay? Welche Preis Freiheit? Whatever the language, violence does not equal freedom!

Is violence, vicious acts of hostility, abuse, neglect and hate, an effective, suitable, societal response to gender self-determination? Should gender freedom be salaried by lost access, insurgency, psychological diagnosis, removal of children, and love eradicated? Is this reasonable?

Violence! There is a minute description of what violence means in the dictionary, yet violence plays itself out within a trans-person's life in a very large way. Violent behavior is physically, emotionally and spiritually engulfing to the perpetrated.

As a woman of transexual experience I've been appalled with the violence that I and so many like and unlike me but of trans-experience themselves have had to contend with just because we wanted to possess our freedom.

I transitioned at sixteen years old but I knew who I was by the age of five. Let me give you some insight as to what I've tolerated at the launching of my transition when all I wanted was to activate my freedom, activate my core identity.

This song title is extracted from Clarissa Estes's women who run with the wolves, "Hambre del alma, the song of the starved soul." My soul, my core, my spirit has always been starving for consciousness, yet this society that we live in has been ravenously unconscious.

Violence
- At sixteen I was thrown out of high school because I began my physical gender modification

Violence
- At sixteen I went from a middle working class family with a roof over my head, a shower, and always food in my belly, to the Baron, the Strand, and the Landseer Hotel, malnourished sleeping in Central Park and the Port Authority

Violence

- At sixteen I turned my first trick. He robbed me of my only ten dollars. He raped me and made me consume my own feces. He then made me clean up the mess, threw me out of his car and drove off with my clothes. The sanitation workers across the street began to applaud and then laugh when they identified me to be someone who wasn't worthy of their assistance

Violence

- At seventeen years of age I went to my first underground surgeon because there was no information on the streets around safe and effective health care providers performing quality, affordable surgical procedures. I will never breathe, swallow, or speak appropriately because of these inept practitioners

Violence

- Going through a transexual puberty I was harassed by Jehovah's Witnesses, business owners, street people, the gay community, street venders, religious groups, hoodlums, as well as being disowned from my family of origin-

Violence

- As I became more and more attractive and sexually promiscuous I learned the power of objectifying the color and shape of my skin. I began to sing "hambre del alma" on a daily basis. What was to become my freedom from the constrictions of gender and a celebration of me became the forfeit of my opportunities to be educated, the forfeit of opportunities for a safe adolescence, the forfeit of opportunities to be with family and reside in a home

Violence

- On a less self-centered intensity*

Violence

- Not being aptly represented on a local, state and federal level

Violence

- Not having our identities legitimized within the medical, psychological and scientific domain

Violence

- Not having much of a voice within the legislative process

Violence

- Not having policies and procedures in place that are progressive and nurturing to our identities

Violence

- Not being integrated into mission statements and board representation within community based organizations and progressive queer organizations

Violence

- Not having city, state and federally granted money allocated specifically to transgender health care, transgender substance use and abuse treatment, social services and the legalization of all our trans … identities

And last, but not least,

Violence

- Having a large percentage of our trans … communities silenced and invisible because they do not identify as gay or lesbian, or as scholars or as activists.

This will all change because I believe in all of you! And I don't believe in the violence. I trust that the truth will someday set us all free.

How interesting, though, through all this, with all these obstructions, we all, on some subconscious level, own ourselves, own our bodies, our wardrobes, our core, our freedom.

But at what price, freedom?

We, the people, across this unearthly fabulous continuum of trans identities, are experiencing greater freedom just by being ourselves, and that pisses a lot of people off. Please know we are teaching this society how to acknowledge their own freedom. Look around you and know that these are our allies, our friends, our supporters, our mirrors, even though sometimes it doesn't feel like that. We have a long fight ahead of us. We've all experienced the violence! Now let us celebrate the freedom! Be strong, learn to love again, and please take care of each other.

© 9/28/00

2001 Rosalyne Blumenstein MSW
Director, Gender Identity Project LGCSC
Evening Clinician, Housing Works Inc.
Member: 4 years, Prevention Planning Group NYCDOH
Member: 1 year, Mental Health Rehabilitation Alcoholism Services
Member: LGBT NYPD Police Council
Member: LGBT Liaison to Manhattan Borough President C Virginia Fields

Eleven years ago a Gender Project was formed within the Lesbian and Gay Community Service Center.

The strategy behind the inception of this project was multi-faceted:

1. to meet the needs of gender different, transgender, and transexual people in crisis
2. to share information and to create visibility
3. to community organize across difference focusing specifically around class, race, gender status and sexual orientation
4. and to restructure an archaic system

- The desire of the project was to enhance social functioning. The desire was to legitimize and support these individuals' identities.

At the time the focus was completely about healing, the project had no idea we would gather together here in front of the city council to testify for equal opportunities.

'Gender' 'Gender' 'Gender'
Ask any progressive scholar their opinion about gender and identity and they'll explain that on some level gender is fluid and complex.

But within this city, many gender fluid, complex, gender different, transgender, and transexual people, are consistently denied housing opportunities, denied access to substance abuse treatment, denied medical care, denied beds, denied the opportunity to flip hamburgers, clean restrooms or just get a job simply because of their gender expression, identity or presentation.

I have experienced tremendous frustration around the homelessness and violence that my clients and my communities have to put up with. You see the way the system works and the way in which the laws are written, discriminatory case managers, intake workers, line workers, landlords, supervisors and hiring staff can make it so difficult that transgender, gender different and transexual people often give up.

Now, if I look back, there has been incredible growth within the communities as well.
Community members have taken this work to new and exciting heights.
The lesbian and gay communities have owned their connection with the bisexual and transgender communities.
Leaders within the transgender communities have expanded this work and have taken the responsibility of organizing for political change.
And the most oppressed within the gender different, transgender, transexual communities have been finding their voice and using that voice to take care of themselves and others.

This amazing work is happening within communities that have no protections. These are amazing individuals, people within the grips of despair, homelessness, people living with HIV/AIDS or dealing with addictions, people dealing with hostility, intolerance, and violence on a daily basis. In spite of all this people are able to grow, excel, nurture and support one another, community organize across difference, build and reconstruct institutions, understand the law and work with community leaders in an attempt to challenge this oppression.

In addition, our communities are not only seeking to change the law to protect only ourselves, we seek to protect all citizens, not only those that are transgender or transexual identified. But to enlarge the description of gender will ultimately challenge sexism, lookism, homophobia, biphobia, transphobia, and racism as well.

Through my work as a director of a gender program, a social worker, a community organizer, a clinician, and as a woman with a transexual history I've the opportunity to work with many other social workers, clinicians, doctors, lawyers, political figures, community organizers around gender/transgender education and discrimination. But we can only accomplish so much without laws that make people accountable for their personal discriminations, their personal ignorance and their personal hostility to the complexities and fluidity of gender within our society.

Past and presently our social order threatens these individuals that are gender different looking, transgender or transexual identified.

Through the brilliance of NYAGRA, MGN, STAR, Housing Works, GIP, PHP, IKQNY, AVP, Harlem United, ALP, and so many community activists that have been struggling for this moment since 1969, as well as the tireless work of the honorable council members, this bias will now be legally confronted.
It is time to expand the social agenda
It is time to expand civil rights and liberties for all
It is time to redistribute this power and its resources so that all may benefit.
It is now time to challenge and hopefully stop gender-based discrimination by using the appropriate definition of gender.

I'm a social worker, so why do I always feel like I'm fighting a war.
The war is with this archaic system, folks.

This city is a melting pot.

This state is full of vibrant hues.

But to paraphrase a colleague Lynn Walker, "We are discriminated against because of the shape of our skin."

We must protect every one with a law that gives us all equal opportunity no matter what we look like or how we are perceived and then stereotyped.

I ask you, but if necessary, I beg you to change the explanation of gender to include all.

****

A morning in the life of a Gender Project Administrator

It's 8 a.m. There's an eighteen-year-old transgender woman sleeping in front of the building. She'd rather sleep there than in the men's shelter system where she is constantly raped, verbally abused and physically harassed by other clients, as well as workers, within the shelter system. She tells me her dreams of being Miss America, of having a husband, of adopting a child, of working, of living, of thriving. Little does she know, and dare I tell her, that the odds are against her ever experiencing these dreams.

It's 9:15 a.m.. This is one of many calls from some youth facility stating that they do not want to house gender different, gender questioning, transgender, pre-op, non-op youth within their facility. Although some have attempted to make space, few institutions assist our youth successfully. These young citizens go back to the streets and sit in front of the center, hoping to connect with a face, a friendly face, a face that won't objectify them, sensationalize them, de-legitimize them or dehumanize them. The odds are against them.

It's 9:30 a.m.. A man of trans experience is calling out of breath, inconsolable, he's screaming he's been 'Outed' at work, harassed and humiliated in the lunch room and his foreman is trying to get him off his work detail.

It's 10:30 a.m. I get a call asking to assist a civil service worker, a civil service worker who has worked eighteen years for this city. How do I help this person transition successfully when their health insurance will not cover any of their medical needs? When their supervisor is trying to get them fired. When their spouse of three years can use this to take away their kids

307

and throw them out of the house. When their gender presentation is used against them to deny them other housing opportunities.

It's 11a.m. I go to the Internet and read this:

A young woman in leather coat, jeans and short hair is stalked, verbally harassed, and then physically assaulted for looking "too butch."

A young student at a western university is beaten senseless by two assailants who target him in part because he is blond, slight and gentle.

A child in the boys locker room is humiliated and then beaten by older boys who accuse him of being "faggy" and "a sissy."

Again, the war is with this archaic system. The system must change!
© 2001

Note:

So much has changed since I wrote these speeches. And so much hasn't. Many gay dominated institutions have embraced LGBT as a new way to market their movement, organization, the informal mission. But LGBT stands under the heading of 'GAY' and that is not what these populations consist of. I am grateful that things are changing but I am so disappointed concerning the direction and exclusion of what B and T truly represent. When I first began this work there was very little organizing going on in NYC for T specific issues. Now there are so many brilliant leaders. I wish them all the luck, energy, support, and my prayers are with them that they get through to the hierarchy 'a day at a time.'

Paper

The Construction, Deconstruction, and Reconstruction
of Gender Identity Mergers
and the Power of Language

A delicate meta-narrative

By Rosalyne Blumenstein CSW
© Copyright 11/2000. All Rights Reserved
RMBLUMENSTEIN@aol.com

Enjoy these four segments of this project from my heart to yours ...

What is the underlying truth about the correlation between language usage
and internal/external freedom? Is there any? So, when one looks at the
socialization of people deconstructing and reconstructing gender identity,
sexual orientation, and sexual fluidity, does language have the power to
impinge upon the individual's ability 'To Be?'
I claim myself not a linguist:
You know, the kind of scholar who discovers and describes the rules that
govern individual language (Farb, p.4)! However, within my social working
hat, my intuitive ear muffs, my streetwise scarf, my deviant denim, my soul
searching turtleneck, my out-reaching gloves, my activist under garments,
and my grounded in humility, thigh high boots, I shall confront the
"queerest of queer" language[1]. I will construct, deconstruct, and reconstruct
the emotions behind the linguistics so that the representation will be
revolutionized.

Brief history
The power of Language

Employing the 'King's English,' as well as a mixture of slang and
informalized linguistics, I evaluated the history and present oppressive or
supportive language centering on the transgender experience within
medicine, the news, the political arena, the media, as well as within the more
organized queer movement.

For this section of this appendix I compiled and revised four sections from
my master's thesis. In addition, this investigation will drape around the neck
of narrative expression. Let us not choke on the word 'transgender,' but

309

share it in a way that is empowering to all. Because of our diet constraints we will consume only a portion at this time.

Many people in the United States have heard, or at some point, utilized the verse 'sticks and stones may break my bones but names will never harm me.' Some feel this world-renowned verse decreases the pain that particular language presents. However, do labels and language empower or oppress an individual? Or is it the individual empowering or oppressing themselves, with language being secondary?

How does language impinge upon individuals who are not receiving encouraging information with regards to who and what they are?

At different points of their existence, people of transgender experience (anywhere on the continuum) have been verbally terrorized via religious entities, academia, peers, families, friends, even strangers on the street, by language that was/is torturous. Therefore, is this verse 'sticks and stones' actually propaganda? Does language have power? Or are these particular groups experiencing pain via this torturous language, just an addition to their already complex pathology?

Let's look at language, disparaging language, in most instances extremely hurtful and hateful language:

> **Bitch, Mockey, Kike, Nigger, Spick, Dago, Ginny, Crip, Freak, Cunt, Homo, Fag, Bull-Dagger, Dyke, Sick, Pervert, Ho, Lowlife, Ruskie, Retard, Moron, Dick, Scumbag, Cracker, Jew, Chink, Gook, Gimp ...**

In some cases these discriminatory wounding lexis are also utilized to empower the individual, depending on context, depending on tone, and depending on who is pronouncing the slur.

Yes, the power of language is as intense as Mayo Angelou's thought process [2]. She knows 'why the caged bird sings,' but do we?
So why does our society attempt to hide that pain, that grief, that hate, that celebration, the life and death of words by stating they are not as piercing as an ice pick to the skull? If Maya's words can take us to new and different heights within our psyche, if Bibles turn many of our lives around, if a powerful speech renders some of us to tears or laughter, how can words not be viewed as armory?

So can one safely assert that language is sometimes used as weapons or as a means to keep others insurgent?

Does language have the power to mobilize or oppress components of the transgender communities?
Pauline Park, a transgendered leader and the head of New York Association of Gender Rights Advocacy (NYAGRA,, a New York Statewide organization dedicated to the rights of transgender, gender variant/gender different people) [3], asserts; that given the profound transphobia and the various diagnosis around gender fluidity, or gender construction/reconstruction, these groups of people are one of the most marginalized populations. The pervasive discrimination, harassment, abuse and violence ,in addition to the utilization of oppressive language, plays a role in keeping a component of these 'queer' communities insurrectionary [4].

The heart of my paper examined the word "transgender," focusing on professional practice, ethnography and ethno-linguistics. What I attempted to prove (most of it subjective, but valued and justified) is that the word "transgender" is defined, deconstructed and reconstructed in ways that are disempowering, problematic, and delegitimizing within many areas of academic, medical, and scientific practice.

Some unfavorable History
Gender Fluidity/Gender Change/Transexuality

> *The range of trans-identity is confusing. And the history is confusing. Although people have challenged gender constraints since mythology, classical history, the Renaissance era, we are not sure if these issues we're discussing were about 'change of sex,' 'change of dress,' or 'change of societal attitude.' What we are sure of is that there is a negative connotation connected to the identity.*
>
> *In Greek mythology, the Venus Castina was sensitive to the "feminine souls locked up in male bodies (Green p.13)." Sex changes were discussed not from a desirable perspective, but as a form of punishment. "For example, Tiresias, a Theban soothsayer, is reported to have been walking on Mt. Cyllene when he came upon two snakes coupling. He killed the female and for this act was punished and changed into a woman (Green p.13)." Among the histories of Roman Emperors there was report of change of sex execution. Emperor Nero was one of the people who demanded his soldiers to change the sex of a slave and then married the slave (Green p.15).*

The Umbrella
come rain or come shine
Transgender, who classifies?

1} Fundamental Terms
Gender identity and sexual identity are independent of each other. **Transgender** is utilized as an umbrella term encompassing many gender and sexual identities. These identities challenge on some core level society's belief around what is *appropriately* male and what is *appropriately* female. In this sense some believe that deviant gender and sexual identity are one and the same. This is due to lack of clarity around what it is 'to be' when there is no legitimate, supportive language to describe someone's experience. Therefore **transgender** is used to describe those that deconstruct or reconstruct what it is to be in a deviant sexual or gender identity. **Transgender** is now used medically, politically and socially to categorize specific people. But who gets to choose how to define their deviant identity label, or is it a choice?

An effeminate gay man can be perfectly comfortable with his gayness and his manhood. But an effeminate gay man might also identify as someone on the transgender continuum. His sexual identity, or orientation, is now recognized as 'normal,' and his gender is identified as the norm if he chooses to identify as male. However, if he indicates that he falls somewhere on the transgender continuum, his gender identity is diagnosed as deviant, creating a negative correlation with his sexual identity.

Why is his sexual orientation seen as normal and fluid (read Alfred Kinsey, Kinsey scale) but gender presentation is constricted, employing gender specific societal rulings?

Because of the political climate, and where queer people are within their own internalized self-acceptance, many gay men, even those who do drag or identify themselves as drag queens, do not identify as transgender, although they may be perceived to fall somewhere on this continuum.

Within the hierarchy of oppression, transgender is on the bottom. For instance, why would a gay white man identify as transgender when he can claim some false privilege just by being male and being white? And why would an African-American man identify as gay when he can own some false privilege by identifying his sexual practices as men who have sex with men - MSM[5].

Oppression/language/power! The same might be true for women who identify as lesbian, butch, gender ambiguous, femme, gender-fucked and/or gender fluid.

When one speaks about 'the transgender experience' one should always focus on inner and/or peripheral gender identity, sex, sex-role, and gender exploration. Transgender in itself is not used as a self-identity for many along this continuum.

"A person may express any variation of all of these identities, and that is where it gets confusing." (Nangeroni, GenderTalk)[6]

"Gender identity is more fluid then our society identifies. To discourage the free expression of identity is to impose a damaging burden of conformity." (Nangeroni)

The challenges that sexually insurgent groups face on a daily basis can be devastating to the homeostasis of that individual.

If someone is identified at birth as **female**, but sees his body, mind, and/or spirit as **male** in all respects, their sex/gender identity is **male**. Such a person may consider himself an (FTM) transexual, a male, a male of transexual experience, a cross-gendered person, etc. Now, in our society, we only have two ways of identifying sex. But you can see just from this example how fluid and/or complex sex/gender identity can be if we legitimize language that people use to self-identify.

The Transgender umbrella term encompasses this and much more. Within a linear equation some identities that fall under the umbrella are, but are not limited to …????(questioning), drag queen, Cross dresser, butch, feMALE, feminine man, female to male, male, FTM, MTM, New Woman, MTF, FTF, cross gender, of transexual experience, Butch queen, female, transgenderist, queen, TS, femme queen, queen, gender fucked, bi-gender, trannie fag, non-op, TV, transexual, pre-Op, male to female, drag king, post-op, new man, TG, phallic woman, masculine, intersex, female, ????. (NYC GENDER IDENTITY PROJECT, TERMINOLOGY).

One can see how many identities are listed here in addition to male and female.

Although some social workers, clinicians, health care providers, scientists, city, church and state might question the legitimacy or validity of these identities, these are identities of many constituents within the queer and non-queer identified arenas within society.

GENDER IDENTITY
How you see yourself socially (remember - gender is a division of appearance and behavior): *Man, woman, feminine, masculine, or a combination of (Nangeroni).* One may have a penis and feminine secondary sexual characteristics and relate socially as how we identify how women relate in our society, whatever that means (see how complex this is to try to explain?). One may have a vagina and masculine secondary sexual characteristics and interact socially as a man. Some might prefer to be fluid, relating sometimes as a man and sometimes as a woman. Others might not identify as either, relating androgynously. As an alternative to a bipolar gender system, some opt for transgender as a way to identify their challenging gender identity and presentation.

Transgender, as an idiom, has been utilized by the organized queer communities for the past ten years. It is a term that dates back to Virginia Prince who used transgenderist to identify herself [7]. The word transgender has roots within the more powerful academic transgender activists/academicians communities. Social work practitioners working within the field of HIV/AIDS, substance use, grass roots public health officers, progressive community based organizations, our own HBIGDA, as well as harm-reduction treatment programs, have been using the word "transgender" as a label for all persons who are gender different. This is problematic to some who fall within the continuum. Some have stated that "transgender" as an identity is a diagnosis or a discriminatory label, which negates their identity[8]. To others it is quite empowering. To date there is no universal definition of this word, even though people think they know what it means. It is still within an interpretation stage, which to many can, again, be problematic and emotionally disruptive.

Medical Constructs and the power of Language

I would like to make a few significant points in this section that might make some of you defensive. Please read the section, hear me out, don't take the section personally, and try to understand how our language usage has influenced the communities, the populations that we serve.

The medical/psychological profession employs language to diagnose, define and 'otherize' the 'transgender experience,' which to some extent dehumanizes, desexualizes, and sets up precedence for lack of opportunities to engage self-love, take delivery of that love, and be present with love.

On the other hand, one can only be grateful to these brilliant individuals for their yearning to specialize and create ways in which to realign genitalia to correspond with primary and secondary sexual characteristics of those 'transexual' identified folks who experienced incongruence in these areas. For whatever reason surgeons came up with these techniques around genital reconstructing or endocrinological hormone-based realignments, I am personally and professionally grateful.

Let's begin by confronting the linguistics of the medical communities with a message from Cheryl Chase, Executive Director of the Intersex Society of North America (ISNA) [9].

> *I was born with ambiguous genitals. A doctor specializing in intersexuality deliberated for three days - sedating my mother each time she asked what was wrong with her baby - before concluding that I was male, with a micropenis, complete hypospadias, undescended testes, and a strange extra opening behind the urethra ... When I was a year and half old my parents consulted a different set of experts who admitted me to a hospital for 'sex determination' ... Doctors told my parents that a thorough medical investigation would be necessary to determine (in the first sense of that word) what my 'true sex' was. They judged my genital appendage to be inadequate as a penis, too short to mark masculine status effectively or to penetrate females. As a female, however, I would be penetrable and potentially fertile. My anatomy having been relabeled as vagina, urethra, labia and outsized clitoris, my sex was determined (in the second sense) by amputating my genital appendage (Chase 1998: 193 Valentine 2000:168 [10]).*

315

Now let's look at what some of the national TG/TS activists assert:

In 1996 the newly founded GenderPac (a National Organization dedicated to Racial and Gender Equality) [11] picketed in front of the offices of the American Psychiatric Association (APA). The protesters were accusing the APA as being afflicted with "Gender-PathoPhilia," defined as an "unnatural need or desire to pathologize any transgender behavior that makes you feel uncomfortable."

Very few within the medical community offer advanced techniques around genital surgical procedures*. However, this extremely expensive - and not just financially, psychologically – and systematically available Sex Reassignment Surgery, or GRS[12] procedure, is not enough. Although surgical procedures are available, we need to look at the language surrounding these surgeries, as well as how we identify the issues and support, empower or devalue the trans-person's experience and/or the identity.

Transgender is now practical shorthand in describing non-normative genders (Valentine, HBIGDA, DOH, CDC, PPG, GWG et al.) [13].

The word, the umbrella, the continuum labeled - transgender, be it noun or adjective, is now utilized within Harry Benjamin International Gender Dysphoria Association (HBIGDA) as a name instead of some of the past medical terminology.

This shows

Growth within the medical communities to listen to, adhere to, and/or acknowledge the power of the communities that came up with the term

or

How people tend to follow the majority, the power, or are forced to do things differently

or

The true complexity of gender and sex challenges us so that we are looking for another way to box people in

or

The medical/psychological establishment (those who are willing to participate in this discussion) is acknowledging sociolinguistics, psycholinguistics, the ethnography of speaking, the sociology of language and allowing communities to provide a new way to view language (Farb, p.4).

*Very seldom covered under any health insurance policy, non refundable non reimbursable, in many states not recognized or legitimized.

We know that the specialists who work with 'transgender' people include, but are not limited to, endocrinologists, psychiatrists, psychologists, social workers, surgeons, sex therapists et al. Transexuality, Gender Dysphoria,

Gender Identity Disorder, are terms with medical origins and meanings (Valentine p.150). Many from the transgender communities use these descriptives and many do not.

Has activism or progressive thinking within the trans-communities changed the way in which the medical communities identify, acknowledge, support, or legitimate the experience?

I'm not so sure.

Valentine, in his dissertation, argues that the transferring of linguistics around the trans experience is because health care professionals are increasingly having to respond to the demands of transgender-identified activists, and the new language that has emerged over the past decade, not just the utilization of the word transexual and the degree in which a person identifies with their discomfort (Valentine p. 150) [14].

> *Within the medical communities, let us look at a few ways in which the language is utilized and contest why this language is problematic.*

Medical usage:

Transexualism – within a 1992 undergraduate abnormal psychology book it states that these people, mostly males, believe that they truly belong to the opposite sex (Bootzin, p.346) [15].

1. MTF - Male to female
2. FTM - Female to male
3. Male transexuals - male to female, are men who have had sex reassignment surgery to **BECOME** female
4. Female transexuals - female to male, are females who have had surgical and/or hormonal reassignment to **BECOME** male.

Contesting the language

When we use a tool to identify a person as MTF (male to female) or FTM (female to male), we are not giving that person the opportunity "to be," be in their skin, be who they are. Female to Male on some level is never allowing that person to be male and vice versa. Although many in the communities utilize these acronyms, it is usually the newly transitioned person that accepts this acronym as their identity.

When the literature speaks about a male transexual (and vice versa), it is referring to someone who was birth identified as male and has gone through treatment and surgery to self-identify as female. If the medical community cites the identity this way it has ultimately a negative effect on the person's sense of self. Even with the amazing technological procedures, the way in which this person is engaged is injurious.

When one identifies another's experience only as a belief and not a reality, our legitimate perception of who they are is questioned. There is not enough information scientifically or biologically to truly state that genitalia or chromosomes are the precise way to identify someone's sex. These are merely markers to which a social meaning is attached (Davis, C. 2001). Also, when you take into account that you are sexing (stating someone's assigned sex) a definition of a transexual, you see there is no true legitimacy around the person's identified sex.

The medical community and/or, the gay community, or society does not identify gay people as straight to gay (STG) or hetero to homo (HTH) or as healthy to sick (HTS) or as young to old (YTO) or as insured to noninsured (ITN). We are not allowing the person to live in their reality, medically, psychologically, spiritually or legally for that matter. In New York State, when one has sex or gender realignment surgery, one's sex is removed from the revised birth certificate. This is not supportive to identity on many levels.

Examples of problematic language
Within the Office of AIDS Research (OAR) a response to a Request for Proposal (RFP) went out to the Center for Disease Control (CDC) to conduct an "Interventional Epidemiological Study." (I have worked with this office in the past around language attempting to move them to a place that supports the trans-person's identity) [16]. Within the OAR's concept paper to the CDC it explains the Ball scene and its transgender participants[9]. The concept paper identifies fem-queens, transgender women, non-op or pre-op transexual women as "men who have sex with men," "men banding together to compete for prize money," "surgical gender," and "minority transgender men" (Torian, 2000, OAR Proposal). Although Torian is willing to confront the CDC with this provocative concept paper, the utilization of language around the trans-identity is awkward, disempowering, transphobic and, to some within the ball scene, hateful, delegitimizing and discriminatory [17].

Politics and the Power of Language
I have entered this section because I feel it relevant for you to understand how language is exploited within the lesbian, gay, bisexual, transgender (LGBT) political discourse. Language can be supportive, problematic or oppressive within this discourse depending on how one uses and explains LGBT issues within the political circle. I discuss these political communities because these are the groups of people that many along the transgender continuum have utilized and/or sought solace within at some point in their

lives. I share sections of local and state politics along with a mention of the West Coast to give you an idea of what is happening within a progressive LGBT agenda.

Hillary Rodham Clinton (New York State senator) was recently interviewed by Lesbian/Gay/New York (LGNY, a local gay identified paper) [18].

Let's play a game! What's missing?

{Hint: there are identities missing within this newspaper's title. Guess what they are?}

Here is the excerpt ...

The Journey Pauses in Brooklyn

"One of the challenges that the gay community faces today as we try to get a hate crimes bill passed, and the employment nondiscrimination act, is a challenge from other members of our community, transgender people and people with gender variations, pushing to try to make some of the language in these proposals more inclusive ..." The interviewer went on to ask Hillary... "One of the things the transgender community points to is that on hate crimes in New York State, the entire coalition for hate crimes held out to have gays and lesbians included in it.(LGNY Sept. 2000)

The trans communities are asking to be included within this hate crimes bill by utilizing language that states 'perceived gender, gender identity and expression [19]'."

Hillary replied, "No one who's a leader within the gay and lesbian community has asked me to do that." (LGNY Sept. 2000).

Language is influential within the political arena and the political arena utilizes this language to support and protect its constituents.

Within this excerpt there are points of interest to note.

Hillary employs the "T" word. She publicly made a statement including the word 'transgender.' Today we have politicians using the "T" word in the context of rights, human rights, legislation, discrimination, hate crimes, and this is groundbreaking. This is a monumental year. The language being utilized surrounding queer issues is shifting. This indicates a societal alteration. However, does Hillary know what transgender means? Has Hillary been educated by her advisors around the continuum of gender different identities? Or is the "T" the most outlandish subdivision of LGBT whereas Hillary might identify the "T" as those gays and lesbians that cross the gender boundaries and that is all?

Hillary states that the leaders of the gay and lesbian movement haven't advised her to wait to first change the language to include 'gender identity and expression' before this law is pushed any further. LGNY also uses language within this article stating "... the gay community faces ..." and

319

then goes on to say "... transgender people are ..." under the heading of 'the gay community,' which to many would assert that transgender is a subheading of the gay community.

The politics of language!

Gay is not the umbrella term for LGBT peoples, yet that is how the leading local, state and national politicians are taught via the 'Gay Agenda.'

LGNY News – Gender Activists Push Issues Center Stage

The New York Association for Gender Rights Advocacy (NYAGRA. See Appendix A and also Pauline Park under brief Hx) "... Urged the Hate Crimes Coalition, made up of a wide array of groups statewide, to add language that would explicitly protect individuals victimized because of their gender expression ... Some law enforcement professionals, particularly the district attorneys of Brooklyn and Westchester, were also advising the coalition that the existing language would suffice to protect transgendered crime victims (LGNY August 2000)."

Within this statement one can't help but think about the politics around the wording transgender and what it means to the district attorney's office in Westchester and Brooklyn. Do they get the concept around transgender? Again, who has educated them around gender different issues? How is transgender interpreted within current events and the political field?

LGNY went on to report ...

The controversy over this brings much surprise to the larger queer communities that "gender activists have managed to move key issues of concern far closer to center stage of queer politics, on a city, state and national level, than anyone might have imagined just a couple of years ago." (LGNY August 2000)

LGNY discusses a grant awarded to the New York Association of Gender Rights Advocacy (NYAGRA), a $10,0000 Capacity Building Grant. NYAGRA has assumed a more prominent public role in recent months. On June 5, the group led a press conference on the steps of city hall to announce introduction of an amendment to the city's human rights ordinance that will add protections against discrimination based on "gender identity and expression." The amendment, which already has the support of 25 of the council's 51 members in NYC, would be the first major change in the human rights ordinance since sexual orientation was added in 1996. (LGNY June 2000)

Here we view a few things happening.

LGNY feels that $10,000 is newsworthy because it is a grant to a transgender-specific statewide advocacy group. This can be considered positive or negative depending upon how one examines the glass, empty or full?

Negative: *a small amount of money is allotted to a trans organization. This gay paper is so impressed that anyone would give some money to 'transgenders' that it becomes newsworthy.*

Positive: *LGNY is utilizing space within their newspaper because they are so delighted that money was finally being allocated to these important issues that they want to start a domino effect around funding by publicizing this.*

Now, let's read from the NY Blade, another gay-identified current events newspaper.

A Call for Inclusion

In an article within the New York Blade, Thom McGeveran (a writer who has written a lot about transgender issues in the past two years) quotes an extremely bright, talented and attractive social worker ...

In the wake of a recent killing of an African-American woman who was transgendered Blumenstein states, focusing on how the murderer should be tried, "Why wasn't there language that would protect all people within the Hate Crimes Bill that was finally introduced?" Blumenstein goes on to say, "On some level this is the best and worst of times, because it's finally come to a point that when a person of transgender experience is murdered it is newsworthy. But people are still being murdered and it is because of their gender presentation or others' perception about their gender and not about their sexual orientation." (NY Blade, July 2000)

Let's have fun with some mind-reads around News and Politics within the LGbt movement.

Empire State Pride Agenda (ESPA) produced a 2000 Statewide Voter Guide [20]. Nowhere in this guide does it discuss the transgender experience. It also doesn't look at how voting for different politicians would affect people along the transgender continuum. The guide looks at

1. Hate Crimes Law for Lesbian/Gay (LG) peoples

2. Sodomy Law

3. The Sexual Orientation Non-Discrimination Act (SONDA)

4. The Dignity for all Students Act (DASA). The Dignity for all Students Act, **All Students**, which many trans-leaders have fought and fought to finally be included in this legislation. However, it is stated within ESPA's pamphlet **"the DASA will protect students from harassment, including HOMOPHOBIC harassment within Public Schools** (ESPA, 2000). There is nothing stated around transphobia or transphobic harassment.

Let's go west within the United States for a second

321

California Alliance for Pride and Equality (CALCAPE) [21]
CALCAPE avows that it is a nonprofit, grass-roots-based organization solely devoted to ensuring the dignity, safety, equality and civil rights of all lesbians, gay, bisexual and transgender Californians.
On its website it discusses what is at stake within this election.

1. It discusses anti-GAY Laws
2. FBI data shows anti-gay hate crimes around gay, lesbian and bisexual ranking third in reported hate crimes (when did bisexuals become gay)?
3. *The 'Don't Ask, Don't Tell' policy that challenges gays and lesbians to serve openly in the military.*
4. *Nothing is discussed around trans-inclusion except for the "T" at the beginning of the website.*

The National Gay and Lesbian Taskforce produced a "What's At Stake" journal for the Gay, Lesbian, Bisexual and Transgender Community in the 2000 Presidential Elections[22].
1. *On the very first page it discusses same-sex marriage, relationships and families but utilizes LGBT as if all LGBT relationships were same sex ones.*
2. *It discusses LGB people in the military.*
3. *It discusses only sexual orientation discrimination.*
4. *It discusses equal benefits for same-sex partners.*

To be fair: The voice of ESPA's winter agenda ...
1. *Under Legislative and Policy Agenda, Trans was listed under Human Rights.*
2. *Under Lesbian and Gay Families, Trans was listed under equal parenting rights.*
3. *Under the initial **LG** Policy Agenda, ESPA discusses the safety of lesbian and gay students, but the,n under Human Rights ESPA states that they promote and are attempting to secure legislation for LGBT students ... **Is this confusing????***

To take this discussion to another level let's center, for a moment, on a motivational speaker named Samuel Betances (a Latino-identified educator) and his discussion within his diversity curriculum "Harness the Rainbow" [20]*.*

At one point in his motivational speech Betances asserts:
"I grew up Latino with mixed blood, where one part of my family was light and had straight hair and the other part of my family had tight, nappy hair. One day, we were entertaining guests and we kept my darker skinned, nappy

haired grandmother in the kitchen while the lighter skinned, straighter haired grandmother came to greet the guests." (Harness the Rainbow, 1994)

The analogy;

Within most of these articles from LGNY and the NY Blade lesbian and gay leaders were astonished to see that gender (meaning transgender) activists had the audacity to come out from the kitchen and challenge the dinner discussion. My assumption is that they were hoping not to have to deal with their own homo and transphobia by keeping their gender different, gender challenged, gender dysphoric, brothers, sisters, heshes, hirs, s/hes and those of transexual experience, silent and hidden (Blumenstein, 1999, Feinberg, 1996, Valentine 2000, Wilchins, 1999 et al.).

Towards the end of Betances' training he discusses celebrating the richness of his skin and the power of his hair texture. These physical characteristics assist him in recognizing his amazing ancestry, i.e. self-acceptance.

I don't think that politically, socially, and/or psychologically the lesbian and gay movement celebrates all of its constituents. I come to this hypothesis from following the political discourse. The news reported within LGNY, the NY Blade, ESPA, and the National Lesbian and Gay Task Force assisted me with this assumption. If transgender identities were included in this "a-gender" agenda, wouldn't the names of these papers be different? Wouldn't Hillary understand the importance of inclusion within the new legislation? Wouldn't lesbians and gays truly want to experience sitting down to dinner, all together?

So here we have some of the political linguistic issues and concerns via local newspapers, a statewide political assemblage, and a national gay and lesbian organization. Our society is beginning to recognize transgender as more than a sensationalistic ideation of 'man into woman or woman into man.'

However

The power of language is such that within the political discourse one cannot be sure about what transgender really means, but one can be sure about how our political leaders are being educated.

Does transgender have the same political meaning to Hillary Clinton as it does to Thom Duane, Out/Gay state senator in Albany?

Does transgender have the same meaning to Pauline Park (NYAGRA), to writer Thom McGeveren (NY Blade) or Paul Shlindler (LGNY), or to this author Rosalyne Blumenstein (GIP, Housing Works Inc.)?

The complexities surrounding these communities, the lack of power around their ownership of the language and definitions, is alarming! And to see, hear and read from the leaders within the queer political arena sometimes including **T** and **B** and many times not explaining the identities, making them a subheading of an orientation that might have nothing to do with *who they are or who they love, not giving these matters space, and never prioritizing the issues, is disconcerting.*

Simply throwing it in to fulfill the sandwich (LGBT) doesn't work!

So as one can read:
A trans person's experience following the reaction to language is far more complex than one might at first think, with all people attempting to come to terms with the idea of fluidity around gender identity and presentation. Awareness of the variations of identity, along with acceptance of those differences, will reduce the extent to which one on the trans continuum will feel disenfranchised or stigmatized by our system. From this, positive interactions and individual resolution can be promoted.
Although we've made great strides medically and psychologically, linguistically there is work to be done on so many levels in order to support the person who is 'living' or 'acknowledging' their trans-experience.

Notes
1
Carrie Davis, GIP counselor (NYC) utilized the expression "the queerest of the queer" on a video I directed and co-edited called "Gender Variance Perception, Yours, Mine, Ours." Carrie utilized this expression to identify people of transgender experience within the LGBT movement 10/99.
2
Maya Angelou is a famous poet who looks at oppression and stigma, light, reflection, and hope.
3
I was involved with NYAGRA at the very beginning. However, the key leaders of this were Carrie Davis, David Valentine, Paisely Currah, Donna Cartwright, Melissa Sklarz, Pauline Park, et al. in New York City. Pauline Park Ph.D., with Paisely Currah had utilized their expertise in political science within the local and state political arena. Pauline used to teach political science and Paisely is still a professor. Together, with the support of this amazing group, they have been instrumental in getting key players within the political arena involved as much as possible to look, or at least listen to, 'transgender oppression.'
4
I use the word 'queer' here to identify those within the activist communities, those within social services, and those within the organized movement that identify as LGBT S/M etc. However, if you ask some older gays and

lesbians what they might think of the word queer, they might be horrified by the use of that language. Language changes and evolves constantly. Meanings change and evolve. But the "power" of the language still has great impact depending on what the words bring up internally.

5

MSM is used as a transmission category identifying men who have sex with men but are looking at men who do not identify as gay. Men who have sex with men include, but are not limited to, men in prison and African-American or Latino men who do not identify with the label gay. Within the New York State Department of Health (NYSDOH) and the New York City Prevention Planning Group et al., MSM is used as a 'target population' which is a priority setting tool within the initiation of the HIV prevention community planning process.

6

Nancy Nangeroni used to be the Executive Director of the Internation Federation for Gender Education (IFGE)

7

Virginia Prince has been known for her work within the TV/cross dressing communities since the early 1960s. Virginia identifies herself as a transgenderist who has not used medical or surgical interventions to live her life as the woman she identifies as. She is one of the first public trasngenderists who began this gender political movement.

8

Many people along the "T" continuum do not identify as transgender, e.g. people of transexual experience, drag queens who identify as gay men, femme queens who are not involved with the more political movement et al.

9

Cheryl Chase is the founder and Executive Director of the Intersex Society of North America. As part of the project of undermining the Western epistemology of sex and gender, she is at present working with historian Alice Dreger on a book that juxtaposes medical narratives of hermaphrodites with their personal narratives.

10

Removal of the clitoris is the removal of an opportunity to experience orgasm. Not only language is a grave concern here ...

11

The Transexual Menace was a group headed by Riki Anne Wilchins (current Executive Director of GenderPac). Riki would show up with a group to challenge whatever was going on around trans issues that were oppressive, discriminatory, hateful and archaic. Riki later founded GenderPac to first challenge oppressive issues of the trans identity and now GPAC's mission is focused around 'gender' issues and concerns on a national level.

12

Sex reassignment, as it has been called, identifies the doctor or the medical practitioner or the surgeon as the one with the power to reassign the patient. Gender realignment surgery takes that power away from the medical professional and puts it in a more progressive context.

13

Not a full explanation of these institutions or groups but here is short statement and what the acronyms stand for.

HBIGDA – Harry Benjamin International Gender Dysphoria Association (of which I am a member), the creator of guidelines for treating people with GID.

DOH – Department of Health under the guidance of the mayor's office and the health commissioner.

CDC – Center for Disease Control out of Atlanta, creates the money for studies, research, prevention and education ...

PPG - Prevention Planning Group (on which I have served four years). Community members get voted in to serve with the PPG and DOH to collaborate around figuring out HIV prevention and education priorities. The PPG and DOH attempt to concur on a yearly basis on a cooperative agreement that is sent to the CDC for the next year's funding.

GWG - Gender Working Groups, of which there are two currently in NYC (I am a member of both). They are the adult **GWG** that meets at Columbia Presbyterian Hospital and the **GWG** for Youth, which meets at Callen Louder Center, St Luke's Roosevelt Hospital, Mt. Sinai, and the LGCSC. This is a youth gender questioning, TG/TS focus group. Both groups are for medical professionals, psychologists, psychiatrists, surgeons et al. working with these populations.

14

Excerpt from The Transexual Phenomenon 1966

Type 1 Transvestite Pseudo Masculine

Type II TV Fetishistic Masculine

Type III TV True Masculine (but with less conviction)

Type IV Transexual No Surgical Undecided. Wavering
Between TV and TS

Type V True Transexual Moderate Intensity Feminine.
("Trapped in a male body")

15

First, let's look at this language. When the Abnormal Psych book states that this is mostly in males, what they are talking about are people who identify as female. Their utilization of language is extremely oppressive. In addition to this there are a lot more men of TS/TG experience out and visible than there were in 1992. "Men" in our society are not judged or objectified as

327

women are. Therefore, men who were born identified as women have an easier time passing through society. Therefore, they are not coming "Out" and being visible. They are just living!

16

NYC did their first needs assessment within the transgender communities focusing on HIV/AIDS. I was an integral component, along with Dr. Barbara Warren, LGCSC Director, MHSS, in making this happen. Kelly McGowan MPH, was the PI and she did an extremely thorough job. This was the first of its kind in NYC. Kelly's work was wonderful. However, there needs to be an epidemiological study so that Community Based Organizations that work with these communities have numbers to point to within answering RFPs. It is great that Torian is attempting to do this work within the DOH, however, the language is disrespectful to those within the "Ball" communities.

17

The Balls are where predominantly African-American and Latino/a communities (involved with this scene) compete for prizes, trophies and money. The Balls have a culture identified as a 'house,' where people participate against other houses. A 'house' consists of a mother and father and their children. The mother and father train their children to compete within the Balls. Some of the categories within a Ball consist of, but are not limited to, face, body, movement, realness, best corporate look, etc. Gender is skewed within the houses and there are femme queens and drag kings and butch lesbians and fem gay men involved within the houses. The transgender study is supposed to be focusing on the 'women,' the 'femme queens,' the 'phallic women,' the non-op or pre-op transsexual women, the women of transsexual experience, as well as the men. However, Torian writes about these groupings as if they were all men.

18

One of two leading local gay papers in NYC

19

For a full explanation of inclusion within the Hate Crimes Bill see NYAGRA's website @ www.NYAGRA.org

20

'Harness the Rainbow' is used within the Office of Alcoholism and Substance Abuse Services curriculum around Ethnic, Racial and Cultural Diversity for which I am a certified trainer. It is a video that some show within a two-day CASAC accredited training program

21

B and T are often recognized as a subdivision of LGBT. CALCAPE does this on their website

22
The website address for the National Lesbian and Gay Taskforce is www.ngltf.org. NGLTF is an amazing organization that has been supportive to B and T inclusion. On their website you can find 'Transgender Equality.' However, something is still very wrong, something is missing!

Bibliography

Abramovitz, Mimi (1991). <u>Putting an end to Double Speak about Race, Class, Gender, and Poverty</u>. An annotated glossary for social workers. Journal of Social Work 36 5 September 1991 380-384

American Psychiatric Association (1994) <u>DSMIV Diagnostic Statistical Manual of Mental Disorders</u> (4th ed. Rev.) Washington, D.C.: American Psychiatric Association

Betances, Samuel (1990) <u>Harness The Rainbow</u> video component of the racial ethnic diversity curriculum OASAS: NY

Bockting, Walter, Coleman, E. (1992) <u>Gender Dysphoria interdisciplinary approaches in clinical management</u> Haworth Press: Washington DC

Bootzin, R., Acocella, J., Alloy, L. 1993 <u>Abnormal Psychology</u> current perspectives sixth edition Mcgraw Hill: NY

Cahill, S. (Fall, 2000). <u>What's at Stake for Gay, Lesbian, Bisexual, and Transgender Community in the 2000 Presidential Election</u> NLGTF Washington D.C.

CAPE California Alliance for Pride and Equality [On-Line] Available: http://www.calcape@c-esystems.com
Davis, C. (2001) discussion in supervision NYC NY

ESPA Agenda (Winter 2000) <u>The voice of the empire state pride agenda</u> NYC: NY

ESPA (Fall 2000) <u>Statewide Voter Guide</u> NYC:NY

Farb, Peter (1973) Word Play Vintage Books: New York

Feinberg, L. (1996) <u>Transgender Warriors</u> Boston: Beacon Press

France, David (May 2000) <u>The War Widow</u> New York Times Magazine (section 6)

Freire, P. (1996) <u>Pedagogy of the Oppressed</u> Continuum: New York

Green, J., Currah, P. (2000) Transgender Equality;a handbook for activists and policymakers. NLGTF Washington D.C. [On-Line] http://www.ngltf.org

Green, R., and Money, J. (1969) <u>Transexualism and sex reassignment</u> Baltimore: John Hopkin University Press

Heritage of Pride Rally (6/11/1999) <u>The Official Guide</u> RND Enterprises (Volume 6 issue 48)

Klein, Fritz MD. (2001) <u>The Journal of Bisexuality</u> Haworth Press: NY

Krafft-Ebing, R. Von (1894) <u>Psychopathia Sexualis</u> Philadelphia: F.A. Davis

LGCSC (Fall 2000) <u>Membership Committee</u> women at the Center LGCSC:NY

LGCSC (Fall 2000) <u>An E*Trade Evening</u> benefiting the LGCSC:NY

McGeveren, T. (7/21/2000) <u>A call for inclusion</u> New York Blade (p.3-5)

Nataf, Zachary 1996. Lesbians Talk Transgender London Scarlet Press

New York City Department of Health Office of AIDS research/HIV Sero-survey The NYC Ball Scene Epidemiological project Lucia Torian, PhD

Park, Pauline PhD. Issues of transgendered Asian Americans and Pacific Islanders

Priesing, Dana. (1997) <u>Transgender/Transexual Lobbying Day</u> Washington D.C.

Queens Winter Pride QLGPC Saturday 1/5/00 Astoria World Manor

Raymond, Janice 1979, The Transexual Empire, the making of the she-male Boston Mass. Beacon press

Schenden, Laurie 1999 what is Transgender Advocate, the national gay and lesbian news magazine 5/25/1999

Schlindler, P. (07/2000) Gender Activist Push issues center Stage LGNY News (p4-34)

Schlindler, P. (10/2000) The Journey Pauses in Brooklyn; Hillary Clinton talks to LGNY LGNY [On-Line] http://www.lgny.org.archives
Stryker, Susan et al. (1998) The Transgender Issue; a journal of lesbian and gay studies. Duke University Press:NY

Swan, Wallace. (1997) Gay/Lesbian/Bisexual/Transgender Public Policy Issues;a citizen's and administrator's guide to the new cultural struggle. Haworth Press:NY

Valentine, David (2000) "I Know What I am": "Transgender"; and the Space between gender and Sexuality Dissertation Anthropology NYU: NY

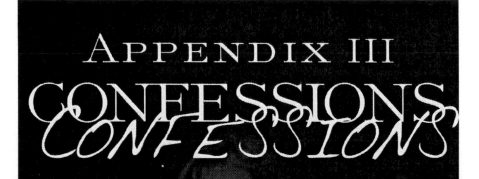

APPENDIX III
CONFESSIONS

Confessions

You hear a lot of people with 'self-esteem' assert:
... I don't care what anyone thinks of me.
... I live for the 'I' and I am OK with my own opinion.
... No matter what anyone says, I know my feelings towards myself will not be stirred!

On some deep level I truly understand that belief system. No matter what occurs in my life that makes me question or challenge my own convictions, somewhere inside there has always been a voice that says Roe, Roz, Rosalyne, you're OK, you are you and you are who you are. But few comprehend 'the who' that I am.

Society wants to challenge my sex, my gender when I am 'Out.'
The ignorant want to challenge my life quest 'to be.'
The academician/the politician/the moral majority/the professional want to silence me.
The so-called democratic lesbian and gay community want to disown, compress, diffuse and deny 'me.'

Do I believe myself to be a victim? If I identified all 'self' a victim, powerless, harmed, and beaten individual, I wouldn't be around discussing these issues. I would be dead.

But I am a victim, since I have always desired for the kindness of strangers and kindred spirits alike.
I am a victim since I have always needed attention, accolade and support from friend and foe.
I am a victim since I have always judged my outside by the appearances of others.
I am a victim.
But every day of my life I challenge these grounded blockades, for they are truly demonic. That is not to say they do not offer me anything emotionally or spiritually. They remind me that I am needy. They remind me that I love, and want to be loved by others. They remind me that my opinion cannot be measured in depth if there are no others, and that I will always be a competitive, self-loving, self-absorbed, uptight, unpretentious, humble, impatient, ageist industrialist.
Am I claiming myself a victim?
No, but I do not deny its power in my world.

Confessions

My belief is one can be smart, conservative, moralistic, upstanding, refined, political, academic, sexy, glamorous, on the edge, showy, stripped off, coarse, provocative, respected, and taken seriously.

I will not hide my past in order to be accepted within the academic, political and professional society. But I am still in desperate need of your acceptance and not hiding disrupts the acceptance within the professional and personal social order.

However, my belief is that I will always be an exhibitionist as long as I feel I can carry the tune.

Writers present literature, scientists prove a hypothesis, thespians display theatrics, artists represent on canvas, and I celebrate armor.

I have a need, a desire, a bleeding ulcer that yearns for people to see, 'see me,' love me, adore me, and appreciate the hard work it must have taken, and does take to present this live body to the world.

My desires are deeply imbedded in my need for you to see me, see the real me, naked and exposed. But the other side of that request is that you see me through my eyes, not some preconceived, stereotypically emotionally brainwashed, ignorant acumen. My requirement is that you move out of your box and acknowledge me, the 'me' that I am.

So how does one live one's life when one is essentially not fulfilled, not whole if one is not validated by EVERYONE for who she is?

One suffers.

At times one feels hopeless.

One feels betrayed.

One feels angry.

A systems therapist I've worked with for quite a few years stated that anger is energy, anger is alive, and anger can be felt and contained.

How I've adored, respected and been angry with this woman.

In opposition of this belief system some 12-step lingo states that 'self-righteous anger' kills the addict, the alcoholic, and can have lethal consequences. How that judgment has angered me, puzzled me, and guided me with my every so often uncontrollable and undeniable, self-righteous anger.

So why call this 'CONFESSIONS?'

I confess to you,

The curious, the intruder, the admirer, the confused, the disbeliever, the voyeur, the traveler, the oppressed, the oppressor

I confess to you,

My admirer, my supporter, my friend, my foe, my heart, my classifier, my peeps, my communities ...

CONFESSIONS

I AM A HUSTLER
I AM A SALES WOMAN
I AM A SOCIAL WORKER
I AM A TEACHER
I AM A TRAINER
I AM A WORK OF ART
I AM A WHORE
I AM AN ACHIEVER
I AM AN EDUCATOR
I AM AN EXTROVERT
I AM ALTERED
I AM BEATEN
I AM BECOMING WRINKLED
I AM BROKEN
I AM COMPETITIVE
I AM CRAZY
I AM CURIOUS
I AM DEEP
I AM DIRTY
I AM FEARFUL
I AM FEARLESS
I AM FUNNY
I AM FURIOUS
I AM GREEDY
I AM HOPEFUL
I AM HOPELESS
I AM HUMAN
I AM HOT
I AM HORNY
I AM IGNORANT
I AM JEALOUS
I AM JEALOUS
I AM LIFE
I AM LONELY
I AM LONELY
I AM MUSCULAR
I AM NASTY
I AM ON EDGE
I AM REAL
I AM REAL
I AM RESPECTABLE
I AM SCARED
I AM SHY
I AM SIZZLING
I AM SURGICALLY ENHANCED
I AM SEXUAL
I AM SMART
I AM STRONG
I AM SUPERFICIAL
I AM TRUSTWORTHY
I AM UPTIGHT
I AM VERY WORTHY
I AM WARM
I AM WOMAN I AM

LIFE IMITATING ART

PHOTOS BY LOREN CAMERON

337

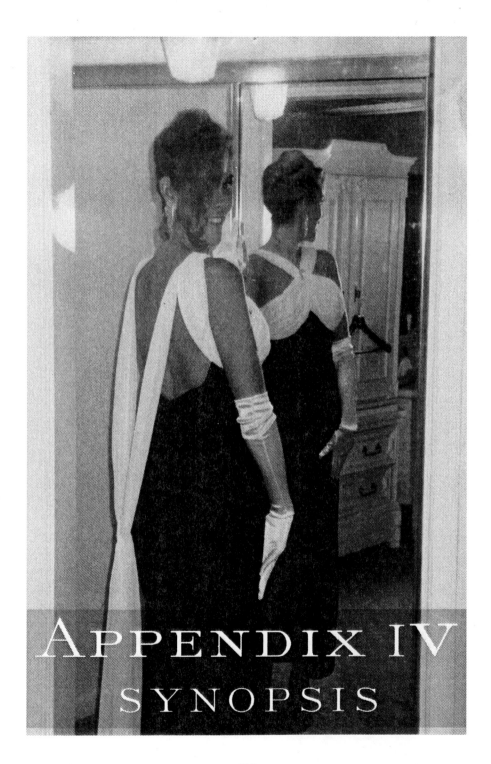

APPENDIX IV
SYNOPSIS

Synopsis

In 1987 I went to my first Narcotics Anonymous World Convention in New Orleans. The theme was 'LIVE YOUR DREAMS.'
Life is too short not too, don't you think?

Rosalyne Blumenstein's "Branded T" is vivid testimony to the power and significance subjugated voices play in the movement to contest and end oppression. As a consequence of this oppression, Rosalyne has been gendered as "other" and is "Branded T[rans]" by the dominant culture that insists her personal understanding of gender is a deception, both to herself and to others, setting the stage for a conflict between two knowledges, one purporting to know universal truths and a second knowledge scaled to the individual, Rosalyne's knowledge of herself.

The knowledge that oppressed peoples have of themselves and their lived bodies has a power and value beyond the individual. This narrative perspective recovers a subjugated knowledge that offers a potent and under utilized resource for community development, as well as for the development of the practical knowledge needed to share space with these communities. Rosalyne's narrative contributes to the drawing of a countermap of trans-experiences as normative. When seen as normative, the adaptive strengths that trans, gender-different and gender-othered people accumulate, the communities they create, and their different sense of fit, become valued components in a cohesive sense of identity. Recognition of subjugated knowledge is integral to supporting this as a normative identity. The subjugated position of Rosalyne's developing narrative often reveals an acute sense of insurgency. Not content to express her vision of the oppression that she and her cohorts endure, her narrative explores action, small resistances, internal triumphs and hidden victories.

The insurgent use of the narrative knowledge as a healing device then becomes a form of action knowledge or action narrative. "Branded T" can then be seen as a potent addition to this developing body of knowledge, a knowledge that is aggressively maneuvering to shift the vision the trans-communities from one based on a global knowledge structured in diagnosis and pathology to one ordered on identity, management of stigma, and creation of community using the subjugated knowledge the trans-communities themselves create and value. In this context, Rosalyne's voice vitally reclaims the power of self-knowledge and has discovered another meaningful way to proclaim, "I am real." – Carrie Davis, MSW, Group Services Coordinator/Gender Identity Project Coordinator
The Lesbian, Gay, Bisexual & Transgender Community Center NYC

Glossary of Unfamiliar Terms

Acting out- fooling around sexually

Axis I – DSMIV clinical disorders, not to be confused with Axel Rose

Axis II – personality disorders, not to be confused with current political administration

Beat – robbed – fooled - gotten over on - see asshole

Break luck - turn your first trick - make money, not to be confused with winning BINGO

Breaking Night – not sleeping and hanging out

Carrying on – acting silly

Change – term for 'sex-change,' not to be confused with "Do you have any?"

Chutzpah – Jewish testes – Balls – Guts – Courage

Cop – buying drugs on the street, not to be confused with Officer Krupky

'D' – dope – heroin – opium – See drooling, nodding out, unconscious, Divine

Detox – kicking drugs – physical withdrawal – see misery

Deuce – 42nd Street before the attack of Disney

Drag - having fun with gender and/or social presentation - see my left foot when I'm not getting schtupped on a regular basis

Fab – fabulous

Heron – heroin

Hir – her – not you, but her with a little him in her – not to be confused with fucking

Huzband – main boyfriend – Old Man – See good lay

IVDU – Intravenous Drug User, not to be confused with Planned Parenthood

Keppelah – yiddish for head – see on top of

Juice - power

L & G - lesbian and gay – See exclusion

Meth – Methadone, not to be confused with a fake story

Meth – methadone, a drug used to help heroin addicts with their withdrawal symptoms

Mitzvah – good deed

Ovah – fabulous – magnificent – See my picture

Passable – blending in as the gender you identify as

Peeps – Place where there are live naked ladies/men and booths – or close family of same culture

Pre-op – old term used to describe nonoperative transexual

Real – not fake – look passable

Relapse – use drugs again – Slip – Have a difficult time staying positive

Run – looking for drugs, buying them, and using them, not to be confused with diarrhea

Scotomas – blocking in your beliefs and blocking out other beliefs

Shady – being mean – reading – tacky – trying to be funny – See Milton Berle

She-male – derogatory way of marketing TS women with penises in the sex industry

Schtupped – being fucked – See me if you want to be

Sil – silicone – substance used for filling in – See my cheeks and …

Snapping on each other – verbally picking on one another

Spooked – someone figuring out you are transexual or have that history, not to be confused with Casper

Stray – a man unfamiliar to me. A man one gets intimate with in a hurry

Taking myself out/Take me out - killing myself, not to be confused with dinner 'alone'

The Center – The NYC LGBT Center - see attempting inclusion

Tranny – a person who identifies as Transexual – See club scene

Transexual – One 'S' used to politically own the word by community and not the medical profession

Transgender- a term used to throw all trans people into a box and not have to look at or respect the individual's identity. An umbrella term that should be used to celebrate diversity and inclusion

Transition – moving from one societal/fashion/gender role to another

TS - Transexual

Tuinals – A pill used as a prompt and sustained sedative and hypnotic – See nasty

Tuiys – Tuinals – See a lot of them/See more drool

'Wepts'– the art of too much weeping

Wiglet – half of a wig, see Fall, see Cher and Dolly's closet, see my mom's casket

IN LOVING MEMORY

In Loving Memory

I honor Lynda Roberts, my surrogate mother, my big sister.

I met Lynda when I was seventeen and she was in her late twenties or early thirties. For some reason she took me under her wing, she nurtured me, supported me, and loved me. Don't get me wrong. Lynda was not maternal. She was a hard woman living a fast and hard lifestyle. But within that milieu she brought class, talent, and a sense of sophistication like no other. She taught me many new approaches and acculturated me into my new life.

Lynda and I met at a disco. It was the 'Studio 54' era and Lynda was newly separated from her husband Vinny. She was a loose canary and she was ready to fly and party. Lynda was a snow-white beauty. I have never met another woman with skin like hers. She was so smooth and hairless she was even able to tweeze the few hairs off her legs. She was in great shape and her aura just added to all of who she was. She had male suitors all over the place. She was highly respected and admired. She was showered with presents and adoration. Lynda was so hot she was sizzling. She even entered a beauty contest against women ten to fifteen years her junior and placed in the finalists. Lynda was a vision and so were her wit and talents.

But with all that she had, all her ability, all her desires, she would always put her passion to the side for a man, and later on, for me.

She had so much talent and creative capability but never really got the break that she needed to truly shine.

Without delay, Lynda took a back seat to dress me up and make me shine. Too many drugs and too many problems, later our friendship ended for four years.

Lynda and I reconciled our differences and reinstated our friendship when I was 27. I was clean and sober and beginning a different kind of life, and so was she. She worked hard and long in an oppressive factory. I went back to school and began to achieve a lot of success. Lynda began to dress me up again for political functions and for fundraising events. She took up right where she left off and never complained about being behind the scenes instead of in front of them.

The years were not kind to Lynda

Her life was not easy

Her road was long and lonely

But together we laughed, I cried, she watched

Together we lived, discrete lives, but we lived.

Although Lynda did not achieve the success she should have

She lived

She lived her dream

She lived her life as Lynda

She lived out who she was without much support from her family of origin

Lynda was: A seamstress, A mentor, A performer, A stage mom, A big sister to both me and Marlene, A multi-talented, vibrant, sexy woman, A demanding woman, A perfectionist, A party animal, A bitter woman who lit up and let go.

Lynda wanted to be recognized out there in the spotlight but she decided to use her energy to support me in my venues. Few people are that selfless.

I thank her, for without her as part of the foundation in my life I would have never survived the toughest of those years.

I have buried too many family members, lovers and friends. There have been too many to count. But Lynda's death has hit me as hard as my mom's. After all, she took over where my mother left off. God bless you and keep you in peace!

Lynda, although your physical being is but ashes in a canister, you have touched my heart, my soul and my spirit in a way that will live on forever. I will love you and miss you more than anybody will ever understand. And as corny and hokey as it sounds, you most definitely were the wind beneath my wings.

NAMASTE

The Saint Francis Prayer:

Lord, make me an instrument of Your peace.

Where there is hatred, let me sow love

Where there is injury, let me pardon

Where there is doubt, let me breathe faith

Where there is despair, let me hope

Where there is darkness, let me show light

Where there is sadness, let me celebrate joy

O, Divine Master, grant that I may not so much seek to be consoled as to
console

To be understood as to understand

To be loved as to love

For it is in giving that we receive

It is in forgiving that we are forgiven

It is in dying that we are awaken again to eternal life.

ROSALYNE BLUMENSTEIN MSW

About the Author

Rosalyne Blumenstein, MSW, now resides in Southern California and is working with and for:
HIV+ substance users and misusers, cancer patients, the TG communities, and she also coaches folks in need of support surrounding incremental/substantial life transformation.
In New York City Rosalyne spearheaded and implemented programs catering to the needs of people along the transgender continuum at the LGBT Center. She assisted in the development of an evening program at Housing Works, Inc. (NYC), a program dedicated to the needs of the HIV/AIDS populations that deals with homelessness and substance use and misuse issues.
Rosalyne's work centers around, but is not limited to:
HIV Prevention and Education, Harm Reduction, Addiction and Recovery, Post Traumatic Stress Disorder PTSD Diversity, Inclusion, and Representation, Marketing Strategies Focusing on New Programming, Outreach to the Sex and the Body Worker Populations, LGBT Communities, Communities of Color, Indigent and Disenfranchised Populations, Youth at High Risk for HIV/AIDS, other STDs, Addiction, Exploitation, and ways in which to celebrate Self-Empowerment

Rosalyne is a member of:
The National Association of Social Workers NASW
The National Association of Alcohol and Drug Professionals NAADAC
Harry Benjamin International Gender Dysphoria Association HBIGDA
International Federation for Gender Education IFGE

She is a Certified Trainer with:
The Office of Alcohol and Substance Abuse Services
National Development Research Institute
Harm Reduction Training Institute/Harm Reduction Coalition on the East and West Coasts

Rosalyne co-directed 'Safe-T-Lessons' with Dr. Barbara Warren (1996), a film focused on HIV Prevention and Education
Rosalyne produced and directed 'Gender Variance Perception ...YOURS/MINE/OURS,' a film shown at the NGLTF Creating Change Conference as well as the NY Film Festival (1998).

Rosalyne produced and directed "Gender Identity Mergers and the Power of Language" for HBIGDA's biannual conference in Galveston Texas (2001).

Rosalyne has been seen on 20/20, the A&E special 'The Transgender Revolution,' and Rosa Von Preunheim's 'The Transexual Menace.' She assisted with the development of the films 'Boys Don't Cry' and 'Southern Comfort.'

Rosalyne has been written up in the NY Times, Pride Magazine, NY Magazine, Time Out, The Advocate, The NY and Washington Blade, New Yorker Magazine, LGNY, San Francisco Frontier's Magazine, and the Village Voice.

Rosalyne is available for lectures and speaking engagements and can be contacted at WWW.RMBLUMENSTEIN@AOL.COM

Printed in the United States
24629LVS00003B/40-60